D1747912

# CROSSING EUROPEAN BOUNDARIES

# New Directions in Anthropology

General Editor: **Jacqueline Waldren,** *Institute of Social Anthropology, University of Oxford*

**Volume 1**    *Coping with Tourists: European Reactions to Mass Tourism*
Edited by Jeremy Boissevain

**Volume 2**    *A Sentimental Economy: Commodity and Community in Rural Ireland*
Carles Salazar

**Volume 3**    *Insiders and Outsiders: Paradise and Reality in Mallorca*
Jacqueline Waldren

**Volume 4**    *The Hegemonic Male: Masculinity in a Portuguese Town*
Miguel Vale de Almeida

**Volume 5**    *Communities of Faith: Sectarianism, Identity, and Social Change on a Danish Island*
Andrew S. Buckser

**Volume 6**    *After Socialism: Land Reform and Rural Social Change in Eastern Europe*
Edited by Ray Abrahams

**Volume 7**    *Immigrants and Bureaucrats: Ethiopians in an Israeli Absorption Center*
Esther Hertzog

**Volume 8**    *A Venetian Island: Environment, History and Change in Burano*
Lidia Sciama

**Volume 9**    *Recalling the Belgian Congo: Conversations and Introspection*
Marie-Bénédicte Dembour

**Volume 10**    *Mastering Soldiers: Conflict, Emotions, and the Enemy in an Israeli Military Unit*
Eyal Ben-Ari

**Volume 11**    *The Great Immigration: Russian Jews in Israel*
Dina Siegel

**Volume 12**    *Morals of Legitimacy: Between Agency and System*
Edited by Italo Pardo

**Volume 13**    *Academic Anthropology and the Museum: Back to the Future*
Edited by Mary Bouquet

**Volume 14**    *Simulated Dreams: Israeli Youth and Virtual Zionism*
Haim Hazan

**Volume 15**    *Defiance and Compliance: Negotiating Gender in Low-Income Cairo*
Heba Aziz Morsi El-Kholy

**Volume 16**    *Troubles with Turtles: Cultural Understandings of the Environment on a Greek Island*
Dimitrios Theodossopoulos

**Volume 17**    *Rebordering the Mediterranean: Boundaries and Citizenship in Southern Europe*
Liliana Suarez-Navaz

**Volume 18**    *The Bounded Field: Localism and Local Identity in an Italian Alpine Valley*
Jaro Stacul

**Volume 19**    *Foundations of National Identity: From Catalonia to Europe*
Josep Llobera

**Volume 20**    *Bodies of Evidence: Burial, Memory and the Recovery of Missing Persons in Cyprus*
Paul Sant Cassia

**Volume 21**    *Who Owns the Past? The Politics of Time in a 'Model' Bulgarian Village*
Deema Kaneff

**Volume 22**    *An Earth-Colored Sea: "Race," Culture and the Politics of Identity in the Postcolonial Portuguese-Speaking World*
Miguel Vale de Almeida

**Volume 23**    *Science, Magic and Religion: The Ritual Process of Museum Magic*
Edited by Mary Bouquet and Nuno Porto

**Volume 24**    *Crossing European Boundaries: Beyond Conventional Geographical Categories*
Edited by Jaro Stacul, Christina Moutsou and Helen Kopnina

**Volume 25**    *Documenting Transnational Migration: Jordanian Men Working and Studying in Europe, Asia and North America*
Richard Antam

# Crossing European Boundaries

*Beyond Conventional Geographical Categories*

Edited by
Jaro Stacul, Christina Moutsou and Helen Kopnina

*Berghahn Books*
New York • Oxford

Published in 2006 by

*Berghahn Books*

www.berghahnbooks.com

© 2006 Jaro Stacul, Christina Moutsou and Helen Kopnina

All rights reserved. Except for the quotation of short passages for the purposes of criticism and review, no part of this book may be reproduced in any form or by any means, electronic or mechanical, including photocopying, recording, or any information storage and retrieval system now know or to be invented, without written permission of the publisher.

**Library of Congress Cataloging-in-Publication Data**
Crossing European boundaries : beyond conventional geographical categories / edited by Jaro Stacul, Christina Moutsou and Helen Kopnina.
   p. cm. — (New directions in anthropology ; v. 24)
Includes bibliographical references and index.
ISBN 1-84545-150-3 (alk. paper)
   1. Multiculturalism–European Union countries. 2. European Union countries–Social conditions. 3. Europe–Economic integration. I. Stacul, Jaro. II. Moutsou, Christina. III. Kopnina, Helen. IV. Series.

HN377.C76 2005
305.8'0094–dc22                                                           2005048252

**British Library Cataloguing in Publication Data**
A catalogue record for this book is available from the British Library.

Printed in the United States on acid-free paper.

ISBN 1-84545-150-3 (hardback)

# Contents

| | |
|---|---|
| **List of Illustrations** | vii |
| **Preface and Acknowledgements** | ix |
| 1. Crossing European Boundaries: Beyond Conventional Geographical Categories<br>*Jaro Stacul, Christina Moutsou and Helen Kopnina* | 1 |

### Part I: Institutional Crossings

| | |
|---|---|
| 2. Crossing Boundaries through Education: European Schools and the Supersession of Nationalism<br>*Cris Shore and Daniela Baratieri* | 23 |
| 3. Neo-Liberal Nationalism: Ethnic Integration and Estonia's Accession to the European Union<br>*Gregory Feldman* | 41 |
| 4. The European Left and the New Immigrations: The Case of Italy<br>*Davide Però* | 64 |

### Part II: The Experience of Immigration

| | |
|---|---|
| 5. The Grand Old West: Mythical Narratives of a Better Past before 1989 in Views of West-Berlin Youth from Immigrant Families<br>*Sabine Mannitz* | 83 |
| 6. Invisible Community: Russians in London and Amsterdam<br>*Helen Kopnina* | 103 |
| 7. Merging European Boundaries: A Stroll in Brussels<br>*Christina Moutsou* | 120 |

8. Bosnian Women in Mallorca: Migration as a Precarious Balancing Act
   *Jacqueline Waldren* — 137

**PART III: LOCALISING EUROPE**

9. Claiming the Local in the Irish/British Borderlands: Locality, Nation-State and the Disruption of Boundaries
   *William F. Kelleher, Jr.* — 153

10. Boundary Formation and Identity Expression in Everyday Interactions: Muslim Minorities in Greece
    *Venetia Evergeti* — 176

11. Negotiating European and National Identity Boundaries in a Village in Northern Greece
    *Eleftheria Deltsou* — 197

12. Claiming a 'European Ethos' at the Margins of the Italian Nation-State
    *Jaro Stacul* — 210

**Notes on Contributors** — 229

**Index** — 233

# List of Illustrations

| | | |
|---|---|---|
| 3.1 | Non-Estonian woman standing alone, appearing alienated, and facing against the movement of the crowd. | 57 |
| 3.2 | Sitting apart, gazing at two Estonian women who socialise near the Estonian National Theatre. | 57 |
| 3.3 | Holding a copy of Estland, a pictorial guide to Estonian nature and rural life. | 58 |
| 3.4 | Finally conversing with a group that includes one of the Estonian women from Figure 3.2. | 58 |
| 7.1 | The nineteen boroughs of the city of Brussels. | 127 |
| 10.1 | Map of the village of Mikrohori drawn by its inhabitants. | 186 |
| 12.1 | Tyrol: Pathway to Europe (Photo: Jaro Stacul). | 215 |

# Preface and Acknowledgements

The present volume brings together recent ethnographic studies on Europe at the turn of the millennium. It addresses a variety of theoretical issues that have become relevant in anthropology as the boundaries of Europe are being redrawn. Like many other academic works, it was conceived outside the 'ivory towers' of academia: the idea of an edited book on Europe was originally developed in the course of a meeting within the informal context of a cafeteria in King's Cross Station, in London. The book subsequently grew out of a workshop entitled *Crossing European Boundaries. Beyond Conventional Geographical Categories*, held in Cracow at the 6th Biennial Conference of the European Association of Social Anthropologists (EASA) in July 2000. The aim of the workshop was a discussion of the meanings attached to the idea of 'crossing European boundaries' in a post-national era in various social contexts, and of the contradictions with which this idea is replete. We are very grateful to the colleagues who enthusiastically contributed to the debates, especially to those who participated in the workshop.

We would like to thank the granting bodies whose financial support made the organisation of the workshop possible; particularly the EASA, which assisted with EU funding. A debt of gratitude is owed to the Department of Social Anthropology of the University of Cambridge both for its financial support, and for providing desk space and the infrastructure that enhanced the completion and production of this book. In Cambridge our thanks are also due to the Computing Centre of Cambridge University for technical support. Helen Kopnina wishes to thank King's College, Cambridge, for funding, and Christina Moutsou and Jaro Stacul express their gratitude to the British Academy for awarding Overseas Conference Grants. Finally, we are deeply grateful to an anonymous reader whose comments and constructive criticism became the basis for the final revisions of this book, and to Engelbert Fellinger for providing the cover illustration.

Helen Kopnina, Christina Moutsou and Jaro Stacul<br>
London, December 2004

# Chapter 1
# Crossing European Boundaries: Beyond Conventional Geographical Categories

Jaro Stacul, Christina Moutsou and Helen Kopnina

### A 'New Europe'?

If anthropology represents an 'uncomfortable discipline', as Firth (1981: 200) phrased it over twenty years ago, perhaps there are grounds for suggesting that Europe has played the role of the 'problematic subject' within the 'uncomfortable discipline'. As an area of anthropological research, it is not as 'exotic' as the locales most anthropologists prefer, and its appearance in the canons of major ethnographic sites has been relatively slow. As Parman (1998: 2) wrote, Europe has been deployed 'as a conceptual construct, as a vehicle of Occidentalism, to define and enforce the boundaries and hierarchical inequalities of Occident and Orient', and served as a testing ground for the distinguishing features of the discipline. 'The role of Europe in the anthropological imagination has been complex, sometimes paradoxical, often provocative' (Parman 1998: 3). Despite its slow appearance in the discipline, now it is agreed that the anthropology of Europe can challenge hierarchies of representation previously taken for granted.

These days, writing about Europe from an anthropological viewpoint is far from being an easy task, for Europe can no longer be studied in its own terms. September 11th and the terrorist threat were not confined to one area of the world, but had considerable impact in Europe. Moreover, the addition of ten member-states to the European Union (EU), which occurred on 1 May 2004, has yet to reveal new political dynamics of inclusion and exclusion. New alliances are being formed, new disparaging lines are being drawn between nations, and new legal mechanisms and policies come into place. While the idea of the bounded nature of the nation-state used to rest on the assumption that it is a territorial entity with its own borders encompassing a national 'culture', nowadays Europe presents us with some new and unexplored issues: it represents an entity in which borders are removed as a result of the neoliberal idea of the single market, and where certain categorical distinctions (West/East, North/South, Left/Right) that have so far been taken for granted are subsequently blurred. By contrast, some national borders have become increasingly important and sometimes conflict with or take over identities created by other, non-national boundaries. The development of communications has meant that Europe is becoming increasingly interconnected with the political as well as ideological sentiments elsewhere, be it in the Middle East, the United States, or the Far East. A sense of Europeanness becomes problematised, challenged and recreated as new boundaries are being redrawn or eliminated. The Cold War partition of Europe for example provided Western Europe with a supposedly solid base-line for its project of regional integration. Yet in the absence of such a negative yard-stick, imposed from outside, the boundaries of Europe become unclear, and so does the definition of a common cultural space that people would willingly adopt as their collective frame of reference.

Since its inception, the anthropology of Europe has been faced with the shifting role of its object of analysis, which is a consequence both of the political changes from the aftermath of the Second World War onwards, and of the theoretical shifts in the discipline that ensued. We will not go into all the details of anthropological studies of Europe in the last fifty years. Suffice it to say, for the purposes of our debate, that at its inception the main theoretical issue of a Europeanist anthropology was that of modernisation: national governments and international organisations were encountering various problems in implementing strategies for development (Goddard *et al.* 1994: 2), and anthropologists were well equipped to provide answers and spot the roots of some of these problems. It is in this context that a tradition of studies of peasantries flourished: the Mediterranean became the preferred geographical area for testing theories and formulating hypotheses, and the 'community' acted as the central unit of investigation.

The crisis of structural-functionalism in the 1960s–1970s, the political unrest that characterised that period and the emergence of Marxism in anthropological theory entailed a shift in theoretical focus: studies of rural communities became less popular and anthropologists paid increasing attention to the interrelationship between the local and the national, most notably to macro social processes of state formation and bureaucratisation, even though they continued to focus on the Mediterranean area. In the 1980s, by contrast, the theoretical framework around which most of Europeanist anthropology was built (i.e. that associated with 'positivism') came under attack from the postmodernist approach, which gave primacy to deconstruction, textuality and the politics of identity (Goddard *et al.* 1994: 19). It is within such a context that anthropology started focusing on European identities rather than on 'communities' (see e.g. Macdonald 1993) and, more recently, on European integration and its paradoxes (see e.g. Bellier and Wilson 2000; Holmes 2000; Shore 2000).

Although this brief summary does not do justice to the development of a Europeanist anthropology and its complexities, it seems safe to suggest that there is a common thread, a pathway running through this body of studies: this is a progressive expansion of scale, from what used to be considered social realities with clear-cut boundaries to entities in which boundaries decline in significance or are redefined. It is against this changing background that the anthropology of present-day Europe should be located. At the turn of the millennium, Europe becomes a pervasive concept. This is suggested not only by the rhetoric of politicians who place considerable emphasis on the necessity to be part of it, but also by the fact that it is appealed to by various regionalist movements which are no longer particularistic in character, but make competing claims to 'Europeanness'. The expansion of the EU is a case in point, as already noted. Likewise countries previously labelled as 'outside Europe' are in the process of rewriting their national history. For some of these countries rewriting history means establishing a relationship with Europe, that is to say claiming a European history. Yet establishing such a relationship is also a political act, for it entails crossing a boundary.

## Anthropological Dilemmas

The significance that the idea of 'crossing' recently acquired in Europeanist anthropology is the outcome of a progressive expansion of scale that goes hand in hand with major theoretical shifts in focus aimed at transcending rigid categorisations. The articles in this book are intended to argue the theoretical significance of the expansion of scale in anthropological studies of Europe. They set out to explore the variety of (often contrasting) meanings associated with the act of 'crossing European boundaries' by looking at locales as diverse as Belgium, Estonia, Germany, Greece, Ireland, Italy, The Netherlands, Spain and the United Kingdom. What unites most of them is a focus on a paradox inherent in the act of 'crossing European boundaries': if one of the ideas that the current concept of 'Europe' conveys is removal of boundaries, it also involves ways of establishing new ones.

Somehow crossing boundaries forms an integral part of the anthropological project. Traditionally, an anthropologist crosses the boundary of his or her own culture by entering the 'field', although some may argue that a subtle cultural boundary remains. Nowadays the societies anthropologists study are no longer perceived as bounded but rather as open and constantly changing: alongside boundaries, previously reified notions such as identity, ethnicity, class and community are undergoing a process of redefinition. What reflecting on the anthropology of Europe brings to the fore is the question of whether anthropology has really changed or has only moved in theory, developing its own debates but not our understanding of the world it presumes to study. To answer this question, we need to ask ourselves where anthropology stands in the contemporary world. To follow Geertz, anthropology is what its practitioners do, so the answer to our question depends on anthropological practices. Anthropology at the beginning of the millennium attempts to adjust itself to a rapidly changing world, not only to defend itself against attacks from other academic disciplines (initiated in part by competition for funding) but also to regain confidence and passion for its own chosen subject. Thus, anthropology's task is a process of continuous accumulation, updating the previously studied data and entering new areas, both theoretical and geographical.

Anthropology has been blamed for indulging in a kind of 'Orientalism', simultaneously exoticising and distancing its subjects. Throughout the twentieth century, Social Anthropology came to be known as the study of non-Western societies. Just like the skull-measuring treasure hunters entering the land of 'savages', anthropologists were blamed for looking at their subjects as the 'other', observing and recording odd cultural antiques and colourful rituals. The 'natives' were often presented against pristine settings devoid of all-too-visible signs of Westernisation. Western influence itself, mostly felt through economic and industrial imports, was often described as intrusive and alien to the 'native' culture. It was not until the early 1970s that a systematic study of the supposedly homogeneous Western culture started to appear in anthropological writing. But once the West was 'discovered' by anthropologists the technique of describing 'tribes' or 'urban minorities' presented curiosities similar to aboriginal skulls and poisoned spearheads. Recent work in anthropology attempts to bring the subject to the fore, to see the 'native' and his 'culture' as an actor on a global stage, starring in a local performance (Johnston *et al.* 2002). As anthropologists notice the plight of impoverished farmers in remote Altain villages, or follow the truckloads of refugees smuggled into Scandinavian ports, or observe the Londoner's easy stroll, our view of Europe expands. We no longer see the 'villages' of the 'other', but we observe modern life in all its human complexity, and we record living history in the context of larger temporal and spatial processes.

Anthropology has been based on ethnographic research and theoretical models as a means of exploring its subject. The British anthropological school has consistently favoured fieldwork as the distinguished method of anthropological research. However, there has been a persistent dilemma within the history of anthropology as to how to integrate theory with practice. The often-observed split between the two has been applied to the anthropology of Europe. There has been a general agreement between anthropologists studying Europe that we need to go beyond strict functional and/or structural models in order to understand current European society. A response to this realisation was the rise of postmodern anthropology, which was an attempt to deconstruct pre-existing anthropological categories, taking a literary and philosophical turn. The problem remained, however, of how to write anthropology in a flexible way so as to reflect complex social processes and offer an in-depth understanding of specific social phenomena.

## Conceptualising Complexity in Europe

There is an increased social and geographical mobility within Europe with which anthropological writing has to come to terms, which goes hand in hand with the dissolution (or remaking) of other boundaries that were central to the definition of social groups. If anthropologists' concern with European identities largely reflects the significance of boundaries in the discipline, the removal of boundaries within the continent makes Europe a privileged context for the observation of the effects of a process that is occurring across the globe: it represents the site of a complex, overlapping, disjunctive order, to follow Appadurai (1990: 296). Once the cradle of nationalism, which conveys ideas of divisions, much of Western Europe now represents a political and territorial entity in which frontiers can be crossed freely without going through checkpoints. Although it would be contentious to postulate that a European identity has the potential to replace national and regional identities, it seems clear that concepts such as 'nation', 'region', 'locality' as well as ethnicity, identity, class and community (to name a few) have now to be redefined in relation to this expanding entity.

The idea of 'crossing boundaries' nicely describes this process of expansion: it is the product of an epoch, and comes to the fore at a time when national boundaries are materially removed and deconstructed in anthropological theory. Nowadays this idea is central to the definition of 'Europe': the act of crossing boundaries, by its very nature, conveys ideas of mobility and, to a certain extent, of placelessness too. As Jacques Delors once said, mobility and cooperation are at the heart of the European ethos (Barry 1993: 314): objects, people and knowledge move across boundaries with a speed and frequency that was unimaginable until a few years ago. Technological change, information production, standardisation and regulation are all notions around which the European Union, as a technologically regulatory State, is built and continues to develop, and the reduction of spatial barriers is an important means to augment social power (Harvey 1989: 232–3).

The idea of 'crossing European boundaries' encapsulates the increasing importance of economic and cultural mobility within the continent (Barry 1993: 317). It expresses a novel reading of European space through which territorial space no longer has the same significance to the activities and organisation of the state. Given this situation of flux and movement, the process of Europeanisation begs various questions. It may be asked, for example, whether it will eventually bring about a significant levelling between eastern and western Europe or a more homogeneous and cohesive whole, as Goddard, Llobera and Shore (1994: 24) suggested. Yet while the association of Europe with mobility and the act of crossing boundaries is largely an expression of the neo-liberal discourse of the single market, as discussed, the meanings attached to it remain largely unexplored. If this idea were taken at face value, we would be led to assume that social actors across the continent are passive recipients of it, and would overlook the fact that crossing European boundaries may mean different things to different people. For those at the centres of EU decision-making, the act of crossing may be tantamount to cosmopolitanism, just as for others it may entail establishing a relationship with a 'European' culture in order to stress distinctiveness.

In this book we seek to distance ourselves from the 'top down' perspective, which has informed many recent anthropological studies on Europeanisation (see e.g. Borneman and Fowler 1997; Bellier and Wilson 2000; Shore 2000; Shore and Abélès 2004). Instead, we take on board the idea that by bringing human agency back into Europe we can make sense of the multiple and often contrasting ideas that the act of 'crossing European boundaries' conveys and assess this act's pervasiveness. The focus on human agency raises various issues. These include the associations individuals make between themselves and an entity in which boundaries can be crossed; how this idea is accommodated to local-level discourses (both in the City of London and in a 'remote' mountain village); how it is received and understood; how far a European identity can coexist with national, regional and local identities; and (last but not least) whether the act of 'crossing European boundaries' represents an accommodation to the power structures that permeate this act or a way of resisting power itself.

A reconsideration of the role of social actors in making sense of the world they live in may seem at odds with recent trends in the discipline, most notably with a tendency to concentrate more on institutions and legal texts than on actor-centred research. This interest in officialdom stems both from the emergence and consolidation of supra-national institutions like the EU, and from the idea, borrowed from Foucault, that power relations permeate all levels of society. This emphasis on power relations has involved increasing attention to the processes and techniques whereby institutions and national and supra-national agencies govern and discipline populations (Ferguson and Gupta 2002). In this regard, Europe is no exception. Complexity in Europe, for instance, has been conceptualised by focusing on large socio-economic and political processes or by paying attention to the shifting boundaries of what had been viewed as bounded communities. Many authors have pointed to the significance of the ideas introduced by the EU to the lives of individuals, but there are not many detailed ethnographic accounts of what it means to social actors to live as 'Europeans' in a particular context.

McDonald's work on the European Commission (1996) forms part of the latter intellectual tradition. In her analysis of the concept of 'unity in diversity' she highlights that the philosophy behind the establishment of the EU is one that juxtaposes itself to the idea of fixed borders linked to nationalism and the nation-state, and seeks to create a 'new Europe' with permeable boundaries. McDonald argues that such a philosophy seems to claim that defeating nationalism makes us better human beings. She also points out that as a result of that, it has become difficult to talk about Europe without automatically referring to the EU. McDonald's paper was published at the same time as other anthropological studies on globalisation and the city (see e.g. Hannerz 1996, Howes 1996, Westwood and Williams 1997). These and other studies confirm that the history of the EU's establishment, putting aside the financial and political reasons behind it, seems to parallel a global sense of the world having become smaller, and regional borders being more frequently transcended. However, McDonald's argument focuses on the social actors and points out the limitations and inaccuracies of conceptualising recent political and social changes as a process separate from everyday life experience.

This volume follows McDonald's example in that it sets out to argue that the question of the EU's placement within Europe and its handling of the concept of Europe does not necessarily need to be viewed from a top-down perspective (see also McDonald 2004). In other words, what seems to be lacking in recent anthropological studies on Europe is a reflection on human agency and social actors. People do not simply enact culture but interpret it in their own ways and through their own cultural categories, and they adapt to a situation of rapid change and flow in ways which are often at odds with the politics of European integration. Like transnationalism, European integration does not simply involve the movements of capital, people and goods, but 'is also made and unmade in the dynamics of intimate spaces and moments of everyday life' (Raj 2003: 20). In this respect, Europeanness may be reinterpreted in the context of everyday life, as Moutsou's chapter (this volume) suggests in relation to Greek and Turkish immigrants in Brussels. Although relations between places are continually shifting as a consequence of the political and economic reorganisation of space in the world system, these shifts can hardly be made sense of unless we acknowledge the fact that social actors make their own space to come to terms with this reorganisation, and are not passive spectators in the face of global processes.

## European Boundaries at Issue

An interest in European boundaries and emphasis on human agency may seem mutually exclusive. After all, the association of Europe with boundaries usually evokes the image of the national border, which conjures up ideas of power. Borders, by their very nature, exist as physical, 'official' realities: they usually convey the idea of a checkpoint one has to go through when leaving one country and entering another. They embody the idea of the State as 'above' citizens (Ferguson and Gupta 2002: 982), and constitute techniques for disciplining and limiting the movement of citizens themselves. There is a vast body of anthropological literature on borders (for details see Donnan and Wilson 1999), which has thoroughly covered the ground on their significance in the discipline, and it is outside the scope of this book to add more material to the existing debate. Suffice it to say, for the purposes of this work, that the anthropology of borders, like that of institutions (and EU institutions), shares much with anthropological studies of elite cultures and power, where researchers try to 'study up' (Bellier and Wilson 2000: 6; Shore and Nugent 2002; see also Nader 1974; Wolf 1974).

Yet even the anthropology of borderlands is not just about State borders, but also about the conceptual, metaphorical boundaries involved (Alvarez 1995: 448). Kelleher's contribution (this volume) makes this point very clearly. Borders are a form of boundaries, but boundaries are not necessarily borders, and they are not only material. While Europe represents the context within which national borders decline in significance, it is also the site in which various other kinds of boundaries become blurred. As already noted, the title *Crossing European Boundaries* is intended as a reflection on the relationship (or tension) between the act of crossing frontiers, as an expression of the neo-liberal ideology of the single market, and the blurring and remaking of other boundaries that is the result of (or goes hand in hand with) this act. This tension is clear, for example, in Però's examination of the Left/Right dichotomy in Italy (this volume), and in the analysis of the redefinition of the boundary between the 'local' and the 'European' in Stacul's chapter on the Italian Alps (this volume).

Boundaries (mainly the social boundaries that inform social relations) have been the subject of a vast body of anthropological literature for a long time. As Donnan and Wilson (1999: 21) have observed, the history of British Social Anthropology and American Cultural Anthropology is characterised by a shift from an interest in what a boundary encompasses to an interest in the boundary itself. The boundary is an element that embodies a sense of identification with a group of people as well as a sense of distinction vis-à-vis other groups, and is the element marking the beginning and end of a community (Cohen 1985: 12). But whereas boundaries used to be of interest because of the practices and beliefs that they encompassed, in late modernity they become problematic because of their changing nature, both in the geopolitical space and in anthropological writing. Kopnina's contribution in this volume, for instance, shows that the idea of 'boundary' is central to Russians' self-representation in Amsterdam and London. The problematic nature of boundaries, though, also stems from the fact that the boundedness of culture they evoke has been questioned by recent postmodern theory. In taking on board the idea that in late modernity boundaries are crossed, some scholars have suggested that in anthropological writing boundedness represents a kind of narrative device (Gupta and Ferguson 1997: 2) or literary fiction (Clifford 1988: 10). It is a device to map the world as a series of separate, territorialised cultures.

Writing about the act of crossing boundaries does not necessarily mean subscribing to a view of the world as fragmented and boundless. Although it seems clear that boundedness cannot be taken for granted, it must also be noted that the ethnographers' practice of assuming the cultural homogeneity of the people they studied and their boundedness replicated the nationalist consensus that prevailed in their home societies (Grimshaw and Hart 1995: 52), and so it should be looked upon as the product of an epoch in which social and political realities were more 'bounded' than they are nowadays. More importantly, 'boundedness' is not at odds with the state of flux and flexibility (Harvey 1989: 339) that is seen as central to the definition of the condition of postmodernity, and Mannitz clearly makes this point in her chapter on the Turkish community in Berlin (this volume). If anything, 'boundedness' is often the reaction to the situation of instability that flux and flexibility themselves involve.

Thus, stressing the act of 'crossing' does not involve discarding boundedness altogether: while certain boundaries are crossed and do fade, others (sometimes more powerful or of a different nature) come into being or are recreated, even in political discourse. The boundaries focussed on in this work are not necessarily marked in geopolitical space only, but include those elements informing social relations (e.g. class, race and gender, to name just a few) that are redefined as a result of the dissolution of those associated with officialdom. The boundaries represented by gender, race or class or even those of territorial communities appear as permeable and transient as those of European states (see e.g. Waldren's contribution in this volume): what 'crossing European boundaries' involves is a swaying back and forth between dissolution and remaking in the geopolitical space (as Feldman demonstrates in his analysis, in this volume, of Estonia's accession to the EU) as well as in social relations. In Deltsou's and Evergeti's contributions on Greece (this volume), for example, it emerges that geographical boundaries are linked to human interaction.

Using the term 'boundaries' instead of 'borders' also has methodological implications. Cohen's (1985) definition of the term illuminates this point:

central to his theory (but see also Barth 1969) is the idea that boundaries are called into being by the exigencies of social interaction, that they play an important role in the definition of a human group, and that they encapsulate its identity. However, he also makes it clear that not all boundaries are objectively apparent: rather, some may exist in the minds of their beholders. The significance of boundaries also lies in their subjective dimension, yet the fact that they may be metaphorical instead of material does not rule out the possibility of their acquiring a political dimension. Fernandez (1997: 726) convincingly makes this point in relation to the North/South dichotomy in Europe: popular cosmologies, he argues, represent category systems that at least potentially contain their own frontiers, which are at odds with a Europe without borders. Europeans do make their own Europe in the way they want, 'but partly in ways that respond to deeper and older geopolitical imaginings'.

Aside from frontiers, even the highly mobile citizens inbred in the European Schools make their own Europe in the way they wish, which can also be very exclusive and barrier-creating in nature. Shore and Baratieri's chapter (this volume) offers such evidence. This idea seems to agree with a recent sociological study on student mobility in Europe (Murphy-Lejeune 2002), which points out that at a time of high European mobility and monetary-union students moving between European countries are still a small minority. According to the author, 'EU citizens are by and large not accustomed to mobility. The right of residence in another member state offered to every European citizen is more an ideal, and European mobility more a dream, than a reality' (Murphy-Lejeune 2002: 51). Mobile students between European countries are almost always strongly encouraged by a social and family background of mixed nationality and/or a history of parents' mobility for career purposes.

The term 'boundaries' is also extensively used in psychology and psychoanalysis to indicate human interaction in relationships. It was introduced in psychoanalytic theory and philosophy more recently than other terms and presupposes an understanding of human beings' interconnectedness. Ego psychology, whose influence is still widely felt, nowadays seems to advocate the individual as a complete and separate entity. As Hacking (1995) demonstrates through his analysis of the false memory syndrome and other contemporary debates about psychological distress, what he calls the 'sciences of memory', i.e. disciplines studying the human mind and emotional states, are deeply embedded in the capitalist culture of the nineteenth and twentieth century. Western society has claimed to be composed of individuals, and, within it, childhood has been turned into a special category and an object of research because of its lack of autonomous function. On the contrary, the use of the concept of boundaries in more recent psychoanalytic studies serves to support the idea of intersubjectivity, a term introduced by Merleau-Ponty

(1962) to make the point that human beings function within relationships in which connectedness needs to be safeguarded and limited by the person's boundaries.

According to Merleau-Ponty, human beings are embedded in relationships since their birth, and these relationships do not only include symbolic and social bonds with significant others, but also what is often perceived as their physical and biological entity. He demonstrates how the body is actually social and our understanding of our very existence comes from relationships and being part of a society. Such an understanding comes in contrast to cognition theory in psychology, which has to a large extent influenced anthropology through structuralism and the study of isolated communities, and which advocates that human and social development takes place within specific developmental stages. Therefore, the more recent understanding of 'boundaries' seems to refer not to individuals, but to human beings within relationships.

The above developments within psychology and in psychoanalytic theory are highly relevant to anthropology's recent attempt to focus on the self and emotionality, as a response and challenge to the understanding of society as a bounded system. Although selfhood is also a potentially controversial term, whose understanding goes beyond the scope of the present project, it seems to entail a more fluid conceptualisation of human beings within society. The concept of self allows for exploration of the complex web of relationships and the continuous dance that characterise human interaction. Thus, a focus on both objective and subjective (or mental) frontiers highlights how the idea of the new Europe and the fading and remaking of geographical boundaries coexist with the shifting of mental boundaries and the redefinition of peoples' individual, social and political identities and social practices.

## The Scope of the Volume

If the argument for an anthropology of Europe is straightforward, how to study Europe 'from below' at the turn of the millennium is more problematic. In addressing a variety of theoretical issues, the contributions in this volume seek to provide some answers by examining themes as diverse as education, immigration, ethnicity, local and national identities, and conceptualisations of work, to mention just a few. Despite this variety of themes, what unites them is a common thread, namely, a concern with what crossing boundaries entails, both in terms of physical movement of peoples and at the level of perception. They imply that, despite the recent emphasis on the necessity of studying systems and relations of power that are not always visible, fieldwork remains not only a research tool, but anthropology's distinguished method of comprehending the context and fluidity of social phenomena. In this respect, it should not be regarded as a means of simply producing or validating theory, but as the essence of anthropological writing. It is often the case that extensive and sensitive ethnographies are more reflective of social complexity than theoretical debates about them. After all, what made anthropology a distinct discipline since its inception was its capacity to reflect on society through the lived experience and simultaneous positional distancing of the researcher.

The first part of the volume deals with the institutional aspect of the act of 'crossing European boundaries'. It focuses on the institutions, agencies and policies designed to foster this act, and on the paradoxes surrounding the accomplishment of this goal. The chapter by Shore and Baratieri, for example, addresses the issue of education by focusing on the role of European Schools, the institutions providing education for the children of EU personnel, and asks whether the European Schools create post-nationalist or non-nationalist citizens of Europe. Education, they note, shapes the cognitive and cultural boundaries of the nation-state in Europe and that of European identity, and European Schools seem to forge the new kind of European subjectivity. History and Geography classes, for example, are designed to disseminate the 'European knowledge' that is missing in the national curricula by implementing a holistic European viewpoint instead of a national one. In this respect, education enables pupils to cross the boundary of their national 'culture', although this does not displace a sense of national identity. Yet the authors argue that while European Schools seem to dissolve the boundaries of national culture, they create others, that is to say class boundaries: because they are exclusive, they will never accommodate a mass public, and only the few who can afford it will have access to European education.

The theme of exclusion is further developed in Feldman's chapter on linguistic and cultural hegemony in the newly created Estonian State. Feldman's chapter adapts the political science perspective to analysis of the role of State institutions, which draw on ideologically potent themes of individual initiative and economic organization to support and explain Government policies. Official discourse on the 'problem' of ethnic integration, in which all non-Estonians are viewed as problematic aliens that need to adapt to Estonian values, is simultaneously cautious of appearing politically incorrect and employs positive metaphors of construction, solidification and growth. However, the author shows that political discourse enacted through integration policy is simultaneously re-enforcing the construction of a non-Estonian 'other' by constructing a category of 'alienated, disenfranchised and threatening' aliens.

The construction of the 'other' through policies is also examined in the following chapter. Però's contribution explores the inadequacies of discourse at a political-ideological level and the recent deconstruction of ideology in Europe. He examines the example of the Left in Italy as a case of significant discrepancies between ideology and actual social policy. He points to the contradictions surrounding the Left's construction of the question of migration and multiculturalism in contemporary Europe in relation to immigrant housing policy. He argues that the Italian Left is characterised by what he terms an 'non-integrating multiculturalism' – a politics that at the level of discourse favours a recognition of ethno-cultural differences, whereas at the level of practice it opposes the presence of foreign immigrants in ways that in the past would have been ascribed to the Right. By focusing on the impact of housing policies on the lives of social actors (i.e. migrants and refugees), Però highlights ideology as a structure often alienated from social happenings and resistant to change, and shows that the blurring of the Left/Right dichotomy disguises the entanglement of the new Left in the legitimation of boundaries along ethnic lines.

The second part of the volume develops one of the themes touched upon in the previous part: immigration. Yet instead of looking at institutions and policies, the contributions in this part concentrate on how the act of 'crossing European boundaries' is constructed by those who do the crossing, the social actors themselves. They show that a constructive answer to the frequent confusion created by the so-called 'postmodern anthropology' is to look at the question of individual social actors and their immediate relationships as an effective locus for understanding social phenomena.

This point is implicit in the chapter by Mannitz in relation to the aftermath of German unification that dissolved the boundary between East and West. In her chapter she concentrates on the Turkish community living in former West Berlin, and looks at the consequences that the collapse of the Wall brought about. She observes that while before 1989 Turkish immigrants were cast by the German state as an integral part of the human landscape of the city, with unification they were turned into the 'Other'. The 'Grand Old West', the time before the fall of the Wall, is nostalgically evoked by Turkish youths as a time of social harmony: it symbolises a form of membership that does not entail identification with the current ethno-national concept of Germanness that conveys ideas of exclusion for non-Germans at the same time as it does away with the East/West dichotomy. More importantly, she demonstrates how Turkish youths, symbolic outsiders to the idea of 'Europe', situate themselves as insiders in German society in relation to East Germans. She shows how such a positioning is linked to ideas of globalisation, capitalism and the economy of the West as opposed to ideas of nationalism based on descent and the history of the nation-state.

Fluidity, relationships and subjectivity are themes largely dealt with by the postmodernist movement, which has deeply affected and transformed recent anthropological studies. However, postmodern anthropology has created new problems by focusing on the large-scale and the social power structures, thereby paying considerably less attention to ethnography. In other words, postmodern anthropology left the discipline and anthropologists powerless by putting a distance between them and the essential means of practising anthropology, i.e. sound and detailed ethnographic research (Bloch 2000). It also initiated a constant questioning of the validity of social research findings in respect of the anthropologists' authority to represent their subjects. Fieldwork though, constitutes a very effective means of understanding change, fluidity and the role of subjective processes by placing one self in midst of social happenings. In this regard, Kopnina's chapter stands as a critique of postmodernism from within. In studying Russian immigrants in two large Western European cities (Amsterdam and London), Kopnina asks the question of what constitutes a social unit, i.e. a community. She wonders whether one can define a community through 'objective' traits, when the social actors themselves do not claim to feel part of an ethnic community. However, through the process of fieldwork it emerges that the concept of community is something largely understood and constructively used by social actors themselves, and therefore the invisibility of the Russian community itself is what constitutes an important subject of anthropological inquiry.

The idea of 'unity through diversity' is examined in Moutsou's chapter based on fieldwork in Brussels, the city symbolically representing Europe. Moutsou argues against the idea of the nation-state imposing a homogenised view of people's identity and in favour of the concept of 'cultural intimacy', pioneered by Herzfeld (1997). She shows that the concept of 'cultural intimacy' allows us to glimpse at identities of social actors from a 'bottom-up' perspective, and to witness how abstract and cumbersome ideas of Europe become interpreted, evaluated, integrated and challenged by the local population. The Greek and the Turkish migrants in the city of Brussels find themselves encompassed by sometimes imposed, sometimes self-generated 'cultural intimacy' through widespread stereotypes of urban space and through their reactions to political processes taking place in the 'capital of Europe'. Social actors thus find themselves in a very complex urban space, where ideas of Europeanness get re-interpreted in the context of migrants' everyday lives.

Waldren uses instead a different approach in her chapter on Bosnian immigrants in the Spanish island of Majorca. Central to her exploration is the act of crossing social boundaries as a result of crossing borders. She addresses issues such as how identity is formed and reformed in different circumstances and settings, how gender differences can be built into future policy and planning, and how local activity relates to global politics and processes. In recounting the experiences and perceptions of migration of a Bosnian woman, the author shows that for women migration means not only movement, but also crossing gender boundaries: movement entails gender dislocation, and migrant women have to take on new social roles. In making the point that crossing boundaries constitutes both a physical and a symbolic act, she shows how global economic and social trends are carried out in local encounters.

The third part of the volume continues the exploration of the act of 'crossing European boundaries' as constructed by social actors, yet it moves to an examination of the redefinition of the 'local' that this act involves. Although some of the chapters in this part develop the examination of minority groups started earlier, they concentrate on geographical areas usually described as the 'periphery'. Yet the authors show that the 'periphery' is also directly affected by the act of 'crossing', albeit in different ways from the 'centres' of Europe.

In anthropological studies the concept of 'boundaries' has often been used to indicate social permeability as well as a focus on individual social actors. The distinction between 'border' and 'boundary' is examined in Kelleher's chapter, which refers to 'borders' rather than boundaries to indicate an unresolved national issue and conflict-ridden area in Northern Ireland. Yet Kelleher's approach focuses on the narratives of an individual female actor, who tries to discover the truth of her brother's death, to highlight the inappropriateness of the concept of 'border' when it comes to peoples' everyday lives in conflicted areas of Europe. He shows how research on transformation requires an understanding of how social actors seek to rebuild a new order with the instruments of the 'old' (i.e. 'tradition'). In recounting the narratives of how women make their own space in the context of global changes and contest the State's organisation of meaning, he argues that women have also resisted some of the projects of the powerful, and further asserts the significance of the 'local' in understanding the 'global'.

The concepts of intersubjectivity and interpersonal relations as a locus for the political are central in Evergeti's work. Evergeti's chapter makes an important shift from the official and contradictory discourses about the Muslim minority in Greece to an actual detailed study of people's ethnic identities in space. After examining the many contradictory accounts of what constitutes the so-called 'Muslim minority', their origins and multiple and often mutually exclusive links with Greece, Turkey and Islam, Evergeti deconstructs the politics behind such discourses. She focuses on the social actors and the complexity of their lives and interaction. This study enables her to draw the conclusion that geographical boundaries are actually closely linked with human interaction. In leaving aside official discourses surrounding Muslim minorities, she highlights how identity formation and living with others in a space are all about a flexible but also resilient interpersonal bargaining.

Deltsou's chapter is instead an example of an anthropological understanding of selfhood through fieldwork. Deltsou studies the interaction and stereotyping of immigrants from the former Soviet Union in Greece in relation to the ambivalent political position of Greece towards the idea of Europe.

Not only does she demonstrate through ethnography how political debates about the East and the West in Europe are understood through social actors' definitions of self, but also how such definitions are fluid, contradictory and negotiable according to the particular social context and interaction. Her conclusions are illuminating for the micro/macro level debate in anthropology: she observes that personal and social boundaries are highly permeable when it comes to casual social interaction, but become rigid and fixed when it comes to establishing one's authority and power over an-other, in other words when an official discourse is at play.

Ideology as a structure supporting ideas of cohesion and solidarity in Europe is internalised, interpreted and enacted by social actors. Conceptualisations of Europe by social actors is the main theme of Stacul's chapter, which addresses the tension created by discourses on modernity and other neo-liberal ideas by the social actors, the members of the nation-states. In his paper on the geographical margins of the Italian nation-state, Stacul argues that by adopting the 'bottom-up' approach in the exploration of the concept of Europe, we discover that collective European identity can coexist, in the minds of the social actors, with the ethic of individualism that is the product of a postmodern era. This coexistence is made possible by evoking the image of a supposedly depoliticised 'community of autonomous workers' living at the margins of the nation-state. This community, although territorialised, cannot be easily bound by conventional notions of collective identity, as the social actors comprising it are continuously engaged in a debate about their place in Europe as well as their understanding of modernity. Ideas of European unity and solidarity are thus challenged and the symbolic boundary as well as 'objective border' demarcating the Italian nation-state are being questioned and re-asserted by the social actors.

Thus, despite the variety of issues addressed, the chapters in this volume illustrate the potential contrast and constructed discrepancies between the political discourse versus the everyday experience of living in Europe, the social construction versus the self and intersubjective interaction. They show that there are different ways of thinking about Europe, and the idea of 'Europe' itself can be locally appropriated and manipulated in ways that are often at odds with the politics of European integration. This exploration, through creative and engaged participant observation, draws the conclusion that, as a matter of fact, the political and social are almost always embedded in the experience of self and the ordinariness of everyday life. In pointing to this significant aspect, this work shows that even an understanding of power has to allow for human agency, and therefore it cannot overlook the role of people as actors in larger social and economic processes. More importantly, this rich array of the practice of hands-on anthropology seems alone to constitute a satisfactory response, through setting an example, to the debates that have been initiated by postmodern anthropology.

The concept of 'boundary' has been extensively used in the anthropology of Europe to demonstrate change as well as the supposedly individual character of ethnic phenomena. Yet the contributions in this work show that a focus on European boundaries and a consideration of human agency are not mutually exclusive, but that they contribute to an understanding of one another. It is the ordinariness of everyday life that forms the background against which larger economic and social processes, like the act of 'crossing European boundaries', are debated and understood. In highlighting the multiple meanings attached to this act, the studies in this volume attempt to explain why Europe is a pervasive concept or why it is contested. Although the act of 'crossing' reduces the distances between the local and the global, it is the peoples in local settings that are directly affected by this process and respond to it through their own cultural categories. This volume shows that in ethnographic research 'boundaries' mean no more than the many ways in which social actors negotiate their position in complex and changing settings. In this respect, geography becomes crucial, not as a definite category, but rather as the very situational context in which people live and come to terms with a situation of flux and change. Therefore, boundaries are not abstract notions, but are time and space specific. They constitute the means through which human agency can be brought back into Europe.

## REFERENCES

Alvarez, R. 1995. 'The Mexican-US border: the making of an anthropology of borderlands'. *Annual Review of Anthropology* 24: 447–70.
Appadurai, A. 1990. 'Disjuncture and difference in the global cultural economy'. In *Global Culture*, ed. M. Featherstone. London, Sage.
Barry, A. 1993. 'The European Community and European government: harmonization, mobility and space'. *Economy and Society* 22, no. 3: 314–26.
Barth, F. 1969. 'Introduction'. In *Ethnic groups and Boundaries*, ed. F. Barth. London, Allen & Unwin.
Bellier, I. and T. Wilson. 2000. 'Building, imagining and experiencing Europe: institutions and identities in the European Union'. In *An Anthropology of the European Union*, eds I. Bellier and T. Wilson. Oxford, Berg.
Bloch, M. 2000. 'Postmodernism – The nature/culture debate in just another guise?'. *Irish Journal of Anthropology* 5: 111–15.
Borneman, J. and N. Fowler. 1997. 'Europeanization'. *Annual Review of Anthropology* 26: 487–514.
Clifford, J. 1988. *The Predicament of Culture*. Cambridge, MA, Harvard University Press.
Cohen, A.P. 1985. *The Symbolic Construction of Community*. London, Tavistock.

Donnan, H. and T. Wilson. 1999. *Borders: Frontiers of Identity, Nation and State*. Oxford, Berg.
Ferguson, J. and A. Gupta. 2002. 'Spatializing states: Toward an ethnography of neoliberal governmentality'. *American Ethnologist* 29, no. 4: 981–1002.
Fernandez, J. 1997. 'The North-South axis in European popular cosmologies and the dynamic of the categorical'. *American Anthropologist* 99, no. 4: 725–28.
Firth, R. 1981. 'Engagement and detachment: Reflections on applying social anthropology to social affairs'. *Human Organization* 40: 193–201.
Goddard, V., Llobera, J. and C. Shore. 1994. 'Introduction. The anthropology of Europe'. In *The Anthropology of Europe*, eds V. Goddard *et al.* Oxford, Berg.
Grimshaw, A. and K. Hart. 1995. 'The rise and fall of scientific ethnography'. In *The Future of Anthropology*, eds A. Ahmed and C. Shore. London, Athlone.
Gupta, A. and J. Ferguson. 1997. 'Beyond "culture": Space, identity, and the politics of difference'. In *Culture, Power, Place: Explorations in Critical Anthropology*, eds A. Gupta and J. Ferguson. Durham, N.C., Duke University Press.
Hacking, I. 1995. *Rewriting the Soul: Multiple Personality and the Sciences of Memory*. Princeton, Princeton University Press.
Hannerz, U. 1996. *Transnational Connections: Culture, People, Places*. London, Routledge.
Harvey, D. 1989. *The Condition of Postmodernity: An Enquiry into the Origins of Cultural Change*. Oxford, Blackwell.
Herzfeld, M. 1997. *Cultural Intimacy: Social Poetics in the Nation-State*. London, Routledge.
Holmes, D.R. 2000. *Integral Europe: Fast-Capitalism, Multiculturalism, Neo-Fascism*. Princeton, Princeton University Press.
Howes, D. 1996. *Cross-Cultural Consumption: Global Markets, Local Realities*. London, Routledge.
Johnston, R.J., Taylor, P. J. and M.J. Watts eds. 2002. *Geographies of Global Change: Remapping the World*. Oxford, Blackwell.
McDonald, M. 1996. '"Unity in diversity": Some tensions in the construction of Europe'. *Social Anthropology* 4, no. 1: 47–60.
McDonald, M. 2004. 'Debating the EU. A response to Shore and Abélès'. *Anthropology Today* 20, no. 3: 24.
Macdonald, S. ed. 1993. *Inside European Identities*. Oxford, Berg.
Merleau-Ponty, M. 1962. *The Phenomenology of Perception*. London, Routledge.
Murphy-Lejeune, E. 2002. *Student Mobility and Narrative in Europe: The New Strangers*. London, Routledge.
Nader, L. 1974. 'Up the anthropologist: Perspectives gained from studying up'. In *Reinventing Anthropology*, ed. D. Hymes. New York, Vintage.
Parman, S. 1998. 'Introduction: Europe in the anthropological imagination'. In *Europe in the Anthropological Imagination*, ed. S. Parman. Upper Saddle River, N.J., Prentice-Hall.
Raj, D.S. 2003. *Where are you From? Middle-class Migrants in the Modern World*. Berkeley, University of California Press.
Shore, C. 2000. *Building Europe: The Cultural Politics of European Integration*. London, Routledge.
Shore, C. and M. Abélès. 2004. 'Debating the European Union. An interview with Cris Shore and Marc Abélès'. *Anthropology Today* 20, no. 2: 10–14.

Shore, C. and D. Nugent, eds. 2002. *Elite Cultures: Anthropological Perspectives*. London, Routledge.

Westwood, S. and J. Williams. 1997. 'Imagining Cities'. In *Imagining Cities: Scripts, Signs, Memory*, eds S. Westwood and J. Williams. London, Routledge.

Wolf, E. 1974. 'American anthropologists and American society'. In *Reinventing Anthropology*, ed. D. Hymes. New York, Vintage.

# Part I: Institutional Crossings

# Chapter 2
# Crossing Boundaries through Education: European Schools and the Supersession of Nationalism

## Cris Shore and Daniela Baratieri

**Introduction: European Schools as Pioneers of 'Europeanisation'**

Modern man is not loyal to a monarch or a land or a faith, whatever he may say, but to a culture. And he is, generally speaking, gelded. (Gellner 1983: 36)

Our generation grew up in a framework of national consciousness. The television programmes we watched, the newspapers we read, the history, geography and literature we were taught – all these things shaped us to think in national terms. It is not easy to lose that. I don't know if a 'European consciousness' exists among EU staff here in Brussels. That is something that will probably develop in future generations. Our children are perhaps the true Europeans. (Comment by EU fonctionnaire, Brussels 1996)[1]

The two quotations above highlight the central problem addressed in this chapter; namely, the role of education in shaping the cognitive and cultural boundaries of the nation state in Europe and, by association, the boundaries of European identity and Europe itself. The first quote by Ernest Gellner sums up the main thesis of his book, *Nations and Nationalism*, that nations are social and historical constructs of relatively recent origin; 'a distinctive form of patriotism ... which becomes pervasive and dominant only under certain social conditions which in fact prevail in the modern world, and nowhere else' (Gellner 1983: 136). Recent and arbitrary as the rise of nations may be, nationalism still dominates the modern imagination and the nationalist principle, however challenged, remains the fundamental basis of political legitimacy. The second quotation, from an official in the European Commission, sums up the hope of many in the EU that a new political order might one day be created to transcend the logic of nation-states and nationalism and, in the words of one of the EU's founding treaties, lay the foundations for 'a destiny henceforth shared'.[2] That is what the EU, through its project of 'European construction', has set out to achieve. The paradox, however, is that while substantial progress towards that goal has been made in the areas of economics (reflected, for example, in intra-EU trade and the creation of the single market, European Central Bank and monetary union), politics and law (notably the expansion of European law and increasing Europeanisation of policy-making among member states), integration among the peoples of Europe has lagged behind visibly. The EU has created a formidable array of institutions for governing what it calls the 'European economic space', but it has been unable to create a corresponding 'European public'. The key problem the EU faces today, which potentially threatens its very survival, is that of what Bruno De Witte (1994) and others call 'cultural legitimacy';[3] how to elicit the active support of the citizens of Europe in whose name the EU justifies its existence? The question of legitimacy is, in turn, intimately bound up with the problem of creating a more salient European identity and demos; that is, a sense of 'We, the people of Europe'.[4]

It is within this wider political context that the issue of education acquires particular significance for understanding the changing boundaries and borders of Europe. Most Europeans continue to be educated in their national languages and national systems of schooling which, either implicitly or explicitly, strive to mould pupils into national subjects. Indeed, the school has long been the primary agent of cultural reproduction as far as the nation-state is concerned. The invention of mass education (one of the hallmarks of capitalist modernity) itself reflects an attempt by middle-class intelligentsias within the emergent nation-states to diffuse national consciousness among the populations over which they sought to govern. As Hobsbawm (1986: 167) observed, '[T]he progress of schools and universities measures that of nationalism, just as schools and especially universities became its most conscious champions'. In short, the idea of 'education for citizenship' has invariably been construed in a nationalist idiom which both reflects and reinforces existing cleavages based on nation and language.

Although small and few in number, the European Schools represent a challenge to this model of education.[5] These Schools also constitute an interesting site for the anthropological study of aspects of the European integration process that have, to date, remained curiously under-researched. Created and funded by the European Community, these schools exist primarily to provide education for the children of EU personnel, yet they also have an important symbolic function as institutions for forging a new kind of European subjectivity. As Desmond Swan declares:

> They are a novel, distinctive and challenging type of school, aiming to achieve things hitherto unattempted in the history of education. These Schools are remarkable primarily because of their unique multi-cultural, multilingual and multinational character and structure. In particular, they are implementing a new kind of pluralism in schooling, and pioneering a new educational paradigm, matched to the emerging identity of tomorrow's citizens of Europe. (Swan 1996: 6)

The aim of this chapter is to explore these claims, in the context of debates about nationalism, identity formation and European citizenship (Smith 1992), from an ethnographic perspective.[6] In what follows, we present the findings of an ESRC-funded anthropological study of the European Schools and their role in promoting what some call 'education for European citizenship' and others have termed 'Europeanisation' (Borneman and Fowler 1997; Shore 2000). Our investigation, carried out over a nine-month period during 1996, focused primarily on three Schools in Belgium, Italy and the U.K., respectively. But what, one might ask, has a study of education and schooling got to do with the wider theme of crossing geographical boundaries in Europe? Our argument is that education is closely linked to definitions and perceptions of State boundaries. Indeed, arguably the most fundamental of all 'categorical boundaries' are those that exist in the mind; in people's 'mental maps' and 'imagined geographies' (Said 1979; Anderson 1983). Almost a century ago, Durkheim and Mauss (1903) made a similar point when they concluded that the 'fundamental categories of thought' – or what they termed the elementary 'modes of classification' – are social and cultural. In fact, they are *political* as much as social (if such an arbitrary distinction can be made). The boundaries of inclusion and exclusion that serve to differentiate 'us' from 'them' tend to be matters less of 'geography' than of politics and ideology. And as historians and theorists of nationalism frequently remind us, the primary agent for reproducing such classifications – and for creating a sense of 'our nation' – has long been mass education.[7] To paraphrase Tom Nairn (1977), mass schooling – along with conscription and taxation – was the major vehicle through which the middle-class intelligentsias of Europe's emergent industrial States 'invited the masses into history' and transformed peasants into national citizens.

In short, ever since the emergence of industrial societies in Europe, mass education has been, and remains, the primary instrument through which the State constructs its nation and achieves what Gellner (1983: 140) called the necessary 'homogenous cultural branding of its flock'. The question we ask is how, if at all, does the European School system challenge this mutually reinforcing and seemingly axiomatic link between culture (construed in a national idiom), State and nation?

## European Schools: A Brief History

Contrary to what is often assumed, the European Schools were not founded in order to instil a 'European identity' but rather, to ensure the preservation of national educational traditions. As the preliminary draft for the creation of the first European School in 1953 declared: 'When their families come to live in Luxembourg, Community officials will want to know that their children can continue their education and in particular the study of their mother tongue.'[8] To quote one of the School's 'founding fathers', 'a comprehensive solution seemed obvious: the setting-up of an entirely new system of education based on an equal partnership and the combining of features from different national traditions.'[9]

While officials from the European Coal and Steel Community (ECSC), then located in Luxembourg, were reluctant to undertake such a responsibility, the driving force behind the first such primary school was an official from the European Court of Justice, Albert Van Houtte. Although its premises may have been shabby, it was reasonably well staffed, with one teacher from each member-state. The satisfied parents then pressed for the establishment of a secondary school where pupils' qualifications would be recognised throughout the member-states of the European Economic Community. For this they had to turn to the authority of the member-states themselves. By 1958 the School had a statute as well as a 'European Baccalaureate'. The European School in Luxembourg had been joined, as EURATOM and the Common Market were created, by one in Brussels (Uccle). Thereafter, other Schools were opened at Mol (Belgium) and Varese (Italy) in 1960, at Karlsruhe in 1962, at Bergen (Holland) in 1962, another in Brussels (Woluwe) and one in Munich in 1976, at Culham (U.K.) in 1978, and lastly another secondary in Brussels (Ixelles) in 1999.

It is worth looking in some detail at the founding document of the European Schools. While there have been many modifications – and, indeed, a new statute agreed in 1994 following the accession of new member-states to the EU – the essentials have remained more or less unchanged since 1954. The philosophy and ethos that form the main 'pillars' of the European Schools are based on three fundamental principles. The first is that education should be in the official languages of the member-states. The second is that the European Schools should have a syllabus and timetable which synthesise the different national systems, allowing any member-state national to feel comfortable coming into it from home or indeed having to go back for whatever reason into the national system at home. The synthesis of member-states' syllabi was a precursor to the European Baccalaureate, holders of which, the statute assured, would 'enjoy in their respective countries all the benefits attaching to the possession of the diploma or certificate awarded at the end of the secondary school in those countries' (Van Houtte 1978: 45). The third pillar upon which the European Schools rest is the idea that these Schools should not merely attempt to integrate the different national systems under one roof, but rather that there should be joint classes 'to encourage ... mutual understanding and cultural exchange between pupils'.[10] In the 1994 statute, which replaced that of 1957, this article reads, 'in order to encourage the unity of the School, to bring pupils of the different language sections together and to foster mutual understanding, certain subjects shall be taught in joint classes'. It also adds that 'the "European dimension" shall be developed in the curricula'.[11]

These principles, which were formulated when the European Community (EC) had six members, have remained in essence unchanged as the Community grew from nine, to twelve and then fifteen members.[12] This is not to say that there have not been ups and downs in the way the Schools have been viewed by the EC or indeed by the member-states. Most significant in this context has been the highly critical report by the European Parliament in 1993, which expressed strong feelings of unease among MEPs and others about the European Schools' lack of accountability, excessive costs and apparent failure to live up to the EU's avowed principle of 'justice for all'; that is, the Schools were charged with encouraging elitism (Oostlander 1993). Nevertheless the Schools continue to grow. On the fortieth anniversary of its foundation one of the Schools' top administrators, seemingly oblivious to this criticism, still felt confident enough to proclaim that '[t]he vision of Jean Monnet has been fulfilled with the European spirit that reigns in the European Schools' (Olson 1996: 136). Among supporters and parents there remains plenty of confidence that the European Schools are not only here to stay but also that they are, indeed, pioneers of a new type of European education.

## Structure, Governance and Funding

The ten European Schools host a total population of pupils numbering over fifteen thousand, ranging from nursery to the end of secondary school age. Over six thousand of these pupils are found in the three Brussels Schools, a further three-and-a-half thousand are in Luxembourg and roughly one thousand each attend the six other Schools. The teacher:pupil ratio throughout the Schools is approximately one:fifteen (a ratio that one only finds, in Britain at least, in the most elite of private schools). The teachers are temporarily seconded from the member-states' national education systems and they are represented very approximately in proportion to the population of the country they come from, except for those from Belgium and Luxembourg.[13] How is this large human resource, distributed over six countries and functioning now in more than nine languages, actually administered?

At the top of the European Schools' administrative hierarchy is the Board of Governors. This body is made up of ministers of education (or their representatives) from each of the EU's member-states, a member of the European Commission, a representative from the Schools' staff and a lay member of the Parents' Association. The latter two members of the Board are permitted to vote only on strictly 'educational' matters (as opposed to more general matters of finance and administration). The Board of Governors is legally responsible for all decisions concerning finance, administration and education in the Schools and, significantly, it is not accountable to the European Parliament. It also consults regularly with ministerial representatives and with representatives of the teachers and parents of all the European Schools, as well as with representatives of associated institutions, which includes institutions that are not part of the EU but nevertheless have the special privilege of being granted places at the European Schools, such as NATO and Eurocontrol. The permanent liaison between the Schools themselves and the Board of Governors is carried out by the Board's Secretary-General and his deputy who together run the central administrative office of the Schools in Brussels. They chair the administrative board of each school and pass on decisions made by the Governors. Servicing the Board is a series of committees and sub-committees that report on financial and educational matters. There is also a Board of Inspectors whose mandate is to bring proposals before the governing body. This Board is made up of two inspectors seconded from each member-state's national inspectorate. Part of its job is to monitor standards in the Schools and contribute to the development of the School's unified curriculum. Regular meetings also take place between representatives of the Parents' Associations of each School. The head teacher of each European School is appointed by the Board of Governors for a period of seven to nine years and, while the idea of 'national quotas' is anathema to the Schools' ethos, there is nonetheless something of a national rota in their preferment. The head teachers themselves do periodically meet up to discuss common strategy and problems. While the Board of Governors proposes each School's annual budget and makes most of the important decisions in the day-to-day running of the School, it is quite clear that, in fact, individual Schools have very little autonomy. Each School, although it may have some particularities, is quite clearly part of a total system.

The buildings that the European Schools occupy are provided free of charge by the member-state in which they are located. Salaries for seconded 'expatriate' teachers are paid at a fixed rate by the member-states from which they are seconded.[14] Teachers receive very generous pay and allowances. Salaries in 2000 were roughly three times that which a teacher in Britain of equivalent seniority would receive. Furthermore, the children of School staff, like those of EU *fonctionnaires*, are exempt from payment of tuition fees. There are also a significant number of locally recruited temporary teachers who are paid at local salary levels out of the general budget of the School. Member-states will also pay for the inspection of the Schools, as well as for any contribution that the Board of Governors deems necessary.

The Schools also receive financial contributions from certain non-Community organisations (such as NATO). These contributions, in effect, buy access to the Schools for the children of employees in these organisations. The bulk of the money, however, is contributed directly by the European Community, which, as Swan notes (1996: 71), amounted to some sixty-eight percent of the total Schools' budget in 1990. Given the small number of pupils that the European Schools cater for, their overall expenditure is extremely high. As the European Parliament's Oostlander Report noted, the average cost per pupil attending a European School is eighty-three percent higher than the average cost per pupil in a Flemish school – and Schools in The Netherlands are themselves extremely costly in comparison with the European norm (Oostlander 1993: 35). Somewhat inevitably, this has led to heated debates and tensions within the European Parliament and elsewhere whenever changes in the School budget or funding mechanism are discussed.

In the European Schools there are two categories of pupil. The first are those from 'entitled' families, that is children of people working directly for an EU institution, or an institution with which the Board of Governors has already concluded an agreement. The second category includes both the children of EU nationals who are not employees of Community institutions, and at one distance further removed, children who are from 'outside' the Community completely. This latter group (who are classified as the 'non-entitled') are obliged to pay school fees and are granted places only when vacancies cannot be filled otherwise. Fees are not very expensive, however. For example, in 1996 sending a child to the European School at Culham in Oxfordshire cost only £659 per year for the nursery, £926 for the primary school and £1,256 for the secondary school. Moreover, the fee for sending a second child to the school is halved.

Considering that the majority of the European Schools' population is located in Brussels and Luxembourg, it is fair to say that the European Schools still cater mostly for the children of people working for the EU. The word 'still' is used here advisedly as the last fifteen or so years have witnessed a gradual decline in the percentage of 'entitled' pupils attending the other European Schools.[15]

### 'Laboratories for Cultivating the European Idea'? Ethos and Ideals

They are a novel, distinctive and challenging type of school, aiming to achieve things hitherto unattempted in the history of education'. (Swan 1996: 6)

To answer the question, 'What exactly do the European Schools stand for?', one must first acknowledge the array of agents acting on different levels that make up these institutions. In this section we will try to describe and analyse what EU officials themselves have to say about the ethos of these Schools, and how these relate to, and rework, the official narratives about the function and ethos of the Schools. One point that was emphasised by virtually all commentators and interviewees was the perceived 'pioneering' and experimental nature of these Schools. As a resolution of the European Parliament summed it up,

> the European Schools are unique in the world in being multilingual and multinational and therefore constitute an irreplaceable laboratory for the creation of a European school system.[16]

The notion of European Schools as 'laboratories' for cultivating the 'European idea' was first expressed by Jean Monnet, the French statesman and EU 'founding father'. As he perceived it:

> Educated side by side, untroubled from infancy by divisive prejudices, acquainted with all that is great and good in the different cultures, it will be borne upon them as they mature that they belong together. Without ceasing to look to their own lands with love and pride, they will become in mind Europeans, schooled and ready to complete and consolidate the work of their fathers before them, to bring into being a united and thriving Europe.[17]

As the same document informs us, these words – like holy relics, have been 'sealed, in parchment, into the foundation stones of all the Schools.' From the point of view of their supporters, the European schools are an 'experiment' in social engineering; what the former president of the European Commission Jacques Delors (1993: 15) called 'a sociological and pedagogical laboratory' the primary objective of which is, as Robert Schuman put it, 'to Europeanise without de-nationalising'.[18]

Co-existing with these ideals and objectives, albeit in striking tension with them, is the reason why the Schools were founded and continue to be financed; namely, as a service for the mobile population of transnational EU employees. Monnet, Schuman and Delors were not the only politicians to entertain high hopes for the European Schools as vehicles for forging 'European consciousness'. According to Egon Klepsch (1993: 13), former president of the European Parliament, the European Schools were designed to 'foster young Europeans' who would go on to be 'the political decision-makers of tomorrow'. The European Schools are thus perceived by their advocates not only as sites for creating a new European identity and subjectivity ('Young Europeans'), but also as a crucible for European political elite-formation (the supposedly denationalised 'political decision-makers of tomorrow').

The remainder of this chapter sets out to examine these claims. It asks: How effectively do the European Schools live up to these ideals and what exactly does education for a post-national European citizenship look like? How do teachers and pupils perceive that education and what difficulties do the schools face in achieving their objectives? What kinds of subjectivity are they helping to foster, and can these Schools provide a model for mass education in the 'Europe of tomorrow'? To answer these questions it is important to examine how certain claims are translated into practice, including what staff and students themselves perceive as the Schools' most salient and distinctive features.

## Teaching Social Sciences in a Foreign Language

> History, geography and general subjects will be taught in two parallel groups: one of the groups will be taught in German and the other in French. Parents will be free to choose which, but all pupils will be obliged to follow these lessons in a language other than their own.[19]

How does this statement, taken from the Recommendations of the School Committee, compare with that of the European Schools foundation stones? Although of the same period and both sanctioned by the School authorities, they stand in clear contradiction. It is, from a theoretical point of view, quite important to stress how contradictions can live side-by-side in the minds of people involved in a project like the constitution of these Schools and can be taken as the main source of inspiration for further speeches or practice. There are practical ways of dealing with contradictions of this sort: one way is to omit the first part of the foundation stone,[20] another is just to leave it in the same magazine and hope that few will notice it.[21] It could certainly be said that pupils do learn 'national history' in their mother tongue before secondary school, so why change this when the pupils are more mature?

Although officially portrayed as a matter of 'language development strategies', perhaps the most noteworthy aspect of this is that the teacher will hardly ever share the same nationality with his/her pupils. At the heart of this decision seems to be an explicit attempt to separate nationality from the teaching of sensitive subjects such as history. As one staff member summed it up: 'My history is my propaganda, your history is your propaganda.'[22] And as Desmond Swan, the most prominent historian of the European Schools affirms: 'Teaching History to non-compatriots may well compel the teachers to question assumptions which never needed questioning on home ground, in order to ensure that the standpoint taken is free of national bias' (Swan 1996: 51–2).

All those teachers of history and geography we interviewed stated, in one way or another, that there is something very special in what they have to do. As one teacher summed it up:

> The difference in being a teacher of history or geography in a European School is that apart from also giving a language lesson we develop a special sensitivity about our pupil's nationalities. You try to include various elements of the history of each nation in your courses, including particular key moments, so that nobody feels left out. ... I

guess the other we do is implement a holistic European point of view rather than a national [one]. [It's] certainly different from teaching British history as something 'separate' from European history. One other thing; we try to select themes or topics which are appropriate to the topics of the European Schools, and that have a European dimension. So, for example, you are unlikely, for example, to sum up arts and crafts of the respective 'Golden age' in isolation [to the rest of Europe].[23]

This extract is also important because it introduces quite vividly a tension lived by these teachers between an 'it ought to be' and an actual 'is'.

Two teachers pondered: 'What resources and information have you got that are particularly outstanding? The books that we use are quite good, but not ... What? ... Special'.[24] The issue of textbooks seems to be a sore point for all the teachers, but particularly for those who end up using the same texts as are used in their respective national education systems. Staff strive constantly to resist this. However, the utility of that resistance is viewed with suspicion. Many teachers see the superficiality caused by the sheer breadth of the Baccalaureate's programme[25] and the problems related to the pupils' command of language(s)[26] as posing overriding difficulties to the project of writing 'proper European textbooks'.[27] As one of the head teachers in Brussels affirmed: 'In History and Geography we take original sources, so you get a view of World War Two through original English, French, German sources. And of course, the kids can read them in the original!'[28] Perhaps lessons dealing with the Second World War constitute a special case. However, lessons on the Cold War observed during this research were a different matter. This 'it ought to be' is something genuinely felt by teachers, but it remains, nonetheless, a slogan that has to be interpreted and put into practice. It is quite clear to the teachers that they are reducing, rather than developing and extending, the premises from which they start. What they seem to be saying is that it is not just about teaching British history 'in a European context', or including a bit of history from all the countries currently in the EU. This, rather than being seen as clumsiness or ineptitude, reflects certain tensions in one of the key arenas into which official resolutions such as 'the introduction of a European dimension in education'[29] become interpreted and reinvented within certain unspoken parameters. The slogan is successful, it is a source of identification, precisely because it is assimilated and taken for granted, and thus becomes a 'naturalised' and unquestioned motor for action.

## Teaching through 'Other' Languages

When somebody says: 'Hey, Gianfranco, will tu sa door even zumachen,' everybody understands it immediately. (Mira Jeukens 6E Secondary School)[30]

You lose interest and comprehension of history because of the hard language.[31]

'Languages' is the European Schools' keyword. The issues linked with languages are all-pervasive. At first sight it appears as if sharing the diverse official languages of other EU member-states is something unproblematic and quite natural on the School's premises, and perhaps it is you, the 'monoglot' outsider, who is the odd one out. However, it soon becomes apparent that this is not the case. As one sports teacher observes:

> We find, especially with the little ones, that we are using two or three different languages to say the same thing. So we get a form of – and I know it sounds absolutely dreadful – 'Eurospeak'. You get just enough sense of communication in one language before you lose the attention of the other pupils. They can't understand you, so you have to shift into another language, and then perhaps a third language.

Added to this, he says, teachers must develop a 'sixth or seventh sense' in order to understand whether classroom noise is pupils helpfully translating what the teacher says for each other or just conventional chatting.[32]

There is a certain amount of 'disfunctionality' in having to cope with different languages at several levels. This lends a very different impression to the image promoted by the Schools themselves, and carefully nurtured through slogans such as 'Unity in diversity'. But what constitutes the strongest bridge between these inconsistencies, and what allows them to coexist in people's minds, is offered in terms of 'experimentation'. That is, any disfunctionality is assigned to the 'Schools' self-image as a 'laboratory'. For the most part, however, slogans about the 'equality of esteem' between languages carry the whole process forward. This, as Swan notes, is a fundamental aspect of the Schools' ethos:

> The equality [of esteem among the member-states and among the major European cultural and linguistic groups represented within them] is established and expressed primarily in the structuring of the Schools into language sections, each of which uses a different major European language as its everyday medium of instruction. (Swan 1996: 10–11)

In practice, however, this 'equality' is a fiction. One is reminded of the Orwellian maxim (summed up in *Animal Farm*) that while 'all animals are equal', some are 'more equal than others'.

This emphasis on 'equality of esteem among the major European linguistic groups' also tends to fade into insignificance when one notes the degree of linguistic diversity that exists within Europe today. As Coulby observes: 'There are nearly two hundred languages spoken by children in the schools of London ... The impact of these [immigrant] populations on the cultural and educational map of the EU is profound.'[33] Equality of esteem among the member-states is also compromised by the creation of a special class of languages, the so-called 'working languages'. Under this heading, English,

French and German become classified as *langues vehiculaires* and occupy a privileged space. This clearly exemplifies the inequalities between what are effectively 'dominant' and 'recessive' European languages. Being *langues vehiculaires* bestows particular prestige and status on these languages. Thus, only 'working languages' are offered as an option for first foreign language, which is the only one taught from a very early age. There is also a tendency for important articles or communications to be written in one of these languages and, as noted above, the teachers and textbooks for History, Geography and Social Sciences will be from the countries where these languages are spoken.

The *langues vehiculaires* policy illustrates the cultural hegemony of the EU's 'core' member-states. It is hard to imagine that schools which do not enjoy the same kind of budget as the European Schools will not reinforce this privileging of certain languages by always choosing to teach the most 'important languages'. One can easily foresee the wide-ranging implications that this trend has, in the accrual of important jobs and not least in the creation of a common identity within the EU.

## Preparation for European Citizenship?

> If at national level, 1% of all children answer this definition [gifted children], we can presume that in the privileged populations of our schools, the percentage will be appreciably higher. (Smith 1995: 7)

The student population of the European Schools is overwhelmingly middle class and privileged; of this fact there can be little doubt. As one teacher puts it: 'Frankly the general population of the Schools has no problem with money ... after all if one is employed by the EU one is middle class!'[34] As such they are, of course, in no way representative of Europe's 'migrant populations'. Guy Neave writing in 1984 summed it up as follows:

> Community civil servants, though it might be indelicate to say so, are a professional substratum of a migrant population numbering around 12,000.000. By according separate establishments for some 10,560 pupils and endowing them with separate status from those attended by the remaining 1,435.000 in the public schools of member-states, the Commission's stance would appear at odds on the one hand with its general policy for the education of migrants' children and on the other, also closely associated with this same group, the principle of equality of educational opportunity. If the public education of host countries is good enough for their nationals and [in particular] for the children of immigrants in manual occupations, there can, in equity, be no case to make in support of special facilities for the children of those migrants whose occupation places them in the professions. (Neave 1984: 132)[35]

Neave underlines the point that a school system created with special resources for a minority inevitably falls into the category of an 'elite' school. This is confirmed in the Schools' very high academic standards as well as their clientele. As one ex-pupil writes:

> If we apply another Darwinian category, the mental (or in our case, academic) one, our school also seems to be extremely fit and healthy. Just last year a record baccalaureate of 9.74 was scored, and many baccalaureates were in the category above 8.5. Many pupils go on to prestigious universities and are successful there. In addition, various pupils' entries in national and international competitions in arts and sciences have been successful.[36]

In 1995 the European Commission proposed that EU member-states should promote knowledge of three 'Community' languages, the aim of which was to create 'a trademark or seal of quality to be bestowed on European classes in schools ... The promoting of such a trademark would give access to further funding from the Member States' (*Commissione Europea* 1995: 70). It does not take much analysis to conclude that the European Schools would have all the pre-requisites for such a mark of distinction. Indeed, the proposal is based largely on the model they provide. Certainly official recognition of this kind tends to boost the sense of purpose and self-confidence that informs the Schools' ethos. The pupils themselves are well aware of being 'special' and are perhaps even a little blasé about it; as a pupil commented: 'we're a European School, that means that many nationalities have to study together'; 'nobody has a clue how lucky they are.'[37]

It could be inferred that most of the pupils feel 'elected' to something very exclusive. Indeed, 10 percent of pupils, when asked: 'What do you dislike about your school?',[38] answered along these lines: 'snobby', 'a privileged cocoon' and 'the mentality people have; they tend to look down on other people'.[39] That said, one should bear in mind that the pupils seem to disagree with the official view of the role of these Schools and with Hoyem's claim that 'the European Schools are political schools. Do not be ashamed to say it loud. We teach new Europeans for a new Europe'.[40] This appears to be confirmed elsewhere. In the section on 'the School' of the questionnaire delivered by the councillors' group 'Ascolto' at the Varese School, some 50–80 percent of respondents agreed that 'This is a European School above all because the teachers and the students come from the countries of Europe', while 'the school prepares you to become a citizen of Europe' was chosen by very few (less than 20–30 percent).[41] Similarly, if the pupils had a say in the Schools' aims the majority would opt for 'preparing people for university and/or the world of work', while only 10 percent would choose 'the development of the social and moral characteristics of citizenship'.[42] Pointing to this discrepancy is important not so much for assessing how 'European' the pupils feel, but for highlighting how the different actors in the school, with their different roles and contradictions, may live and see the same reality in dissimilar ways.

Perhaps it is worth adding that ex-pupils seem to realise and value their distinctive 'European' education once they are confronted with the 'outside world' of university.[43] It is then that they feel *sui generis*.[44] According to one MEP (Elles 1988: 79), 'the European Schools are the blueprint for a future education system for all Europeans. It is incumbent upon all involved with them, therefore, to ensure that they take the lead and set the standards.' This, however, is something that needs to be questioned. There is no justification, certainly even in the official politics of the EU itself, for considering children of people working for EU institutions as in some way more 'citizens of Europe' than, say, the child of a dock worker from Belfast or a shepherd from Sicily. It is surely in being an Ulsterman (and British) or a Sicilian (and Italian) that one expresses one's 'European-ness'. If this is not the case then 'true Europeans' become only those who have access to all those things, '*la valigia per l'Europa*' ('suitcase for Europe'),[45] that go to make up how a model European citizen is defined.

The idea that this 'suitcase for Europe' will be acquired through an education at the European Schools seems to have been internalised by their pupils. When asked where the future was likely to take them, most pupils refused to give a definitive answer, leaving their options open. This kind of answer can only come from young people entering a social class that does not need to worry about obtaining a specific job on leaving secondary school and, perhaps, confirms their status as a highly adaptable and mobile group in the top ranks of Europe's elite in what Swan (1996: 7) calls 'the dawning of post-nationalist Europe'.

## Conclusion

To conclude, let us return to the questions that framed this discussion. Are the European Schools creating non-nationalist – or 'post-nationalist' – Europeans, as some claim? Are the children really free of the cultural baggage of nationalism? Certainly, the schools succeed in making their pupils feel different and special, but they do not necessarily replace or displace a sense of national identity. Children at the European Schools in Brussels, it should be remembered, are still subject to the socialising influences of their parents who, as de-territorialised expatriates, often have an exaggerated and somewhat atavistic sense of their own national identity. Furthermore, the diffusion of cable television in Brussels (introduced over thirty years ago) means that most pupils now have access to their national television channels. Among School staff and pupils there is a rather vague definition of what 'being European' means, although a strong sense of being European prevails. To some extent their European identity is constructed in opposition to the nation-state (seen as the culprit responsible for two world wars) and its 'monoglot' national subjects. It is also founded in part on an appreciation of 'Western civilisation' as the source of Europe's shared cultural heritage. Ex-pupils are also highly mobile, unfettered by traditional boundaries of class and language, and tend to view the whole of Europe as their domestic labour market. However, there is no evidence, as yet, to support the hypothesis that they will naturally gravitate towards jobs in the EU institutions, as their parents have done, although this is a possibility that cannot be ruled out.

Are the European School pupils creating a new type of supra-national European persona? This is perhaps a question that we cannot answer. What they have created is a unique and intensive educational environment the experience of which seems to have a profound influence on the formation and character of its pupils. They are undoubtedly 'hybridised' individuals who have grown up between national cultures, never quite fully integrated or socialised into any single national culture. Mark Leonard, a former pupil at the School in Uccle and currently Director of the Foreign Policy Research Centre in London, summed it up thus:

> If you read some of this rhetoric, it is about creating 'European citizens', but there is no content to European citizenship. What the European Schools do is something a lot healthier, which is to create very mongrelised national citizens. They do eat up more of your life than other schools. They are long days and they try to pack a lot in. In terms of the drawbacks, I think the main one is that you become socialised, but it is very much within an elite group. So you don't necessarily learn much about average opinion in your own country. You miss out on key elements of what your national 'cultural capital' is because you're excluded from it. But all these things are compensated by the fact that you have got highly educated parents who come from particular backgrounds. ... The main problem is simply that you are surrounded by very privileged people. It's also very 'white', because it's the EU. There was only one black guy in our entire year. But I can't think of anywhere I would rather have gone to school in terms of the educational experiences. I've got better educational experience than any of my peers.[46]

Rather than offering firm conclusions, then, we end with a few tentative thoughts that we hope might help to stimulate further debate and research. A key point we have highlighted is the image and identity the Schools project in their discourse about themselves. The most frequently used expressions linked to these Schools, or this 'educational system', are 'pioneering', 'pilot', 'experimental' and 'laboratories'. These terms inevitably presuppose a certain leading role that these School see themselves as having in relation to other schools. When teachers and head teachers were asked if it was foreseeable that this 'pilot' system could be extended throughout the EU, however, all agreed that this was not feasible on account of the Schools' prohibitively high costs.[47]

Despite the construction of another School in Brussels and Mr Van Houtte's repeated calls for the establishment of a European School in every capital of the Union, it is generally recognised that these Schools will never be able to accommodate a mass public. They are, by definition, exclusive and elitist. But then, so too were schools and universities at the dawn of the age of nationalism in Europe.

## NOTES

1. Fieldwork interviews, Brussels 1996.
2. This phrase was enshrined in the preamble to the 1951 ECSC Treaty.
3. See especially Wallace and Smith (1995).
4. For a more detailed analysis of the relationship between European identity and the problem of legitimacy, see in particular Garcia (1994); and Shore (2000).
5. There are currently ten schools. The first, created in Luxembourg in 1953, had seventy-two students and six teachers. By 1993 this figure had climbed to fourteen thousand students and one thousand teachers (Fischbach 1993: 16).
6. This research was carried out under the aegis of an ESRC-funded project on 'EU civil servants and cultural policy' (project number R000236097). The authors would like to acknowledge their gratitude to the ESRC for its generous support.
7. See in particular Anderson (1983), Gellner (1983) and Hobsbawm (1990).
8. Cited in *Schola Europaea* special edition for the 25th anniversary of the European Schools 1978: 74.
9. Marcel Decombis quoted in *Schola Europaea* (1978: 53).
10. Article 4 of the 1957 statute of the European Schools.
11. See the 1994 'Convention Defining the Statute of the European Schools' (London, HMSO: 4).
12. The only significant differences between the 1994 and 1957 Statutes are concerning administration.
13. This information is gleaned from statistics supplied by the Central Office of the European Schools, Brussels 1996.
14. These staff salaries comprise about 22 percent of the European School's overall budget.
15. For a more detailed analysis of this trend, see Swan (1996: 108–11).
16. See OJ No. C 125/64–7 April 1987.
17. European Schools (n.d.): 7.
18. Robert Schuman, cited in Delors (1993: 15).
19. Extract from the recommendations of the School Committee, chaired by Mr. Van Houtte (27 April 1953) in *Schola Europaea* (1978: 75).
20. As in the European Schools Official Brochure (Brussels, 1996: 7).
21. Ole Due, President of the Court of Justice of the European Communities letter, cited in Olsen (1993: 136).
22. Fieldwork interviews, October 1996.
23. Fieldwork interviews with teachers of history and geography at the European School of Brussels 1/Uccle (October 1996).
24. Fieldwork interviews with teachers at the European School, Brussels, October 1996.
25. This was confirmed in interviews with history teachers at the Brussels 2 (Woluwe) European School (November 1996).
26. This, at least, was proposed by staff at the European School at Culham (Fieldwork interviews, June 1997).

27. A point confirmed in numerous fieldwork interviews.
28. Fieldwork interview with John Marshall, headmaster of the European School of Brussels 1/Uccle (June 1993).
29. This phrase recurs throughout official EU documents, reports and statements. See, for example, OJ 20 December 1976, para. iv, sect. 5; G. Neave's essay (1984: 123), 'The European Dimension in Education'; and the 'Resolution of the European Council adopted 24 May 1988 on the European Dimension in Education', reprinted in Hopkins (1998: 123–29).
30. Cited in *Europese School Bergen 1963–1988*, Bergen, 1988: 17.
31. 'A question of identity' (1996–1997: q.n.59: 16, note 7)
32. Interview with teacher at the European School of Brussels 2/Woluwe (Brussels, 7 November 1996).
33. Cited in Sultana (1995: 131).
34. Fieldwork interviews, History teacher at the European School of Varese (Italy), March 1997.
35. However, Desmond Swan is dismissive of these criticisms. In his view, 'this argument would have more validity if the EC as such did, in fact, have full responsibility for the education of all its immigrants, or again if it were ever to be accorded a determining voice in formulating education policy as a whole for the member states. But neither is the case to date' (Swan 1996: 14). The EU's growing role in shaping European education policy is heatedly discussed by Sultana (1995; 1996) and Ryba (1996).
36. Teichmann, S. (a 7th year pupil at the European School at Karlsruhe), 'Birthday greeting to the European School for their 40th anniversary' in *Schola Europaea* 124.
37. 'A question of identity' (1996–1997: q.n.74, n. 2: 4).
38. 'A question of identity' (1996–1997: n.4: 4).
39. 'A question of identity' (1996–1997: respectively q.n.62-36-29, n. 4: 4).
40. Hoyem, T. (headmaster of the European School at Culham), letter to J. Olsen in the occasion of the Schools' 40th anniversary, in *Schola Europaea* (1993: 122).
41. 'The school' (questions 1–10: 1–3) in the questionnaire designed and delivered by Varese School's councillors' group 'Ascolto' for the 5th–7th-year pupils of that school in 1995–1996.
42. 'The school' (question 2: 1).
43. It would certainly be very productive to dedicate a study to the ex-pupils of these schools, since the data available is nearly non-existent.
44. This has been deduced from the material previously discussed, which is perhaps somewhat biased since most of the testimonies come from ex-pupils who chose to write for the Schools' pedagogical bulletin.
45. Steiwer, J., Head teacher of the European School at Varese (1996: 15).
46. Interviews, London, July 2000.
47. Although, in another context Swan (1996: 25) points out that maintaining so many language sections and recruiting high quality staff from abroad is inevitably going to be very expensive.

# References

Anderson, B. 1983. *Imagined Communities: Reflections on the Origins and Spread of Nationalism*. London, Verso.

Borneman, J. and N. Fowler. 1997. 'Europeanization'. *Annual Review of Anthropology* 26: 487–514.

Commissione Europea. 1995. *Libro bianco su istruzione e formazione: insegnare e apprendere, verso la società conoscitiva*. Luxembourg, European Commission.

Delors, J. 1993. 'Letter to the European Schools'. Reprinted in *Schola Europaea: 1953–1993*, Brussels, European School.

De Witte, B. 1994. 'Cultural Legitimation: Back to the Language Question'. In *European Identity and the Search for Legitimacy*, ed. S. Garcia. London, Pinter.
Durkheim, E. and M. Mauss. 1963 [1903]. *Primitive Classification*. London, Cohen and West.
Elles, J. 1988. 'How I see the future of the European School system'. In *Schola Europaea: Culham 1978–1988*, Culham, European School.
European Schools, n.d. *The European Schools*. Brussels, European School.
Fischbach, M. 1993. 'Message aux Ecoles Européennes'. *Schola Europaea: 1953–1993*, Brussels, European School.
Garcia, S. ed. 1994. *European Identity and the Search for Legitimacy*. London, Pinter.
Gellner, E. 1983. *Nations and Nationalism*. Oxford, Blackwell.
Hobsbawm, E. 1986. *The Age of Revolution: 1789–1848*. London, Abacus.
Hopkins K. 1998. *Into the Heart of Europe*. London, Routledge.
Klepsch, E. 1993. 'A Birthday Greeting to the European Schools'. In *Schola Europaea. Commemorative Book, 1953–1993*, ed. J. Olsen. Brussels, European Schools.
Nairn, T. 1977. *The Break-Up of Britain*. London, New Left Books.
Neave, G. 1984. 'The European dimension in education'. In *The EEC and Education*, Stoke-on-Trent, Trentham Books.
Olson, J. 1996. 'Where do we come from? ... And where do we go from here?'. In *Schola Europaea. Commemorative Book 1953–1993*. Brussels, European School.
Oostlander, A. 1993. *Report on the proposal for a council decision on the conclusion by the European economic community and the European atomic energy community of the convention defining the statute of the European schools* (com(93) – c3-0142/93). Brussels, Europ 26262 Session Documents.
Ryba, R. 1996. '"Of facts, fictions and the EU" and "the power of the European union in educational matters"'. In *Educational Dilemmas: Debates and Diversity*, Vol.3, eds K. Watson *et al*. London, Continuum International Publishing.
Said, E. 1979. *Orientalism*. Harmondsworth, Penguin.
Shore, C. 2000. *Building Europe: The Cultural Politics of European Integration*. London, Routledge.
Smith, A.D. 1992. 'National identity and the idea of European unity'. *International Affairs* 68, no. 1: 55–76.
Smith, A. 1995. 'The special needs of gifted children in the European schools'. In *Schola Europaea*. Brussels, European School.
Steiwer, J. 1996. *La valigia per l'Europa: la Schola Europea*. Bergamo, Soroptimist.
Sultana, R.G. 1995. 'A uniting Europe, a dividing education? Euro-centrism and the curriculum'. *International Studies in Sociology of Education* 5, no. 2: 115–44.
Sultana, R.G. 1996. 'The European union and its educational agenda: a wolf in sheep's clothing?' In *Educational Dilemmas: Debates and Diversity* Vol.3, eds K. Watson *et al.* London, Continuum International Publishing.
Swan, D. 1996. *A Singular Pluralism. European Schools 1984–1994*. Dublin, Institute of Public Administration.
Van Houtte, A. 1978. 'The Legal constitution of the European schools'. In *Schola Europaea*, Brussels, European School.
Wallace, W. and J. Smith. 1995. 'Democracy or technocracy? European integration and the problem of popular consent'. *West European Politics* 18, no. 3: 137–57.

# Chapter 3
# Neo-Liberal Nationalism: Ethnic Integration and Estonia's Accession to the European Union

Gregory Feldman

### Introduction[1]

This chapter's aims are two-fold. First, it examines how European Union (EU) accession reinforces, rather than transcends, the nation-state around the issues of citizenship and integration policy. This point is demonstrated by showing how the European Commission (EC) and the Nordic countries actively support the Estonian government's main ethnic integration policy entitled *State Programme: 'Integration in Estonian Society 2000–2007'*.[2] This document, aimed at creating a multicultural society, ironically, seeks the establishment of the 'Estonian cultural domain'. Second, this chapter illustrates how nationalism and the nation-state are not necessarily threatened by the rise of neo-liberal governance in Europe. Instead, Estonia's integration policy demonstrates how neo-liberal strategies of social regulation can be tailored to meet the State's nationalist agenda. This tactic appears in the *State Programme*, and its precursor projects, and it is inextricably linked to three goals shared by the Estonian, EC and Nordic officials involved in its upper-level management. The first two goals are the security of the Estonian nation-state and security in northern Europe. 'Security' in both cases is conceived rather traditionally, as maintaining an isomorphic relationship between territory, nation and State. The third goal is the expansion of markets eastward across the Baltic Sea region. The confluence of nationalism and neo-liberalism generates a certain image of the integrated minority individual: as one whose disorientation in a foreign country renders him/her a social and security threat, but also as one who can still find self-fulfilment and a constructive social role by pro-actively embracing the language and culture of the nation in whose name the State exists.

This chapter begins by describing fieldwork among diplomats, officials and policy elites and by introducing the policy setting in which fieldwork was conducted. It then discusses the main theoretical points, which aim to show that unexamined distinctions between the West European nation (civic, inclusive, good) and the East European nation (ethnic, exclusive, bad) obscure how the nation functions similarly as a key symbol among diplomats, officials and policy elites on either side of the old Iron Curtain. It also discusses how the anthropological study of policy can yield insight into modes of governance in mass society. Next, it sets the broader historical and international context in which integration in Estonia occurs. Liberal Estonian officials and Western officials work together to implement the *State Programme*, while conservative Estonian officials deprioritise it. Despite their differences over the role of non-Estonians in Estonian society, all of these officials strive to make the Estonian language and culture isomorphic with the territorial State. Then, an ethnographic example is given to show how the political dynamics among them leave Estonian officials with much ability to control the definition and pace of integration. Follow-up interviews show that as long as the *State Programme* is on track, Western officials are content with this situation because their interests in the matter share the same nationalist premises as their Estonian counterparts. Finally, this chapter shows how the rite of passage through which 'un-integrated non-Estonians' become 'integrated Estonian citizens' relies on a neo-liberal strategy to effect the nationalist agenda of securing the Estonian nation.[3]

## Fieldwork among Officials

This chapter is based on more than a year of fieldwork at the Integration Foundation from 1999 to 2001. The Integration Foundation is an Estonian NGO responsible for administering internationally-funded ethnic integration projects for the Estonian government. Reporting to the Minister without Portfolio for Ethnic Affairs, it is the central node in a complex array of international, national and local organisations that are all working to strengthen the capacity of the public, private and non-governmental sectors to integrate non-Estonians. From 1998 to 2001, the majority of the Integration Foundation's workload was dedicated to implementing two large-scale projects funded by the EC and the Nordic countries: the *European Union-*

*PHARE Estonian Language Training Programme* (LTP) and the *Nordic/UK/ UNDP Project: 'Support to the State Integration Programme'* (NUUP).[4]

These two projects, which form the bulk of activities for the State Programme, fund a wide range of integration-related activities. Some are aimed at government, such as customer service training for employees at Estonia's Citizen and Migration Board and assistance in designing a new civics exam for applicants for Estonian citizenship. Most of the funds, however, are awarded to private firms and non-governmental organisations that, for example, produce Estonian language training texts, train teachers of Estonian as a second language, run summer Estonian language camps for non-Estonian youth and conduct large-scale public awareness campaigns about the virtues of ethnic integration. Education about Estonian culture and history is built into many of these activities on the assumption that non-Estonians can end their social isolation by gaining familiarity with Estonian society. Integration policy assumes that they could not have known Estonian culture, despite being born in Estonia, because the Soviet Union both repressed it and discouraged Russians from integrating during the Soviet era. The fact that financial support largely derives from the EU and the Nordic countries and is redistributed to the private and third sectors in Estonia testifies to Trouillot's (2001: 132) point that State functions are being redeployed at a number of local, supra-national and transnational sites. Though the State may be dismantling institutionally, more and more actors are becoming responsible for implementing State responsibilities.

The Integration Foundation permitted me to conduct my ethnographic research as long as I provided assistance to their own operations: ethnographic rights for free labour.[5] This arrangement provided extended contact with the officials who oversee the implementation of the LTP and the NUUP. They included advisors to the Minister for Ethnic Affairs, diplomats from the Nordic and other Western embassies, and officials from the Estonian offices of the EC, the United Nations Development Programme (UNDP), and the Organization for Security and Cooperation in Europe (OSCE). My ethnographic fieldwork neither raised their suspicions nor erected barriers mainly because I was able to fulfil a recognisable and purposeful role in their social organisation. Indeed, Estonian and Western officials were accustomed to Western researchers, and many were pleased that at least one was taking an extended amount of time to see the complex issue from their viewpoint. I was permitted to attend steering committee meetings during which these officials reviewed developments and discussed future directions for these projects. I also was given the opportunity to study a range of policy documents and programme statements from the numerous smaller projects funded throughout the 1990s that culminated in the *State Programme*. Invitations to conferences on ethnic relations and EU enlargement were extended. All but a few officials granted lengthy and candid interviews. The UNDP eventually hired me as a consultant to evaluate the LTP and NUUP.

## Towards Theorising Neo-Liberal Nationalism in Europe

The fact that the EU and the Nordic countries so strongly support the goal of Estonia's integration program – the creation of an Estonian cultural domain – raises several important theoretical questions. If the 'West' endorses a culturally homogenous model for a future EU member-state, then does the familiar distinction between Western civic nationalism and Eastern ethnic nationalism hold? How does the rise in neo-liberal governance interface with the nationalist aims of Estonia's (or any European government's) integration policy? How can an anthropological approach to public policy shed light on governance strategies in contemporary Europe? More specifically, how is the policy construction of national minorities bound up with constructions of (inter)national security?

The *State Programme* generates what Trouillot (2001: 126) calls an isolation effect, or the production of an atomised and undifferentiated public modelled for governance. Specifically, ethnic integration policy constructs non-Estonians as a homogenous and alien population whom the Soviet collapse has left disoriented, disenfranchised and threatening to the Estonian State. Integration will transform them into self-fulfilled, proactive, productive and Estonia-centred members of society. If the non-Estonian chooses to learn the Estonian language, then s/he proceeds in a rite of passage that teaches the values incumbent in the language, enables contributions to Estonian society and provides opportunities to maximise his/her personal and productive capacities. This narrative works in the State's advantage. The State can abdicate responsibility for the social marginalisation of those who do not integrate because neo-liberal rhetoric frames the individual's disadvantaged circumstances as the product of their own (in)action. The narrative obscures the structural inequalities between citizens and non-citizens as well as the majority and the minority. Furthermore, securing the 'Estonian cultural domain' – establishing the traditional bond between State, territory and the national majority's putative culture – is to become the responsibility of the non-Estonian. The subordinate status of non-Estonians, thus, cannot be fully explained negatively, or as a result of actions taken against non-Estonians by Estonian nationalists. Rather, the non-Estonian that emerges in the State Programme is a positive expression of how Estonian and West European officials create nations, states and citizens in Europe. The security threat here is located in the cultural 'other' who is unfamiliar with daily life in the host nation. The alien's foreign disposition is to be overcome by co-opting that individual into reproducing the majority language and culture.

Estonian efforts to secure the nation-state cannot be explained through normative claims about 'east' European nationalism. Instead, it must be situated in Estonia's integration with Europe throughout the 1990s. Even discounting Western funding for the Estonia's integration program, Estonian practices regarding language policy, citizenship requirements and minority rights are consistent with those across Europe. They are also approved by international organisations that have monitored ethnic relations in Estonia. Thus, while many anthropologists have focused on how the demarcation of ethnic and national boundaries occurs as a reaction against Europeanisation and globalisation (Foster 1991; Stolcke 1995; Holmes 2000), the present study sees value in illustrating the opposite: how the demarcation of a nation and State rides in the tracks of EU accession. It differs from earlier research on postsocialist transformations which assume that east Europeans must dissolve fundamentally different forms of socio-political organisation so that they can adopt wholesale 'western democracy', 'entrepreneurism' and 'capitalism' (Garcia 1993: 11–12; Smith 1995: 7; Wicker 1997: 32). Instead, it is important to highlight agency on the part of east Europeans as they engage with western trends (Wedel 1998; Burawoy and Verdery 1999; Berdahl et al. 2000). Nonetheless, that engagement occurs within a discourse of nationhood shared by eastern and western European officials, thereby showing the reduced value in stressing 'East–West' boundaries.

Analyses of such discursive fields – which contain acceptable political debate – can occur through the study of public policy. Policy can be read as a cultural text composed of classificatory schemes and rhetorical devices that empower some and silence others (Shore and Wright 1997: 7). Policy analysis illuminates how the subject of governance in contemporary liberal democracy is constructed and linked to globalising trends. In other words, it shows how the State attempts to manage intersecting and conflicting power structures that are localised on its territory but linked to international systems (L. Abu-Lughod cited in Shore and Wright 1997: 13). In this case, the non-Estonian subject is the embodiment of three conflated tiers of socio-political organisation (international, national and local/non-national).[6] Ethnic integration policy constitutes a specific site where geographically dispersed officials conflate levels with the effect of producing governable national minorities, of welding the Estonian culture to the Estonian territorial State, and of securing the Estonian State in the EU. Finally, it is important to recognise that policies, like the statements of officials who write them, are not mere rhetoric concealing ulterior actions. Rather, these are attempts to legitimise observable actions – institutional development, legislative enactments, funding allocations, programme strategies – which are essential to reproducing dominant political structures.

## (Re)independence, Security and the Politics of Ethnic and European Integration

To understand ethnic integration in Estonia it is important to understand the reasoning through which roughly 500,000 Soviet-era Russian-speakers were denied citizenship in Estonia after it regained independence on 20 August 1991 from the Soviet Union. Estonian leaders framed the drive for independence as a movement to re-establish the inter-war Estonian Republic, which the Soviet Union illegally annexed in 1940. Thus, Estonian independence was a legal matter of restoring a State, rather than the messier matter of seceding from another State. The U.S., U.K. and most Western governments endorsed this point as they refused to acknowledge Soviet annexation of Estonia (and Latvia and Lithuania) throughout the Cold War. Built into this principle of State restoration, however, was that of the restoration of citizenship, an implication that the Western diplomatic community accepted. Individuals who held citizenship in the pre-Soviet Estonian republic or descended from such a citizen, automatically acquired citizenship in post-Soviet Estonia. Those who arrived from other parts of the Soviet Union during the period of annexation, and their descendants, were classified as illegal immigrants and were required to obtain residency permits. Nonetheless, the Estonian constitution, drafted with assistance from the Council of Europe (CoE), provides social rights and liberal principles of individual freedoms for all inhabitants of Estonia plus guarantees to develop the Estonian national identity, language and culture (Lauristin and Vihalemm 1997: 101).

Along with the efficient legal logic of State restoration, the demographic changes that Estonia incurred throughout the Soviet era were also important. Soviet resettlement policies and Russification more generally made it easy to justify denying citizenship as Soviet-era Russian-speakers knew very little Estonian and the Soviet Union hardly required them to integrate in the Estonian Soviet Socialist Republic. Between 1940 and 1953 the population of Estonia declined by some 250,000 people through emigration, deportation and execution. In 1934, ethnic Estonians numbered 991,000 (88 percent) out of 1.1 million people living in the country (Raun 1991: 129). The remainder were mainly ethnic Russians numbering 90,000 (8 percent) (ibid.: 247). By 2000, ethnic Estonians numbered roughly 939,000 (65 percent) out of 1.4 million people living in the country. Non-Estonians made up the remaining 500,000 (35 percent) with the vast majority of this group consisting of ethnic Russians (404,000) (Statistical Office of Estonia 2000). Indeed, these changes prompted fear among Estonian officials of the eventual loss of the Estonian language and culture (Ruutsoo 1995; Endre and Laar 1997; Vihalemm and Lauristin 1997: 280).

This situation, of course, looks different from the viewpoint of Russian-speakers. In 2001, approximately 315,000 non-Estonians still did not possess Estonian citizenship (Estonian Government 2000a: 9). Twenty thousand people were naturalised each year between 1994 and 1996. However, the numbers dropped to 8,124 and 9,969 people in 1997 and 1998 respectively. This decrease in people acquiring Estonian citizenship continued with only 4,534 in 1999 and 3,425 in 2000 (Poleshchuk 2001: 6). The dramatic slowdown in naturalisation has mainly occurred because non-Estonians who spoke the requisite amount of Estonian necessary for citizenship have already naturalised.[7] Despite being well-designed and well-managed programmes, the LTP and NUUP have scarcely been able to reverse that trend. The remainder now have to learn the official language – the most difficult naturalisation requirement – for the first time in their lives.

Although it accepted the denial of citizenship, the western diplomatic community, through the mouthpiece of the OSCE's High Commissioner on National Minorities, pressured the Estonian Government to clarify the terms of naturalisation and develop the means for Russian-speakers to learn the Estonian language. The Estonian Government shared this concern, but made it clear that the Government would need Western financial assistance to fulfil this task (OSCE 1993). Less than a year later the High Commissioner wrote to the Estonian Foreign Minister (OSCE 1994) that he was 'aware of the willingness of a number of Governments to assist the Government of Estonia' in its integration efforts. The Government began to outline a full integration programme in 1997 and by 1998 the LTP and NUUP had begun. During that time, Estonia began accession talks with the EC, and one of its criteria for entry was the implementation of a full-scale ethnic integration programme. The LTP and NUUP became the basis for the State Programme, which the Government approved in March 2000. Most significantly, the document framed integration as a security problem by virtue of the co-existence of two cultural-linguistic communities in one State: 'Sociological research conducted in the 1990s clearly points to the development of a model [sic] two societies in one state in Estonia. It is not difficult to see the danger of such a development in the framework of both social and security policy' (Estonian Government 2000b: sect. 3.1). To solve this problem State Programme aims for the creation of 'the Estonian model of a multicultural society, which is characterised by *the principles of cultural pluralism, a strong common core, and the preservation and development of the Estonian cultural domain*' (ibid.: sect. 3.4). Cultural pluralism recognises the Government's commitment to create the conditions to preserve minority cultures and languages. The strong common core involves uniting Estonian society (regardless of ethnicity) around the Estonian language.[8] Indeed, roughly 80 percent of the programme's budget is dedicated to this cause. The preservation of the Estonian cultural domain reflects the constitutional requirement to ensure the reproduction of the Estonian language and culture.[9]

The same year that the Estonian Government passed the State Programme, the EC concluded that Estonia fulfilled the political criteria necessary for accession, including stable democratic institutions and the respect for and protection of minorities (European Commission 2000: 13). The OSCE also determined that Estonia fulfilled its recommendations for citizenship and naturalisation, and closed its mission to Estonia in December 2001 (ibid.:

18). Estonia has signed, ratified and put into force the *Framework Convention for the Protection of National Minorities*. It has not signed the *European Charter for Regional or Minority Languages*. (As of February 2004, only seventeen of the forty-three CoE member-states have ratified and put into force the *European Charter*. Belgium, France, Greece, Iceland, Ireland, Italy, Luxembourg and Portugal are among those that have not put it into force, and several of those countries have not even ratified it.) The Estonian Government's approach to ethnic integration conforms to broader European practices, now that the EC's main concern now is technical rather than political. It is keen to make sure that Estonia develops the institutional capacity to expedite the ethnic integration process, arguing that the government needs to continue efforts 'reinforcing the capacity of public administration' (European Commission 2000: 21). In other words, the EC is committed to ensuring that the Estonian Government establishes the 'Estonian cultural domain', and it shares Estonian officials' concern that their Western counterparts must cover much of its costs.

As such, the major debate between West European and Estonian officials does not pivot on Estonia's treatment of minorities and non-citizens; Estonia is fully 'European' in this regard. Rather, it hinges on west European officials' perceptions of their Estonian counterparts' willingness and ability to institutionalise a sustainable administrative structure through which to implement the *State Programme*. Conservative factions in the Government argue that the State has no moral obligation to provide language training for people who arrived as a consequence of the illegal Soviet occupation. They also contend that ethnic integration is cost-prohibitive because of across the board spending cuts necessary for Estonia's market reforms. Some argue that fundamental cultural differences preclude ethnic integration. In the context of NATO's 1999 bombing of Serbia, Mart Nutt (cited in Kuus 2002: 98), an MP and author of Estonia's citizenship law wrote: 'it is a ruthless fact that a Russian considers a Serb as a brother while an Estonian will remain an alien. Blood is thicker than water ... and this holds true also for the Russian who, according to some sociologists, has been integrated.' In contrast, liberal Estonian officials are committed to implementing the *State Programme*. They maintain that non-Estonians can become 'competent' members of Estonian society if they take the initiative to learn the Estonian language and familiarise themselves with Estonian culture and history. This condition is not in place simply for communication purposes. Instead, integration and naturalisation are constructed as a process whereby one develops an appreciation of Estonian values, culture and history along with loyalty to the Estonian State. Nonetheless, the legal requirements for citizenship involve no demonstration of knowledge of Estonian culture and history, even though Western-funded integration programmes build this knowledge into their specific activities. One NGO leader who is active in ethnic integration explains the importance of this knowledge in his characterisation of the historical relationship between Estonians and Russians:

We do belong to two different civilisations. All our language philosophy and language logics are Finno-Ugric, not Indo-European. In Russian, they have the word *doma*, which means in English 'house' or 'home'. In Estonian, we say [home] with the word *kodu*. We have another word for [the physical structure] 'house', *maja*. We are individualistic and not collectivist [like Russians]. In Estonian the term *peremees* means 'master of my house'. The Russians came here and commanded us; uninvited and in large numbers: it built resistance.

It is important to stress what exactly is the contentious issue between liberal Estonian officials, conservative Estonian officials and Western officials. All three groups agree that a putative Estonian culture and the Estonian language should be made isomorphic with the territorial Estonian State, a goal that calls into question the claim that the EU transcends the nation. They differ on the question of whether an ethnic Russian is capable of conducting him or herself in an 'Estonian' manner. Conservative Estonian officials argue that an individual's ethnic identity can neither be transformed nor concealed and that 'Estonian' and 'Russian' are mutually exclusive with the latter constituting a threat to the former. Thus, they neither believe that it will work nor that it should receive priority over many other aspects Estonia's accession reforms. Liberal Estonian officials and Western officials share the belief that different cultures pose fundamental threats to each other, and thus the national majority must maintain a privileged position in relation to the State, particularly a very small nation like Estonia. However, they argue that the integration process can teach Russians to behave in an Estonian manner. As such, funding integration is foremost a matter of security given such culturally fundamentalist assumptions (Stolcke 1995: 5). However, Western officials cannot always determine which camp has the stronger voice in Estonian Government and, as the next section shows, this situation causes them much stress.

## A Gathering of Officials: Tension over the Administration of Ethnic Integration

Administrators from the Integration Foundation organised a retreat in November 1999 in order to directly update the ambassadors from donor countries on the current draft of the *State Programme*. The Government was keen to present the creation of this programme as an open process, soliciting input from many different angles. The ambassadors, in turn, wanted assurance that the integration projects they funded would lead to a sustainable *State Programme*. They normally receive briefs from their first secretaries who attend LTP and NP steering-committee meetings.[10] In addition to the diplomats from donor countries, the organisers also invited the ambassadors of France, the U.K., Germany, and the U.S. with the aim of soliciting more funds. European Commission and UNDP representatives were also present.

The retreat demonstrated how the tension between west European and Estonian officials over funding and institutionalising the ethnic integration process pivots on administrative questions (How will integration be conducted most efficiently?) rather than political questions (Are the goals of integration just?). It also shows how Western officials appear to be more insecure about ethnic relations than their Estonian counterparts. They have difficulty recognising how committed the Government is to institutionalising the integration process as the coalition at the time was mixed, with both liberals and conservatives. Indeed, the Minister for Ethnic Affairs, who chaired this meeting, was a member of the Moderates which held liberal views on integration. However, the Government coalition was led by the *Isamaaliit* (Pro Patria Union) whose members were former radical nationalists, many of whom in the early 1990s called for the return of Russians to Russia. Funding integration was low on their list of priorities. Western ambassadors were keen to make sure that Minister of Ethnic Affairs could keep integration alive.[11] Importantly, the event illustrates that international relations, often thought of as a practice conducted by faceless non-reflexive States, is quite the opposite. Specific people are authorised to carry out tasks in the name of the State. This introduces the element of contingency to international relations and testifies to the value of ethnographic methods.

The retreat was held in a renovated nineteenth-century Classicist manor house once inhabited by Baltic German landlords. Like many manor houses, this one is now a tourist attraction featuring guides and hostesses dressed in colourful, Estonian national costumes. At least in presentations to Western officials, much of contemporary national identity is constructed upon Estonian peasant life connoting the purity of nature and the Estonian language as well as the virtues of self-reliance. After a welcome reception in the foyer, the participants gathered in an elegant second floor hall replete with parquet flooring, chandeliers, white drapes and ornate window trimmings. The director of the Integration Foundation seated the ambassadors of Finland, Denmark, Sweden and Norway and the resident representative of UNDP in the front line of chairs informally deemed 'ambassadors' row'. The Minister greeted the audience and gave brief introductory remarks. She spoke of an older ethnic Russian man living in Ida-Virumaa.[12] Although the old man cannot speak Estonian, she said, he is still contributing to ethnic integration in two ways: by working as a small merchant and by sending his daughter to take Estonian-medium courses at Tartu University, the country's premier institution of higher learning and main centre for Estonian philology.

This tale is more than rhetorical filler to preface substantive discussion. Rather, it is what Ortner (1979: 95) calls a 'key scenario', a type of elaborating symbol that provides a clear-cut action plan for correct and successful living. It presents the constructive role that the self-motivated and integrated non-Estonian can play in Westward-bound Estonian society. Having concluded that the older generation of non-Estonians is unable and unmotivated to learn Estonian, efforts at language training are aimed mainly at the younger generation. Yet, the old man's employment in small business connotes neo-liberal self-reliance, while his daughter's attendance at Tartu University signifies the connecting links between one's command of the Estonian language, appreciation of Estonian identity, enhanced career potential and economic growth for Estonia. This narrative brings to life the rhetorical mix of nationalism and neo-liberalism, in which the non-Estonian individual can achieve personal fulfilment while simultaneously preserving the Estonian language and nation.

The Minister also lamented the lack of national identity in Estonia. 'When you ask people in Narva where they are from,' she explained, 'they simply respond "Narva", not "Estonia"'.[13] This led to her next point that the *State Programme* will solve the problem by unifying society into a common sphere of (Estonian language) communication. Thus, she reasoned, people in Narva will start to identify themselves as Estonians. The Minister then opened the floor for questions.

Ambassador #1 raised a hand, then prefaced a question with strong support for the long-term goals of the *State Programme*. However, the ambassador noted that the programme had no sub-targets to implement it step by step. 'Where are the stations on the road map?' the ambassador asked, adding, 'The linguistic side is there but not the social and economic aspects. These are not quite as developed.' The Minister concurred that specific activities had not yet been delineated.

Ambassador #2 spoke: '[My capital] would support it, but it needs more specifics. It needs a budget. How will it be funded from Estonia? It should also address how the programme will be administered. It's such a cross-cutting issue.' The Minister added, 'This is an extremely important issue.'

Ambassador #3 had also expected greater stress on the social, legal and economic aspects. The ambassador also called for yearly progress reports, interjecting that 'You, Madame Minister, are the privileged interface with the outside world. This would help clear up many political problems.' The Minister noted that other Government policies addressed these issues.

Ambassador #4, showing frustration, inquired, 'Have we evaluated what has been done before ... Are you ready to take over, and make lasting work in Estonia?' The ambassador did not want the Estonian Government taking foreign aid for granted. He wanted to be able to report to his capital that aid was establishing sustainable institutions in Estonia. The Minister responded that evaluations were needed, and that 'this is a learning process'.

This exchange signifies the Minister's (and the Estonian State's) strong position. The retreat's very location symbolically reinforced the Estonian nation in the forms of the rural manor house and the traditional maidens. The Minister also controlled the pace of the discussion. Her introduction and tale of the Tartu University student consumed thirty-five minutes of a discussion scheduled for seventy-five minutes, thereby reducing the number of questions and comments from the Western officials. When questions were asked, she answered them in a terminal manner. The Minister could even gain rhetorical control over the pace of integration by using west European officials' stereotype of Estonia to her own advantage. Her response to Ambassador #4, 'this is a learning process', allowed her to distance the Government from criticism for hesitating on integration on the assumption that Estonia, a victim of Soviet totalitarian rule, could not be expected quickly to develop the institutions supporting a 'multicultural, civil society'. A slower pace, of course, forces donor Governments to continue supplying funds. Since conservatives in Government are unwilling to allocate more funds for ethnic integration, the Minister does not want to lose foreign support by claiming that ethnic integration is self-sustainable.

Other comments also reflected the ambassadors' uncertainty over the Estonian Government's commitment to implementing the *State Programme*: 'Where's the road map?'; 'It should also address how the programme will be administered'; and 'Are you ready to make lasting work?' The audience, in the words of Ambassador #3, had to push the Minister to communicate with them: 'You, Madame Minister, are the privileged interface with the outside world.' Significantly, the ambassador's frustration is that of a west European official wanting to learn more about the applicant state rather than the applicant demanding the attention of the EU. The Minister's presentation was strategically ambiguous as she must balance her own Party's agenda against that of *Isamaaliit*. Nonetheless, the donor Governments still provided, directly or indirectly, 52 percent of the *State Programme*'s budget for the year 2000.

Overall, Estonian officials were quite adept at converting Western predispositions about Estonia and Estonians to their advantage, a situation complicating the normative claim that the postsocialist transformations involve a direct transfer of knowledge from to West to East (Burawoy and Verdery 1999, Kuus 2004). The leverage that they can exert in this relationship derives from the fact that Western diplomats were keenly interested in ethnic integration throughout the 1990s because the *State Programme*'s goals were in line with their foreign policy objectives in the Baltic Sea region. Capturing the ambiguity of the power relationship between west Europe and Estonia, an Estonian official noted that the '[*State Programme*] is only good for raising money. We can show it to whomever.' The individual then lifted a hand in the air with the open palm facing outward. The gesture carried a double meaning. It symbolised both the presentation of a policy worthy of financial and political support as well as an order to 'Stop! Don't look any further.' West European officials do indeed look further but the compatibility of their agenda with liberal Estonian officials leaves the latter quite assured that the West is more than willing to bankroll the plan that they offer.

## European Interests and the Marginalization of Russian-Speakers

Interviews with diplomats after the retreat provide further elaboration of the geopolitical and economic interests of the donor countries vis-à-vis ethnic integration in Estonia. They also further illustrate the compatible interests of liberal Estonian officials and their Western counterparts. The metaphors through which diplomats convey their respective governments' interests rely both on the notion of a secure state as a container of a particular national language and culture and on a business approach to their handling of integration in Estonia. A senior Nordic diplomat explained the importance of integration in terms of regional stability. 'It is an advantage that the Baltic area have a positive development as well as Russia ... It adds security to us all. The human side, the altruistic side, [*is that*] all countries have the right to determine themselves. The basic fact is that the countries are now independent ... but in a good neighbourhood.' The key point is that self-determination in a good and secure neighbourhood (a Western-oriented Baltic Sea region) requires asserting the cultural hegemony of the nation in whose name the State exists. Another Nordic diplomat explained the matter with more candour: 'Stability is a major part of our [foreign] policy and integration is essential in that context.'

Economic interests closely follow the concern for stability. 'The first concern when the USSR collapsed was certainly stability' another diplomat added. 'Stability' he continued, 'is one area, but also building a market economy is important ... There aren't many controversial issues in the current text [of the *State Programme*].' Another diplomat also stressed the economic dimension of stability: 'Anything we can do to expand our networks across the area must be a plus for everyone in the region ... The goals are market economy, democracy and environment ...' Market economics is the metaphor through which the donors' role in the NP is understood. The diplomat said 'We monitor the process and give advice. We are like the strategic stockholders with interest in the company. The governing board of the Integration Foundation is the board of directors. We step in when our interests are threatened.' They have not stepped in, however, because the interests of the Estonian Government and the donor remain sufficiently compatible.

The diplomats' views oppose those of Russian-speaking leaders who convened their own meeting of the President's Round Table for Ethnic Affairs to discuss the *State Programme*.[14] Most members argued that too much attention is given to language with one describing their concern as 'pathological'. Another commented that 'civil wars also take place among people who speak the same language', challenging the common notion that language unites people while different languages push them toward conflict. One participant then waved a draft of the *State Programme* in the air, and exclaimed,

> What is really behind integration for certain political forces? We have known 'what' and 'how' but not 'what for'. This document is to protect the Estonian language. They would like to create an assimilated not an integrated society. We must find from where these desires come. This is a seven-year version of a [Soviet] five-year plan.

Despite its forceful delivery, his point had little impact on the Western diplomats who were present at the Round Table meeting. Their reaction was to support the *State Programme* by covering over 50 percent of its budget. Other Round Table members adhere to a more radical position that citizenship should not be a reward for loyalty but rather the State should earn the loyalty of non-Estonians by first awarding citizenship. They are aware, however, that this position will not gain acceptance into political debate as it contradicts the basic tenet of the minority-state relations: that the State is fundamentally challenged if non-citizens do not demonstrate loyalty by first naturalising, a rite of passage through which a non-citizen acquires the knowledge necessary to assume the rights and responsibilities of citizenship.

## Neo-Liberal Nationalism and the Construction of the Minority Individual

That rite of passage, of course, is inextricably linked to the broader political and economic processes surrounding Estonia's accession to the EU. Mediated by Western and liberal Estonian officials, these processes simultaneously involve securing the Estonian nation-state and liberalising its economy. These processes bear upon the construction of an ideal minority individual and upon a narrative about their trajectory from Soviet-era migrant in Estonia to integrated Estonian citizen.

Integration policy constructs Russian-speakers quite sympathetically, as alienated, disenfranchised and unable 'to find sufficient opportunities for self-realisation' after the re-establishment of Estonian independence (Estonian Government 2000b: sect. 3.1). While their alien status in an independent Estonian society is appreciated, non-Estonians are also feared as they do not 'mesh' with the cultural fabric of society. The 1998 outline for the *State Programme* framed the matter this way:

> The alienation of a significant number of non-Estonians from Estonian society and an isolation in a world of their own language and mentality. Sociological research conducted in the 1990s clearly points to the development of a model [sic] 'two societies in one State' in Estonia. It is not difficult to see the danger of such a development in the framework of both social and security policy (Estonian Government 1998: 1).

In this context, the purpose of integration is to help reconstitute the alien's mentality from that of an unpredictable outsider to that of an economically productive and Estonia-centred inside member of society. Economic growth is intimately linked to security as productive citizens will avoid the temptation of social disruption: 'The situation among non-Estonian youth is of concern, where many talented young people cannot find sufficient employment opportunities, while growing unemployment provides fertile ground for a criminal subculture' (ibid.). In some passages, non-Estonians' poor Estonian language ability is presented not only as a personal obstruction, but a national one as well, for example, '[lack of Estonian is] the principle impediment to the career potential of non-Estonians and economic growth in Estonia' (Estonian Government 2000b: 20).

However, state downsizing, as a part of the neo-liberal reforms necessary for EU accession, also allows the government to distance itself from the plight of Russian-speakers in Estonia. It is the non-Estonians who must explore Estonian culture and history so that they can re-orient themselves. As such, the *State Programme* presents integration in Estonia not as a state directive, but rather as an opportunity for pro-active individuals to maximise their self-fulfilment. Hence, integration 'is the result of the free choice of the individual, not a decision dictated from "above"' (ibid.). One should not wait for the State to provide individual opportunity, as in the Socialist era, but rather take the initiative to end a seemingly self-imposed lethargy: 'The diffident and passive attitudes widespread among non-Estonians must be replaced by the understanding that each person's prospects for a secure future in Estonian society depend above all on his own activeness and cooperation' (ibid.: 21). Indeed, non-Estonian individuals are the building blocks of an integrated Estonian society.

> The direct subjects of integration are individuals. Integration on the level of the individual shapes the common core in the public sphere of society, and that common core operates on the basis of the Estonian language, common social institutions and democratic values. (ibid.)

Nikolas Rose's critique of Western liberal democracy is instructive in explaining the integration in Estonia. Rose (1992: 147) argues that since liberal democracy depends upon pro-active individuals, then it needs to invent techniques to *constitute* its citizens so they internalise State values as their own. Governing in a liberal-democratic way means governing *through* the freedom and aspirations of subjects rather than in spite of them (ibid.: 142). This arrangement makes the citizen's 'free choice' an instrument in State hegemony. Integration renders the minority individual in Estonia safe, secure, and productive. The non-ethnic other is not so much negatively sanctioned by restricting his or her liberty, but rather co-opted so that this individual's talents contribute positively to the viability of the nation-state and market economy.

Thus, the Estonian Government's nationalist agenda should not be understood as a retention of supposedly exclusive Eastern, ethnic nationalism. Instead, it functions in a very contemporary pan-European mode. The individual is implicitly asked to assume the traditional State tasks of securing the State and stimulating the economy. Through their interaction with reformed institutions that are repositories of the Estonian language and culture, non-Estonians should undergo a reconstitution of the self to acquire the cultural-linguistic knowledge necessary for the positive status of self-fulfilled and productive Estonian citizen. (Recall that the EC- and Nordic-funded projects in support of the *State Programme* are designed to reform these institutions.) He or she is then prepared to assume greater political and economic responsibilities commensurate with the new status (Turner 1979: 242).

This rite of passage is depicted especially well in a series of photographs that appear in the guidebook of the *Estonian Language Training Strategy* (European Union PHARE Programme 1998: 13). The EU funded the design and implementation of the Strategy, which was a precursor project of the Estonia's *State Programme*. Each of its chapters opens with a photograph of a young Russian-speaking woman proceeding through the rite of passage. In chapter one, she stands with her hands in her pockets, positioned against the movement of society (Figure 3.1). She is a nonconformist and a social and security risk. Next, she appears lonely while gazing at two young women, at least one of whom is an ethnic Estonian as signified by her blonde hair (Figure 3.2). In the background is the Estonian National Theatre, a major national icon. Then, she stands at the Estonian literature section of a bookstore, holding a copy of *Estland*, a picture book of rural Estonia (Figure 3.3). She has taken the initiative to end her social isolation by learning about Estonian literature, history and culture. Finally, the Russian-speaking woman is freely conversing with the Estonian woman and four others (Figure 3.4). Ethnic integration has now occurred because of the non-Estonian woman's efforts to learn the Estonian language and culture. The reconstitution of her self is complete; she is no longer a security, and she is happy. Integration would have failed had she clung to an alternative ethnic identity because she would have remained juxtaposed against the Estonian majority. She must internally prioritise competing identities.

More deeply, this young woman's energy and talents must be redirected toward the future EU member-state's political security and economic prosperity lest her social alienation induce chaos. According to the *State Programme*, this is only possible if she herself identifies with Estonianness and acts accordingly in public. True, the Estonian Government cannot force her to integrate, but it can create a situation in which an increase in political and economic opportunities is contingent upon her doing so. Conveniently, the Government is not to blame if she fails to learn the Estonian language because,

*Neo-Liberal Nationalism*

Figure 3.1 Non-Estonian woman standing alone, appearing alienated, and facing against the movement of the crowd. (Photo: European Uunion PHARE Programme 1998).

Figure 3.2 Sitting apart, gazing at two Estonian women who socialise near the Estonian National Theatre. (Photo: European Union PHARE Programme, 1998).

Figure 3.3  Holding a copy of Estland, a pictorial guide to Estonian nature and rural life. The first step toward integration, i.e. the non-Estonian learning about Estonia. (Photo: European Union PHARE Programme, 1998).

Figure 3.4  Finally conversing with a group that includes one of the Estonian women from Figure 3.2. (Photo: European Union PHARE Programme, 1998).

according to neo-liberal logic, this failure signifies her own lack of effort. Failure or success, the 'Estonian cultural domain' will remain either through her active participation in an Estonian-language based society or through her social marginalisation resulting from an inability to speak the official language. Never does her disadvantaged social position enter into the equation. Instead, her disadvantage is her own personal outlook, which only she can correct.

## Conclusion: New Tactics for National Demarcation?

This chapter set out to achieve two goals. First, it aimed to show how the EU accession does not undermine the nation per se, but, in key ways, institutionalises and normalises the nation. This point helps to overcome the East–West dichotomy when conceptualising how the nation functions as a category among diplomats and State officials. Certainly, conservative Estonian officials differ significantly from their Western and liberal Estonian counterparts insofar as they argue that Russians are incapable of conducting themselves in a putatively Estonian manner. They doubt the virtue and efficacy of integration because of this cultural fundamentalism. However, liberal Estonian and Western officials also share the assumption that two cultures in the same State constitute a security risk, but they believe that Russians can adopt an Estonian outlook when interacting in the public domain. The common theme underlying their differences, and reinforced through the process of EU accession, is that a putative national culture must achieve a privileged position within the territorial State. Unlike conservatives, liberals believe that Russian-speakers can participate in that project.

Second, neo-liberal trends in Europe do not necessarily jeopardise the classic equation of nation, territory and State. Instead, neo-liberal modes of governance can be deployed in service of the State's nationalist agenda of welding a particular national culture to the territorial State. Western and liberal Estonian officials posit that the non-Estonian's participation in Estonian society should become self-perpetuating and consummate with his or her own self-identity. The State co-opts the talents of non-citizens by making their economic and political self-actualisation contingent upon their reproduction of the State's official language and national culture. Minorities and non-citizens are ostensibly welcome, but only insofar as they participate in the nation-state's culturally exclusive program. Thus they must subordinate alternative ethnic identities to spaces that do not intrude upon the State's sovereignty.

This chapter also aimed to show the value of an anthropological approach to policy. Policy is the site where hegemonic discourses are condensed and reworked to present an ideal vision of prosperous and pacific society. As such, they speak directly to the issue of how citizens are subjectified and disciplined, and how their interactions are re-ordered for the sake of conformity and productivity. The State Programme re-articulates the relationship between the non-Estonian individual, the State and society in light of increasing ties with the EU. It also demonstrates the dispersal of State functions to a plethora of local, supra-national, and transnational as well as private and non-governmental sites, making the State at once non-localisable and omnipresent.

If the case of ethnic integration in Estonia suggests the limited value of a conceptual boundary between 'East' and 'West' European nation-states, then where might key European boundaries lie? Perhaps new boundaries lie not in geographic space but in State practices, which differ according the extent to which immigrants and minorities are either co-opted (i.e. converted into reproducers of national hegemony) or blatantly sanctioned (i.e. constructed as foils on whom national identity is inscribed). Rather than homogenise the population through such negative tactics as restrictive immigration policy, monetary incentives to emigrate, or the brutal tactics witnessed in the former Yugoslavia, a State's participation in an EU political economy requires at least some use of minorities' and non-citizens' abilities. Perhaps Europe's default mode of socio-political organisation is still set on the nationalist switch, though it relies on new tactics to keep it there.

## NOTES

1. This research was supported by a Fulbright Fellowship (1999–2000) and a David L. Boren Fellowship (2000–2001). I would like to thank Cris Shore for helpful comments on an earlier draft of this paper. I would also like to thank the Integration Foundation, the Estonian office of UNDP, and the Department of Sociology at Tallinn Pedagogical University for assistance with field research and for providing office facilities. Photographs were taken by Jaan Künnap.
2. The definition of 'ethnic integration' underpinning the *State Programme* and policy discussions with western diplomats is the process of cohering Estonian society by providing Russian-speakers with the linguistic and cultural knowledge necessary to participate in the labour market, to feel at home in Estonia, and, if desired, to acquire citizenship. It is also involves the opportunity to preserve ethnic differences, but less emphasis is placed on this goal.
3. 'Non-Estonians' and 'Russian-speakers' can be used synonymously. I use the former in the context of ethnic integration policy because it refers to them as such. Elsewhere I use 'Russian-speakers'. These terms refer to a diversity of people who arrived in Estonia during the Soviet era and mainly speak Russian as a first language. They are mostly ethnic Russians, but also include Byelorussians, Ukrainians, Tatars, Poles, Jews and others. These terms do not include the roughly seventy-five thousand Russian-speakers who held citizenship in pre-Soviet Estonia, or are descended from such a person, because, in contrast to Soviet-era Russian-speakers, they automatically regained citizenship in post-Soviet Estonia.
4. As of February 2004, the LTP is still running and the NP has been reborn as 'Integrating Estonia 2002–2004', which is funded by Great Britain, Sweden, Norway and Finland. A third pro-

ject has emerged called the Language Immersion Centre, which is supported by the Canadian International Development Agency, the Finnish National Board of Education, the Royal Netherlands Embassy and the Council of Europe.
5. I mainly edited quarterly reports for the two internationally funded projects, drafted correspondence to donors and developed funding proposals to international organisations. English is the primary language in the upper administrative levels of ethnic integration because of the prominent role of the EC and EU member-states. Nearly everyone I encountered during fieldwork, regardless of ethnicity or nationality, spoke English fluently.
6. The point is not that these processes determine the subject of policy, but rather they establish a hegemonic framework in which people must negotiate and situate their identities.
7. Chapter six of the law on citizenship passed on 1 April 1995 stipulates that the applicant for citizenship through naturalisation must:
   1. be at least fifteen years of age;
   2. have stayed in Estonia on the basis of a permanent residence permit for at least five years prior to the date on which he or she submits an application for Estonian citizenship and for one year from the day following the date of registration of the application;
   3. have knowledge of the Estonian language in accordance with the requirements provided for in § 8 of this Act;
   4. have knowledge of the Constitution of the Republic of Estonia and the Citizenship Act in accordance with the requirements provided for in § 9 of this Act;
   5. have a permanent legal income which ensures his or her own subsistence and that of his or her dependants;
   6. be loyal to the Estonian State;
   7. take an oath: '*Taotledes Eesti kodakondsust, tõotan olla ustav Eesti põhiseaduslikule korrale.*' [In applying for Estonian citizenship, I swear to be loyal to the constitutional order of Estonia.]

   Citizenship provides the right to belong to a political party, to vote in national elections, to hold public sector jobs and to run for any political office. Certificates documenting Estonian language proficiency are required to work in public and private sector jobs if these pertain to the public good.
8. This passage was written in reference to the *Framework Convention for the Protection of National Minorities*, which aims to protect minority culture within the framework of the sovereign, territorial nation-state. It does not prioritize multiculturalism over the national majority.
9. The preamble of the Estonian Constitution guarantees 'the preservation and development of the Estonian nation and culture throughout the ages' (Estonian State 1992). The official Estonian version uses the term *rahvas*, which in English means 'nation' in the civic sense, rather than *rahvus*, which connotes the ethnic meaning of nation. However, Estonian administrators and officials operate almost entirely on the basis of the Estonian *rahvus* when designing ethnic integration programmes. This testifies to Hayden's (2000: 15) point that nation-states may welcome minorities as citizens while never fully accepting them into mainstream society. For a detailed analysis of the Estonian Constitution as it pertains to citizenship, law and ethnic relations see Ruutsoo (1998).
10. In small embassies, a first secretary is usually the highest ranking diplomat in an embassy below the ambassador. First secretaries are usually the most deeply immersed in the details of an embassy's numerous projects.
11. This Centre-Right Government, composed of the Pro Patria Union, the Moderate Party and the Reform Party, collapsed in December 2001. It was replaced by a coalition of the Centre Party (a Centre-Left party with many Russian-speaking supporters) and the Reform Party (a pro-business party). The following election in March 2003 brought the newly formed *Res Publica* Party into government in partnership the Reform Party.

12. Ida-Virumaa is an economically depressed county in north-east Estonia. The population is 90 percent Russian-speakers (over 125,000 people), mostly blue-collar workers who immigrated to Ida-Virumaa during the Soviet era to work in what was then an expanding industrial sector. Along with the capital city of Tallinn, most Russian-speakers live in Ida-Virumaa.
13. Narva is the largest city in Ida-Virumaa.
14. President Lennart Meri created the President's Roundtable for Ethnic Affairs in 1993. The Roundtable can make recommendations regarding ethnic issues to the Government, but the Government has no obligation to consider them. Its members are mainly Russian-speaking politicians, academics, public intellectuals and heads of national minority associations.

## REFERENCES

Berdahl, D., Bunzl, M. and M. Lampland eds. 2000. *Altering States: Ethnographies of Transition in Eastern Europe and the Former Soviet Union.* Ann Arbor, University of Michigan Press.

Burawoy, M. and K. Verdery eds. 1999. *Uncertain Transitions: Ethnographies of Change in the Post-Socialist World.* Lanham, Rowman and Littlefield.

Endre, S. and M. Laar. 'Valitsus kõigutab rahvusriigi alustalasid [The Government is Shaking the Pillars of the Nation-State]' Eesti Päevaleht, 12 December 1997.

Estonian Government. 1998. The Integration of Non-Estonians into Estonian Society: The Bases of the Estonian State Integration Policy. Tallinn, Integration Foundation.

Estonian Government. 2000a. *Integrating Estonia 1997–2000: Report from the Government of Estonia.* Tallinn, Integration Foundation.

Estonian Government. 2000b. *State Programme: 'Integration in Estonian Society 2000–2007'.* Tallinn, Integration Foundation.

Estonian State. 1992. *Preamble to the Constitution of the Republic of Estonia.* http://www.rk.ee/rkogu/eng/epseng.html#1p.

European Commission. 2000. *Estonia 2000: Regular Report from the Commission on Estonia's Progress Towards Accession.* Tallinn, Delegation of the European Commission to Estonia.

European Union PHARE Programme. 1998. *Language Training Strategy for the Non-Estonian-Speaking Population.* Tallinn, Integration Foundation.

Foster, R. 1991. 'Making national cultures in the global ecumene'. *Annual Review of Anthropology* 20: 235–60.

Garcia, S. 1993. 'Europe's fragmented identities and the frontiers of citizenship'. In *European Identity and the Search for Legitimacy*, ed. S. Garcia. London, Pinter.

Hayden, R. 2000. *Blueprints for a House Divided: The Constitutional Logic of the Yugoslav Conflicts.* Ann Arbor, University of Michigan Press.

Holmes, D.R. 2000. *Integral Europe: Fast-Capitalism, Multiculturalism, Neofascism.* Princeton, Princeton University Press.

Kuus, M. 2004. '"Those goody-goody Estonians": Toward rethinking security in the European Union applicant states'. *Environment and Planning D: Society and Space* 22, no. 2: 191–207.

Kuus, M. 2002. 'European integration in identity narratives in Estonia: A quest for security'. *Journal of Peace Research* 39, no. 1: 91–108.
Lauristin, M. and P. Vihalemm. 1997. 'Recent historical developments in Estonia: Three stages of transition (1987–1997)'. In *Return to the Western World: Cultural and Political Perspectives on the Estonian Post-Communist Transition*, eds M. Lauristin and P. Vihalemm with K. Rosengren and L.Wiebull. Tartu, Tartu University Press.
Organization for Security and Cooperation in Europe, Reference: No 3005/94/L, http://www.riga.lv/minelres/count/estonia/940309r.htm, 1994.
Organization for Security and Cooperation in Europe, CSCE Communication No. 124, http://www.osce.org/hcnm.documents/recommendations/lithuania/1993/02c1243, 1993.
Ortner, S. 1979. 'On Key Symbols'. In *Reader in Comparative Religion: An Anthropological Approach*, eds W. Lessa and E. Vogt. New York, Harper and Row.
Poleshchuk, V. 2001. *Accession to the European Union and National Integration in Estonia and Latvia*. Technical report no. 8. Flensburg, European Centre for Minority Issues.
Raun, T. 1991. *Estonia and the Estonians*. Stanford, Stanford University Press.
Rose, N. 1992. 'Governing the enterprising self'. In *The Values of the Enterprise Culture: The Moral Debate*, eds P. Heelas and P. Morris. London, Routledge.
Ruutsoo, R. 1998. 'Eesti kodakondsuspoliitika ja rahvusriigi kujunemise piirjooned' (Estonian citizenship policy in the context of the emerging nation-state). In *Vene küsimus ja eesti valikud* (the Russian question and challenges for Estonia), ed. M. Heidmets. Tallinn, Tallinna Pedagoogikaülikool Kirjastus.
Ruutsoo, R. 1995. 'Introduction: Estonia on the border of two civilizations'. *Nationalities Papers* 23, no. 1: 13–16.
Shore, C. and S.Wright. 1997. 'Policy: A New Field of Anthropology'. In *Anthropology of Policy*, eds C. Shore and S. Wright. London, Routledge.
Smith, A. 1995. *Nations and Nationalism in a Global Era*. Cambridge, Polity.
Statistical Office of Estonia. *Ethnic Composition of the Population*. http://www.stat.ee/index.aw/section=6579
Stolcke, V. 1995. 'Talking culture: New boundaries, new rhetorics of exclusion in Europe'. *Current Anthropology* 36, no. 1: 1–13.
Trouillot, M.R. 2001. 'The anthropology of the state in the age of globalization: Close encounters of the deceptive kind'. *Current Anthropology* 42, no. 1: 125–38.
Turner, V. 1979. 'Betwixt and between: The liminal phase of the rite de passage'. In *Reader in Comparative Religion: An Anthropological Approach*, eds W. Lessa and E. Vogt. New York, Harper and Row.
Wedel, J. 1998. *Collision and Collusion: The Strange Case of Western Aid to Eastern Europe 1989–1998*. New York, St. Martin's Press.
Wicker, H.R. 1997. 'Introduction: Theorizing ethnicity and nationalism'. In *Rethinking Nationalism and Ethnicity: The Struggle for Meaning and Order in Europe*, ed. H.R. Wicker. Oxford, Berg.

# Chapter 4
# The European Left and the New Immigrations: The Case of Italy

Davide Però

Migration and 'multiculturalism' constitute a crucial context for reflecting on the social, cultural and political changes that Europe has undergone in recent years. Whereas considerable scholarship has gone into the analysis of political institutions (e.g. Shore 1997 and 2000; Shore and Black 1994) and the political Right (Stolcke 1995; Holmes 2000), we know little about how the egalitarian side of the political spectrum, commonly referred to as the Left (Bobbio 1994), has been addressing this phenomenon.[1]

With regard to the political Right, Verena Stolcke (1995) has suggested that its exclusionary discourse in the context of migration and multiculturalism has moved from racism (exclusion on the basis of racial and biological difference) to cultural fundamentalism (exclusion on the basis of alleged cultural incompatibility).[2] Thus, immigrants from poor regions of the world are considered undesirable and detestable not because of their alleged biological inferiority but because they represent embodiments of irreconcilably different cultures and as such they pose a formidable threat to the cultural integrity of the supposedly homogeneous national communities of Europe. Douglas Holmes (2000) has vividly shown, through a multi-sited European ethnography, how anti-immigration, opposition to Europeanisation, and fast-capitalist restructuring constitute crucial elements in the 'counter-enlightenment' battle of the radical Right in defence of the supposedly original and authentic ethnic communities, cultures, identities and traditions of the continent. With regard to the EU, Cris Shore (1997 and 2000) has drawn attention to the fact that many of its efforts to develop a European identity involve the creation of a European 'Other'. This process of 'othering' is carried out through the strengthening of physical and symbolic boundaries, and the political technology of citizenship, as well as through the circulation of an idea of Europe as 'a distinctive bounded region set apart from others by race, religion, language and habitat' (Shore 2000: 62). Shore has described this process as follows:

> Creating the 'European identity', as depicted in EU discourse, entails a degree of exclusion of the Other. Identity formation ... is essentially a dualistic process involving fission and fusion as new boundaries are created to distinguish categories of 'us' and 'them'. 'European identity' tends to become meaningful only when contrasted to that which is not European. As Europe consolidates and converges, and as barriers between European nation-states are eliminated, so the boundaries separating Europe from its Third World 'Others' have intensified – and Islam (particularly 'fundamentalism') has replaced communism as the key marker for defining the limits of European civilisation. (Shore 2000: 63)

All of this indicates that Western Europe is pervaded by a hegemonic ethno-nationalist discourse which both in its illiberal and anti-EU version (Right) and in its neo-liberal and Europeanist one (EU) prescribes congruence of culture, community and territory, and considers immigrants (especially if Muslim) as outsiders when not dysfunctional aliens.

The aim of this chapter is to provide perspectives – i.e. suggest interpretations that are grounded in first-hand analysis of concrete situations and social relations – on how the mainstream European Left has been constructing the question of immigration, highlighting how such constructions have changed in the recent past, and how they relate to those of the other political forces and institutions considered above. The questions being addressed in this chapter include: What does the ethnographic examination of the discourses and practices of the mainstream Left tell us about its treatment of ethno-cultural difference? How are immigrants being categorised by these discourses and practices? Do these categorisations challenge or reinforce the boundaries of inclusion/exclusion being set up by the State and the European Union? How does the Left's recent rhetoric of recognition of ethno-cultural difference relate to its traditional commitment to social and economic justice? How have Left-wing constructions of immigrants changed since the 'socialist era'? [3]

The views put forward in this chapter draw on ethnographic material collected in Bologna, the traditional showcase city of the Italian Left, in the second half of the 1990s. It is argued here that the contemporary mainstream Left in Europe is characterised by what could be called 'non-integrating multiculturalism', that is a politics that favours the recognition of ethno-cultural differences and syncretism (at least at the rhetorical level) but fails to 'integrate' or intersect with initiatives in other fields, such as those regarding socio-economic and gender equality. Partly because of such failure, this politics of the Left is also scarcely contributing to the 'integration' of immigrants.

In addressing how the mainstream political Left constructs the question of migration and multiculturalism in contemporary Europe, this chapter is structured as follows. First it discusses the basic transformations that the mainstream European Left has undergone in recent years. Then it offers a concise overview of the socialist construction of immigrants. After that, it presents the ethnographic case of the construction of immigration by the contemporary Left. This examination entails analysing the official discourse about immigrants and multiculturalism of the Democratic Party of the Left (PDS-DS; the heirs of the Italian Communist Party or PCI and second largest Italian party) and subsequently comparing it with its wider official rhetoric; with the grass-roots discourses of its militants; with the policy practices of the administration of Bologna, and with those of the 'civil society' that collaborated with such administration in policy-making and which forms part of its entourage; and with the views of immigrants. The conclusions formulate theoretical inferences about the contemporary European Left in the context of migration charting its position in relation to the political Right and the European institutions.

## From Socialism to Post-Socialism

In *Destra e Sinistra* Norberto Bobbio (1994) identifies equality (*eguaglianza*) as the main distinguishing feature of the Left. The crucial constant in distinguishing this historical movement from its counterpart has been the effort to remove the obstacles (of class, gender, ethnicity and so forth) that render men and women less equal (1999[1994]: 73).[4] This loose and relative definition of the Left is useful for our purposes because it seems capable of accommodating historical and geographical variations, at least in the European context.

The most significant transformation that the political Left has recently undergone in Western Europe is represented by its 'post-socialist' turn, the process of distancing from the socialist discourse that was initiated in the early 1980s (Meiksins Wood 1986) and that, after the collapse of communism in 1989, accelerated exponentially. This change has been quite noticeable in Italy where the largest communist party in Western Europe – the Italian Communist Party (PCI) – terminated its socialist experience and began a new, 'post-socialist' one with the creation of the Democratic Party of the Left (or PDS-DS). The PDS-DS intended to represent better the plurality of egalitarian demands of the new social subjects of Italian society. However, 'post-socialist' transformations of the Left were by no means restricted to Italy; the U.K. for instance, witnessed a similar transition (though perhaps less radical) which is most effectively symbolised by the decision of the Labour Party to eliminate clause 4 of its constitution (stating the party's commitment to collective ownership) and turn itself into New Labour.

This 'post-socialist' turn, which Ellen Meiksins Wood (1986) describes as the 'retreat from class', has coincided with a growing concern of the Left with questions of identity, cultural difference, citizenship, democracy and institutional reform, economic rationality and efficient-ism, as some of the main ways to pursue greater development and social justice (at least this is what has been repeatedly claimed).

## The Left and Immigration in the Socialist Era

Before turning to the examination of the Left and immigration in the 'post-socialist' era, it is important to consider the socialist construction of immigration. During the socialist era the Left constructed immigrants essentially in terms of class. This construction on the one hand explained migration as the result of exploitative capitalist dynamics and interests and on the other involved the grouping of immigrants and local working classes in the same category, the proletariat (which was counterpoised to that of the bourgeoisie). With class considered the main societal cleavage, the immigrants were thus incorporated alongside the local proletariat in the struggle against the exploitative economic elites. In the case of Italy this inclusionary construction can be seen in the way the PCI framed the massive immigration of poor southern Italians to the industrial North. The following quotation is taken from a popular PCI publication: 'Emigration ... has represented not only an economic but also a political choice of the ruling class which, in the attempt to beat the workers and peasant movement, decided for the forced exodus and rejected both the reform and transformation of agriculture and the industrial development of the South'.[5] These discourses were inclusionary as they incorporated the southerner into the same group as the northern working classes and thereby challenged the existing diffused discourses that considered the southerners as ethno culturally different and alien and therefore excludible (Però 2005).[6]

Although the discourse of the socialist Left about immigrants was overall egalitarian and inclusionary, it had at least two significant limitations. The first is that such discourse was not always applied in practice[7] in both the field of policies and in that of everyday grassroots behaviour. In the former, this discrepancy is evident in the *seuil de tolérance* policies adopted by French communist municipalities during the 1970s which sought to impose a quota on the number of immigrants in their territories and reinforced the xenophobic perceptions of immigrants as a problem (see Grillo 1985 and MacMaster 1990). In the latter, this discrepancy can be seen from the often hostile attitudes of many trade union members in the north-western European countries examined in Castles and Kosack (1973) or from the scarcely inclusionary behaviour of many Communist Party supporters in 1970s Bologna (Kertzer 1980; Però 2005). The second flaw is represented by the general failure to recognise the ethno-cultural difference and specificities of the immigrants who were reductively conceived as mere economic subjects (Però 2005; Pratt 2002). In other words, the Left was revealed as incapable of developing a discourse of recognition of cultural difference within the wider discourse of class. In sum, during the socialist era the mainstream Left operated largely according to a class discourse which generally included the immigrants among the key players of the socialist project of transformation of society but was incapable of recognising as crucial other dimensions of inequality and difference (e.g. ethnicity or gender).[8]

## The Left and Immigration in the Post-Socialist Era

Italy is very interesting for conducting an examination of the Left in the context of migration not only because there the transition to 'post-socialism' has been quite marked (as it has involved a communist rather than a socialist or labour party),[9] but also because it coincided with a significant international immigration flow which turned Italy into a country of immigration after having been for decades one of the main sending countries of the world (King 1993; King and Andall 1999).

Within anthropology, the examination of the Left and immigration has largely been neglected.[10] On the one hand, the established sub-disciplinary tradition of the 'anthropology of the Italian red belt' (Però 1996) stopped with the end of the PCI (with the partial exception of Kertzer 1996 which examined the symbolic aspects of the PCI-PDS transition). On the other hand, the emerging anthropology of Italian immigration and multiculturalism dealt only tangentially with the Left (e.g. Carter 1997; Cole 1997; Grillo and Pratt eds 2002; Maher 1996; Zinn 1994).

### *Immigration and the Official Rhetoric of Inclusion of the PDS: Neglect Unless Otherwise Specified*

The first step in addressing how the mainstream Italian Left constructs the question of migration is to consider the official ideology of its main organisation (the PDS-DS). After the fall of the Berlin Wall the newly born PDS-DS retained an official discourse of inclusion vis-à-vis the immigrants – who were now coming from the poorer regions of the world (King and Rybachzuk 1993; King *et al.* 1997) rather than from the south of the country – but the basis for their inclusion was no longer that of class solidarity; it had changed. The new inclusionary premises were now those of a moral commitment to the recognition of cultural differences and appreciation of multiculturalism. In this way the incorporation of immigrants had become essentially a cultural problem. This attitude can be seen, for example, in the wide range of documents produced on this topic by the Left-wing administration of Bologna during the 1990s and in which it was common to find statements like 'The Municipality of Bologna believes that *differences* (individual, social, cultural, ethnical) are great values and resources to society and that humankind becomes enriched rather than threatened by them' (Comune di Bologna 1998).

This rosy self-representation of the mainstream Left as inclusionary and multicultural has for quite some time gone unquestioned and even enjoyed the accreditation of some academic commentators (e.g. Orsini-Jones and Gattullo 1996 and 2000; Delle Donne 1995). But to what extent can such self-representation be considered accurate? I argue that this question is to be examined in relation to a wider context represented by: the general official rhetoric of the party; the everyday grassroots discourses of its militants; the institutional practices of its local administrations; the activities of the organisations of the so-called civil society (e.g. NGOs) that habitually collaborate with the Left in the provision of services concerning migrants; and the immigrants' perspectives. It is to the consideration of these aspects that the remainder of this chapter now turns.

## *Rhetorical Flaws*

The self-representations of the PDS-DS in relation to immigration and multiculturalism are 'politically correct' and favourable to the inclusion and well-being of the immigrants and to the recognition of their ethno-cultural difference. However, it seems that when not specifically addressing issues of multiculturalism and migration this inclusionary commitment goes out of sight.

An important rhetorical flaw can be found in the foundational document of the then new party, its statute. This statute, in fact, contains no references to the new immigrations, despite the fact that at the outset of the 1990s – as pointed out by Cole (1997) – immigration constituted the single most important issue in public debate. This silence is even more extraordinary since the statute was to mark the embracement of the interests of the new social subjects (as well as the distancing from class politics). Were the immigrants not being considered as part of these new subjects? Were they deliberately left out? Although this lack of reference is probably due more to an oversight than to a malevolent omission, it shows how the issue of the representation of immigrants did not rank very high on the agenda of the party.[11] A second important rhetorical flaw of the PDS-DS has been its recurrent discussion of immigration and criminality in conjunction (see Dal Lago 1999), in much the same way as conservative and xenophobic political organisations have done (although the language, tone and intent of the latter are far more alarmist and deliberately exclusionary). Thus, it seems that when the Left is not self-representing its own official ideological position in relation to multiculturalism (in which it portrays itself as politically correct and inclusionary), it becomes characterised by a less inclusionary attitude.

## Left-Wing Grassroots Discourses about Immigrants

This section intends to provide a sense of the discourses about immigrants that I found among PDS-DS militants. The situation encountered at this level is very ambivalent. In fact, besides some instances of militants who acted inspired by ideals of cultural pluralism and solidarity towards disadvantaged and less-fortunate people who had left their homes and countries in search of better life conditions, I found several instances of instrumental and exclusionary attitudes. Here are a few examples of such attitudes.

The first example refers to a discourse that I recurrently found among the rank and file of the PDS-DS in the 1990s, that of exploitative inclusion. Exploitative inclusion characterises the arguments put forward by Mandolini,[12] a co-director of a social centre for elderly people in Bologna, who after being a partisan had militated first in the PCI and then in the PDS-DS. During a discussion with some elderly members of his centre he defended immigration against those who considered it a negative phenomenon that had brought about greater tensions and insecurity in the city. His defence, however, did not seem guided by ideals of multiculturalism/ethno-cultural pluralism (of the type that characterise the party official rhetoric: 'immigrants are a resource for the cultural enrichment of Italian society'). Neither did it appear to be based on class or even humanitarian solidarity (such as 'they are poor people and exploited victims of capitalism and colonialism who were never given opportunities for self-development in their country of origin and whose interests we must now defend if we want to create a socialist or even only a more socially cohesive and just society'), nor did it reflect a libertarian ideal (of the type: 'human beings are born free and should be entitled to travel and settle down wherever they see the most appropriate opportunities'). Mandolini based his defence of immigration on a utilitarian argument, which is not dissimilar from the one that can be found among 'moderate' politico-administrative and economic elites. He argued that 'immigrants are useful to us because they do the hard and dirty jobs that we no longer want to do, they pay our pension and contribute to our economy because in this way the bosses don't move their business outside Italy where labour is cheaper. So we have to be thankful to the immigrants!'

The second example of how the official rhetoric of inclusion and recognition of cultural difference of the mainstream Left often finds scarce correspondence to everyday life refers to attitudes towards exclusion of immigrants from the moral democratic community. This instance is well illustrated by the comments of comrade Avventura (a middle-aged full-time PDS-DS activist whom I met during the national election campaign of 1996) on the question of conceding voting rights to immigrants. She argued that conceding any such rights to immigrants would be a mistake because, in her view, immigrants suffer from a sort of democratic deficit that she illustrated as follows:

> I know a Chinese doctor who has lived in Italy for many years and who is a very good doctor and an extremely correct person ... but once at a dinner we discussed the Gulf War and he was in favour of Saddam Hussein and against the West. Now how can we possibly give voting rights to these people who are not accustomed to democracy?

This attitude reveals a striking similarity to those that characterise the political Right and xenophobic forces.

The third example of the misfit that often exists between official and grassroots Left-wing discourses about immigrants refers to an attitude of rejection of ethnic diversity in one's own residential surroundings. This instance is illustrated by the following account of how a group of local PDS-DS activists reacted to the City Council's decision to site a group of Roma refugees from the former Yugoslavia in their district for the period of their 'legalisation'. One morning in mid-July 1995 a local party leader of the district in which I carried out much of my fieldwork phoned me to let me know about a confidential party meeting scheduled for the following day in one *sezione* of the district. The meeting had been confidentially arranged by the *consigliere comunale* (member of the city parliament) elected in the district and most of the party leaders of the district (who had arranged for his election and to whom he was somewhat accountable). The purpose of the meeting was to timely inform the local party leaders of the city mayor's policy decision shortly to transfer a group of *profughi-nomadi* (Roma refugees from the former Yugoslavia) from the Reno river bank (where they had been living in the most appalling conditions) into the velodrome located in their district. The meeting was also meant to ask for the active support of the party rank and file in the district because the transfer, being about 'gypsies' and given the diffused anti-gypsy sentiments, was likely to generate protests. The rank and file was thus being invited to prepare the ground, contain the citizens' *malumore* (ill feelings), and ultimately render the policy implementation smoother. 'From a human and social point of view we [PDS-DS] cannot be those who chuck them out ... the question is who will take care of surveillance, as the people [of the neighbourhood] will be terrified of theft and burglaries when they leave their homes for the holidays in August', said the *consigliere*.

The reactions to the *consigliere*'s opening speech ranged from calm and articulated criticism to angry outbursts. Somebody complained that the policy decision had been taken without consulting with that party base whose support was now being sought. Somebody else suggested that the true identity of the refugees was not that of *profughi di guerra* (refugees of war) as they were being presented, but that of *zingari* (gypsies). This person also argued that 'technically speaking' the Council was not in the condition to carry out this operation on its own, and that it indeed needed extra help, but from the *protezione civile*[13] rather than from party *sezioni*. A third party cadre pointed out that it was high time that the Council administration began to be properly supported by the *Prefettura* (the main representative of the central State in the territory), 'as the City Council alone is not able to take care of the entire world arriving in Bologna'. He also explained that the choice of place and time for the operation was *infelice* ('a bad choice') since: these people were 'gypsies' who had lived in sub-human conditions and on socially questionable sources of survival for several years; the location was inappropriate, too close to the local highly populated area (literally under many local residents' windows and in front of their own doors); and the local residents were bound to get really upset to find 'gypsies all over the place' together with the unpleasant surprises the 'gypsies' would generate on the residents' return from their holidays at the end of August.

However, these scarcely inclusionary discourses of control, surveillance, security, protection from disasters, and contention, were soon to appear 'soft' in comparison to the reaction of the party cadre who had joined the meeting late. As soon as he realised the issue being discussed he launched himself into a series of shouts and angry complaints of the following type: 'Into the velodrome! ... are we crazy? ... Leave them down at the river bank where they are!'; 'We have already got the extra-communitarians there, we have already done our duty! [by accepting such a centre on the territory]!',[14] 'In front of my house? I can't believe it!'.[15] In sum, the instances presented in this section have sought to convey a sense of the exclusionary terms in which the immigrants are often talked about and considered by the mainstream Left in everyday contexts, and to highlight how the commitment to the recognition of ethno-cultural difference is often unattended in practice.

## Policy Practices: Immigrant Housing Policy in Bologna during the 1990s

Whereas the question of ethno-cultural recognition often disappears from sight in the everyday grassroots discourses of party militants, in the policies of the Left-wing administration of Bologna it is much more present, although in a problematic way as this section will show. The most important policy effort of the Left-wing administration of Bologna in the context of migration went into the sphere of housing. To confront the difficulty faced by immigrants in accessing housing in Bologna[16] the administration, instead of favouring the immigrants' residential distribution across the city, decided to concentrate them in specific residential structures according to ethno-cultural criteria (i.e. Moroccans with Moroccans, Pakistanis with Pakistanis, Senegalese with Senegalese and so forth). Subsequently the aim of the Council was to turn such centres into 'community centres', each to appoint its own ethnic community leader to act as interlocutor vis-à-vis the City Council.

From the perspective of cultural recognition, the greatest problem with this policy lay in having coupled such centres with very marginalising and exclusionary arrangements, which included: the very poor quality of the buildings, many of which were light metal bungalows; their siting in unhealthy places that often were not served by public transport, such as industrial districts or open fields next to the municipal dog pound; their unhealthy and unsafe conditions (which did not meet the ordinary health and safety regulations); the misuse and abuse of the structures which worsened even further their already dangerous hygienic and safety conditions (e.g. cases of tuberculosis had appeared);[17] their male-biased nature (e.g. ten of the twelve Centres of First Shelter CPAs were for males only in spite of the fact that immigrant women represented almost half of the immigrant population of the city; see Zontini 2001); and their bad administration (characterised by contradictory and patronising when not oppressive management policies).[18] In sum, in Bologna, the official Left-wing commitment to the recognition of ethno-cultural difference became translated into policies that coupled difference with the provision of second-rate and marginalising services, as the case of housing just considered illustrates.

## 'Civil Society'

Now that political parties have lost a considerable amount of significance (e.g. their membership has shrunk, they are less 'present' in everyday social relations and less appreciated as channels of mobilisation), a comprehensive examination of the mainstream political Left must include that part of 'civil society' that forms its entourage and that often collaborates systematically with it in policy-making and practices of 'governance'. My point about the mainstream Leftist 'civil society' in the context of migration and multiculturalism is that it is characterised by a position of essentialism and scarce participation similar to that illustrated in the previous pages. In some cases this similarity is connected to the subordinate position that 'civil society' occupies with respect to formal political organisations and institutions. This seems particularly the case in regimes of 'governance', where 'civil society' organisations are often hired by governments to deliver public services on their behalf in exchange for money and other resources.

To illustrate this point I will provide a brief ethnographic account of the experience I observed during my 1995 fieldwork. At the outset of that year the Bologna City Council as part of its immigration policy contracted out a project of Participatory Action Research (PAR) to one of the main NGOs of the city operating in the sector of migration and multiculturalism and composed by politically engaged 'Leftists'. The official objective was to conduct PAR in two of the main CPAs of the city, in order to facilitate the settlement process of its immigrant residents.

Soon, however, the project revealed itself to be an attempt on the part of the Council (in collaboration with the NGO) to on the one hand bring back to 'acceptable' levels the degenerated situations of the centres,[19] and on the other finally overcome the immigrants' resistance to transforming the CPAs into self-managed centres of community. As mentioned in the previous section, the policy of the Left-wing administration of Bologna had sought to solve the problem of immigrants' homelessness by housing a large portion of the legal immigrants (approximately one thousand) in very cheap and precarious residential structures according to ethnic criteria.[20] After subjecting the CPAs to authoritarian management for some years the Council decided that the Centres had to be self-managed. As this decision had not gone down well with the immigrants, who interpreted it as a sign of abandonment and neglect, the Council sought to impose its policy by withdrawing the provision of assistance (i.e. social workers, security guards, maintenance, rubbish collection and telephone) until the immigrants reconsidered their view and began organising themselves as a 'community' with their own leader to represent them vis-à-vis the Council. Apart from the questionable attempt to set up self-management via top-down decision-making, the choice of seeking to enforce this decision by suspending the provision of assistance not only failed but resulted in an 'explosive' situation characterised by further lowering of the already poor hygienic and safety conditions of the Centre, and by the overall worsening of a degraded social environment.

Realising that the situation had got out of hand and become politically quite dangerous, the Council (whose officials where no longer even recognised as legitimate interlocutors by the CPA residents) identified in the abovementioned NGO-led PAR project an alternative way to set up its new policy of self-management. By agreeing to oversee the logistics of the Council's policy the NGO subscribed, reinforced and articulated the policy of the Left-wing administration that the previous section has described as perfunctorily recognising difference, scarcely participatory, essentialist and paternalistic, when not oppressive.

Of course, this brief account of civil societal involvement in rather exclusionary practices cannot be considered representative of the entire 'third sector', which is heterogeneous (and in which many actors would not regard themselves as being primarily inspired by Left-wing values). Nevertheless, the situation described in these pages is not uncommon in processes of governance and subcontracting public services provision to non-profit-making organisations. By showing the subordination of those sectors of 'civil society' that participate in 'governance' to political parties and public administrations, this section not only highlights how badly official commitments to cultural recognition are translated into practice, but also questions the representations of Italian 'civil society' as virtuous and independent that authoritative commentators have provided (Bagnasco 1994; Ginsborg 2001).

## Immigrants' Views

A final element to consider in an anthropological examination of the discourses and practices of the Left in the context of migration is the view of the immigrants themselves. When presented before a generic choice between the Right and Left the orientation of the majority of immigrants is likely to be more sympathetic to the latter who are comparatively less hostile to them. However, this relative preference for the Left does not necessarily imply a wholehearted positive assessment. On the contrary, in my fieldwork I came across several immigrants who considered themselves on the Left of the political spectrum, but whose experiences in Bologna had disappointed them often to the extent of reconsidering their politico-ideological identity and a sense of belonging.

In some cases the vacuum created by disillusionment with 'progressive' politics seemed to be filled by a growing sympathy or support for radical strands of Islamism. The case of A. is illustrative in this respect. In a number of conversations, A. said that he had been a Communist supporter – although never really an activist – and how he disliked the lack of democracy and opportunities afflicting his country (and how this situation constituted one of the reasons for migrating). He explained how in Bologna he was expecting to find both democracy and socialism but regretfully found neither. On the contrary, his experience of the Left and its 'progressive' policy-making (especially in the field of housing) were regarded as oppressive, and pointed out that the only credible alternative to capitalism and injustice was now for him that of Islamists.

In other cases, disillusionment with the Left led to political cynicism and disenchantment. For instance, B., who had volunteered in local PDS-DS festivals (*feste dell'Unità*) as well as in the immigration office of a trade union, in the light of his experience of the contradictions between the principles and policy practices of the Left bluntly concluded that 'socialism in Bologna is bollocks!' ('*il socialismo a Bologna è una cazzata!*'). To B. there no longer existed a substantial difference between the Left and the Right.

On the specific question of cultural recognition, it was common when asking immigrants if the multicultural initiatives of the Council were adequately acknowledging their ethno-cultural identity to be answered with sarcastic comments. They especially criticised the *feste* for which they had been invited to bring or cook cous-cous, for this was considered a rather hypocritical initiative of marginal importance, compared to the substantial interventions they needed in fields such as housing.

## Conclusion

In seeking to chart the position of the Left on the map of contemporary European political cultures in relation to immigration and multiculturalism, this chapter has suggested that the Left has moved from a rhetoric of inclusion and construction of immigrants merely based on class and socio-economic equality to one merely based on ethnicity and cultural recognition. This chapter has also highlighted how, at least in Italy, such rhetoric has been on the one hand, poorly reflected in everyday grassroots discourses and practices and on the other hand, often translated into marginalising public policies.[21]

Thus, as far as the contemporary mainstream Left is concerned, such public policies express a situation that could be described as 'non-integrating multiculturalism'. This is an attitude that in principle favours the recognition of ethno-cultural difference and appreciates syncretism, but that (apart from being scarcely applied in practice) fails to 'integrate' or combine with other egalitarian preoccupations, such as the promotion of socio-economic justice. Using Brah's terminology (1996) we could alternatively define 'non-integrating multiculturalism' as a politics that operates only along the axis of ethno-cultural differentiation (and with strong limitations) and does not combine or intersect with egalitarian initiatives along any other axis of differentiation. I have chosen this expression to describe the mainstream Left in the context of migration because, while it acknowledges the Left's positive attitude towards multiculturalism,[22] it highlights both its failure to develop a political process that 'integrates' commitments on the various fronts of inequality and its scarce 'integrationist' effects with respect to the immigrants.

'Non-integrating multiculturalism' is not a casual attitude but reflects well the new 'post-socialist' course undertaken by the Left and its attitude of accommodation, rather than opposition, to the contemporary neo-liberal transformation of society. This transformation includes the rolling back of the State, cuts in public spending, the subordination of political powers to economic ones with the consequent exclusion of the economy from the sphere of political intervention, and the incapability of political elites to transcend the national scale (see Bauman 1998). Recognising the position of the Left in relation to this scenario has important implications for how we interpret and represent its position with respect to difference and inequality. The current rhetoric of ethno-cultural recognition of the mainstream Left appears functional to maintain a 'progressive' and 'politically correct' appearance at a time when it has largely renounced confronting the conditions of super-exploitation that so often affect immigrants and that – partly as a result of these changes in Left-wing attitudes – appear as increasingly 'natural', 'normal' and 'inevitable' features of contemporary society. In this new context, those critiques (such as those of the New Left and Cultural Studies) that saw the main problem with the Left as the reduction of all differences and inequalities to those of class appear no longer relevant. Such critiques may have accurately described important sectors of the Left in the past but they no longer serve to describe a Left that seems to have abandoned much of its commitment to socio-economic justice.

In conclusion, the material presented in this chapter has suggested that the 'post-socialist' Left (by privileging cultural differences at the expenses of material justice) is entangled, on the one hand, in the reinforcement of the dominant 'ethnicism' that frames the immigrants in merely ethno-cultural terms and, on the other hand, in the legitimisation of the exclusionary mechanisms, boundaries and representations that characterise both the State apparatuses of 'fortress Europe'[23] and – more brutally so – the organisations of the political Right.

## NOTES

1. The examination of the political Left in the context of migration contained in this chapter has benefited from the helpful comments of the book editors, the anonymous reviewer, Dorothy Zinn and Elisabetta Zontini whom I gratefully acknowledge.
2. Drawing on her U.S. ethnography, Ong (1996) has argued that culture has not replaced race in exclusionary constructions but has developed alongside it.
3. In addressing these questions this chapter will also contribute to revive an important tradition in Europeanist anthropology that was particularly strong in the Italian case until the fall of the Berlin Wall, namely, the study of political cultures, especially the Left (e.g. Kertzer 1980; Pratt 1986; Shore 1990; Li Causi 1993).
4. It is beyond the scope of this chapter to discuss the lively debate that Bobbio's book has generated (see the references contained in its 1999 edition here cited).
5. Grazzani in PCI (1976: 32; my transl.).
6. A good explanation of the in-group/out-group dynamics of inclusion/exclusion in the context of migration in Italy appears in Maher (1996).
7. Today this rhetoric/practice discrepancy is systematic as I have shown in Però (2001) and as will emerge from the remainder of this chapter.
8. For a wider discussion of the Left and immigration in the past see Però (2005).
9. For a discussion of the transition see Ignazi (1992) and Kertzer (1996).

10. A similar situation is also found in other disciplines.
11. The neglect of immigrants is visible in Bologna Futura (1989), a book by the PCI of Bologna on its policy initiatives at the outset of the 1990s.
12. I have used pseudonyms to refer to my informants.
13. The *protezione civile* is the rapid intervention unit of the Italian State specialised in confronting public emergencies like natural disasters and so forth.
14. This refers to a Centre of First Shelter for immigrants, which I have examined in the context of local public policies in Però (1997).
15. For the entire account of the meeting and subsequent grassroots discourses and initiatives see Però (1999a). For the detailed ethnography of the policy intervention see Però (1999a,b).
16. Bologna is a city of approximately 400,000 residents, whose empty flats are estimated to number around 10,000.
17. Many of these buildings had an expiry date of two years and they were being used for most of a decade.
18. For a detailed account of the housing policy of Bologna see Però (1997 and 2001).
19. Such degeneration was in large part due to the inconsistency and flaws in the policy measure adopted; see Però (1997).
20. For a more detailed description of the CPAs and of the PAR experience see Però (1997).
21. Of course, this is neither to deny instances in which the new multiculturalist discourse of the Left has helped to deflate intolerance (as in the case of the pro-refugee committee discussed in Però 1999a), nor to claim that no significant differences exist between Left and Right in the context of migration.
22. Multiculturalism is here to be understood as defined by Touraine (2000), that is to say in an inclusionary, synchretic and pluralist sense and in contrast to 'multi-communitarianism' which envisages the maintenance of different cultures (essentially conceived) as separate and bounded to specific territories.
23. That is, a Europe closed and precluded to those from the poor 'outside'.

## References

Bagnasco, A. 1994. 'La società civile entra in scena: associazionismo quali prospettive?'. In *Lo Stato dell'Italia*, ed. P. Ginsborg. Milan, Il Saggiatore.

Bauman, Z. 1998. *Globalization: The Human Consequences*. Cambridge, Polity.

Bobbio, N. 1994. *Destra e sinistra: Ragioni e significati di una distinzione politica*. Rome, Donzelli.

Brah, A. 1996. *Cartographies of Diaspora: Contesting Identities*. London, Routledge.

Carter, D.M. 1997. *States of Grace: Senegalese in Italy and the New European Immigration*. Minneapolis, University of Minnesota Press.

Castles, S. and G. Kosack. 1973. *Immigrant Workers and Class Structure in Western Europe*. Oxford, Oxford University Press.

Cole, J. 1997. *The New Racism in Europe: A Sicilian Ethnography*. Cambridge, Cambridge University Press.

Comune di Bologna, Istituzione Servizi Immigrazione. *La Città Multietnica*. 1998. http://www2.comune.Bologna.it/bologna/immigra/intreng.htm

Dal Lago, A. 1999. *Non-persone: L'esclusione dei migranti in una società globale*. Milan, Feltrinelli.

Delle Donne, M. 1995. 'Difficulties of refugees towards integration: The Italian case'. In *Avenues to Integration: Refugees in Contemporary Europe*, ed. M. Delle Donne. Naples, Ipermedium.
Ginsborg, P. 2001. *Italy and its Discontents: Family, Civil Society, State 1980–2001*. London, Allen Lane The Penguin Press.
Grillo, R.D. 1985. *Ideologies and Institutions in Urban France*. Cambridge, Cambridge University Press.
Grillo, R.D. and J.C. Pratt eds. 2002. *The Politics of Recognising Difference: Multiculturalism Italian Style*. Aldershot, Ashgate.
Holmes, D.R. 2000. *Integral Europe: Fast-Capitalism, Multiculturalism, Neofascism*. Princeton, Princeton University Press.
Ignazi, P. 1992. *Dal PCI al PDS*. Bologna, Il Mulino.
Kertzer D.I. 1980. *Comrades and Christians: Religion and Political Struggle in Communist Italy*. Cambridge, Cambridge University Press.
Kertzer D.I. 1996. *Politics and Symbols: The Italian Communist Party and the Fall of Communism*. New Haven, Yale University Press.
King, R. 1993. 'Recent immigration to Italy: Character, causes, and consequences'. *GeoJournal* 30, no. 3: 283–92.
King, R. and J. Andall. 1999. 'The geography and sociology of recent immigration to Italy'. *Modern Italy* 2, no. 2: 135–58.
King, R., Fielding, A. and R. Black. 1997. 'The international migration turnround in southern Europe'. In *Southern Europe and the New Immigrations*, eds R. King and R. Black. Brighton, Sussex Academic Press.
King, R. and K. Rybacuzk. 1993. 'Southern Europe and the international division of labour from emigration to immigration'. In *The New Geography of European Migrations*, ed. R. King. London, Belhaven.
Li Causi, L. 1993. *Il Partito a Noi ci ha Dato! Antropologia Politica di una Sezione Comunista Senese nel Dopoguerra*. Siena, Laboratorio EtnoAntropologico.
MacMaster, N. 1990. 'The "seuil de tolerance": the uses of a "scientific" racist concept'. In *Race, Discourse and Power in France*, ed. M. Silverman. Aldershot, Avebury.
Maher, V. 1996. 'Immigration and social identities'. In *Italian Cultural Studies*, eds R. Lumley and D. Forgacs. Oxford, Oxford University Press.
Meiksins Wood, E. 1986. *The Retreat from Class*. London, Verso.
Ong, A. 1996. 'Cultural citizenship as subject-making: Immigrants negotiate racial and cultural boundaries in the United States'. *Contemporary Anthropology* 37, no. 5: 737–62.
Orsini-Jones, M. and F. Gattullo. 1996. 'Visibility at a price? Black women in red Bologna'. *Tuttitalia* 14: 24–38.
Orsini-Jones, M. and F. Gattullo. 2000. 'Migrant women in Italy: National trends and local perspectives'. In *Gender and Migration in Southern Europe*, eds F. Anthias and G. Lazaridis. Oxford, Berg.
Partito Comunista Italiano (PCI). 1976. *Almanacco PCI*. Rome, Partito Comunista Italiano.
Partito Comunista Italiano (PCI), Federazione di Bologna. 1989. *Bologna Futura*. Milan, Franco Angeli.
Però, D. 1996. 'Political anthropology of Italy in action'. *Anthropology in Action* 3, no. 3: 36–8.

Però, D. 1997. 'Immigrants and politics in Left-wing Bologna: Results from participatory action research'. In *Southern Europe and the New Immigrations*, eds R. King and R. Black. Brighton, Sussex Academic Press.

Però, D. 1999a. *The Politics of Identity in Left-Wing Bologna: An Ethnographic Study of the Discourses and Practices of the Italian Left in the Context of Migration.* Unpublished D.Phil. Thesis, University of Sussex.

Però, D. 1999b. 'Next to the dog pound: Institutional discourses and practices about Rom refugees in Left-wing Bologna'. *Modern Italy* 4, no. 2: 207–24.

Però, D. 2001. 'Inclusionary rhetoric / exclusionary practice: An ethnographic critique of the Italian Left in the context of migration'. In *The Mediterranean Passage: Migration and New Cultural Encounters in Southern Europe*, ed. R. King. Liverpool, Liverpool University Press.

Però, D. 2002. 'The Left and the Political Participation of Immigrants in Italy: The Case of the Forum of Bologna'. In *The Politics of Recognising Difference. Multiculturalism Italian Style*, eds R.D. Grillo and J.C. Pratt. Aldershot, Ashgate.

Però, D. 2005. 'Inclusion without Recognition: The Socialist Left and Immigrants in 1970s Italy'. *Focaal – European Journal of Anthropology*, forthcoming.

Pratt, J.C. 2002. 'Political unity and cultural diversity'. In *The Politics of Recognising Difference: Multiculturalism Italian Style*, eds R.D. Grillo and J.C. Pratt. Aldershot, Ashgate.

Shore, C. 1990. *Italian Communism: The Escape from Leninism.* London, Pluto Press.

Shore, C. 1997. 'Ethnicity, xenophobia and the boundaries of Europe'. *International Journal on Minority and Group Rights* 4, no. 3/4: 247–62.

Shore, S. 2000. *Building Europe: The Cultural Politics of the European Union.* London, Routledge.

Shore, C. and A. Black. 1994. '"Citizens' Europe" and the construction of European identity'. In *The Anthropology of Europe*, eds V. Goddard *et al.* Oxford, Berg.

Stolcke, V. 1995. 'Talking culture: New boundaries, new rhetorics of exclusion in Europe'. *Current Anthropology* 36, no. 1: 1–24.

Zinn, D.L. 1994. 'The Senegale immigrants in Bari: What happens when the Africans peer back'. In *International Yearbook of Oral Histories and Life Stories*, eds R. Benmayor and A. Skotnes. Oxford, Oxford University Press.

Zontini, E. 2001. 'Family formation in gendered migration: Moroccan and Filipino women in Bologna'. In *The Mediterranean Passage: Migration and New Cultural Encounters in Southern Europe*, ed. R. King. Liverpool, Liverpool University Press.

# Part II: The Experience of Immigration

# Chapter 5
# The Grand Old West: Mythical Narratives of a Better Past before 1989 in Views of West-Berlin Youth from Immigrant Families

Sabine Mannitz

## Introduction

This chapter examines the creation of new boundaries in the aftermath of the German unification. Without any doubt, the end of the Cold War and the breakdown in the Eastern hemisphere of the political world have meant in the first instance an opening of borders and an erosion of the polarised concepts of East versus West. Particularly in Europe, the new world order 'created a political momentum for change in the direction of political union that was without precedence' (Wiener 1998: 222). At the same time, the events of the 1990s stimulated a revitalisation of the concept of nation state and eventually led to the erection of many new state borders in the former Soviet Union and its satellites. Whether one interprets these developments as complementary effects or as opposite trends, there is no doubt that 'with the end of the Cold War issues of collective identity have become centrally important' and might have 'given rise to xenophobia and a new wave of nationalism' (Katzenstein 1997: 22).

Within these changes Germany represents a special case. Given their status as frontier states, the German Democratic Republic (GDR) and the Federal

Republic of Germany (FRG) were prime symbols of the East–West confrontation. They were therefore neatly integrated in their respective power blocs and had given up national rhetoric to found a collective identity. The catastrophe of National Socialism and the Second World War had after all contributed to a far-reaching disavowal of references to national communion in post-war Germany on either side of the political fence. In these circumstances the opportunity to establish a common state after 1989 was not only unexpected, but also implied the awkward necessity to rethink and redefine the conceptual boundaries that had been established successfully over a span of four decades. The meanings of East and West have shifted, and at the same time a shift in notions has taken place: 'Western Europe' was not a clearly defined region in world politics any longer, and likewise the concept of a politically defined 'Eastern Europe' to start in the GDR was rendered invalid. Since then, parts of the former East tend to be termed 'central Europe', thereby denoting geographical and cultural rather than political aspects. In the case of Germany, 'the geopolitical changes initiated with the collapse of the Berlin Wall had moved Germany almost overnight into the centre of Europe as opposed to its former status of lingering on the eastern margins of Western Europe' (Wiener 1998: 222) – or on the western margins of Eastern Europe, as one should add for the case of the GDR.

How do these conceptual changes affect German society, which has to cope with a former East and a former West within its new borders? I will investigate this question through interviews I conducted with immigrants' children in Berlin – the city that stood for divided Germany as much as divided Germany stood for the East–West divide. After unification, Berlin has remained a focal point, although it has clearly lost this importance in the international political setting. This is not so much due to its regained status of being the German capital, but because of the inevitable confrontation with the history of the German division in the city. Berlin represents a kind of integration laboratory; people from the former East and West encounter each other in Berlin much more than elsewhere.

One may ask why I concentrate on informants with non-German nationality to investigate such a national issue. In fact the immigrant population does not figure prominently in the public debates about post-unification Germany. This seems to be related to the way immigration has been dealt with in the Federal Republic for most of the past forty years. To highlight the particular position of the labour immigrants and their children in German society, the argument starts hence with a brief section on the history of labour immigration to the FRG, its normative treatment and the related nation concept.

With regard to the drawing of boundaries, the first part will focus on a specific ambivalence on the part of the immigrants and their children: whether and to what extent they belong to 'the German people' is a matter of contested interpretation. This implies a certain space where boundaries might be blurred or manipulated and is also the reason why the immigrants' discursive practices concerning the German unification or Germanness are particularly interesting. On the one hand, regarding nationality, theirs is the position of outsiders. On the other hand, most of the immigrant families have been living in West German society for such a long time that they are evidently insiders on this level, even more so in comparison to Germans from the former GDR. To discuss a presumably national issue from the perspective of non-national but socially experienced participants allows thus for a critical reflection of the concepts that dominate the public discourse on in-groups versus others that tend to oppose immigrant minorities to the national majority population.

The different options for constructing national collectivity in terms of social and economic participation as opposed to cultural origin were taken up in a remarkable way by the youths from immigrant backgrounds whom I met in Berlin. In reaction to the large-scale political discourses about the new Germany and the historical tasks it involves, these young people revealed frictions and new boundaries, and constructed the myth of a better past before 1989. In what follows, I will argue that this glorification of the 'grand old West' reveals a strong identification with as well as claims of belonging to German society.

The views I am going to cite were expressed by adolescents (fifteen to twenty years old) from – for the most part Turkish – immigrant families who live in Neukölln and Kreuzberg in Berlin. Both boroughs belonged to West Berlin formerly and were located in the immediate shade of the Wall. My first access to this social space consisted of intensive ethnographic fieldwork in a secondary school in 1996–1997.[1] All the young people who are quoted in what follows were pupils at that school during my research. In addition to data from my fieldwork, I will employ empirical material that was developed in between 1997 and 2001 by means of interviews with some of these – then former – pupils.

## Labour Immigration to West Germany before the Unification

Ironically enough with regard to the topic under discussion here, the construction of the Berlin Wall in 1961 marked the beginning of a new phase of immigration for the FRG. Right after the Second World War, refugees and expelled and displaced persons made up most of the migrants who came to settle in the occupied zones that were to become GDR and FRG. Evidently, these 'migrations' were not voluntary, and historical circumstances must have played a significant role in their acceptance in post-war Germany (see Frantzioch 1987; Münz *et al.* 1997: 23). When the Iron Curtain fell, stopping migrations from the Eastern parts to the increasingly prospering Western zones of occupied Germany,[2] labour immigration from Southern Europe started on a large scale in the Federal Republic: 2.6 million 'guest-workers' came to Western Germany and Berlin between 1961 and 1973 from Italy, Greece, Spain, Portugal, Yugoslavia and Turkey. Most numerous were the immigrants from Turkey (600,000), Yugoslavia (535,000) and Italy (450,000).[3] The then usual term 'guest-worker' indicates the rationale that was applied to labour immigration: hiring labourers from abroad was supposed to work in the style of rotation and to depend on the economic trends and needs in the German 'host society'. In the 1960s this was in fact a consensual matter: most 'guest-workers' themselves had no intention to stay but wanted to earn and save money for a few years and then return to their countries of origin. There were hence considerable moves of temporary immigration as well as returns to the sending countries until the early 1970s (see Münz *et al.* 1997: 35–51).

In the course of the 1960s the idea of rotation gradually lost acceptance. Many of the 'guest-workers' realised that they could not reach their economic goals quickly. Their German employers on the other hand found it easier to keep personnel once it had been trained and had picked up some German language. Last but not least, the social misery of regarding and treating people merely as workforce without granting them any realistic possibilities to lead a regular family life spoke against rotation. The issue was raised increasingly by labour unions and welfare organisations. This referred in particular to Turkish migrants whose terms of duration had been restricted to two years already in the bilateral contract which the FRG had signed with Turkey in 1961. From 1964 the West German Government reacted to the growing dissatisfaction with rotation by issuing working and residence permits that allowed longer periods of stay.[4] More and more 'guest-workers' ended their provisional living conditions, invited their families over and started to settle down.

With the beginning of recession in the 1970s, the federal Government aimed at the consolidation of the economy and reduction of the number of foreign workers who lived in West Germany. The recruitment of labour force from abroad was frozen officially in 1973, and financial assistance was introduced for people who returned to their countries of origin. New regulations were passed to restrict immigration by way of family reunion. Since then, foreigners who move to Germany on the basis of working permits can bring their spouse and minor children of up to the age of sixteen years old. For various reasons, the Government's intention to reduce the number of foreign residents by recruitment freeze and return incentives failed. The fear that further restrictions could follow stimulated family reunions and effected a solidification rather than a drop in immigration flow. From 1973 to the late 1980s was a phase of establishment as far as the former 'guest-workers' and their families were concerned. Yet irrespective of these factual developments, the normative creed remained – until the year 2000 – that 'Germany is no immigration country' and should hence stick to the 'freeze' principles regarding labour immigration. Consequently, the presence of the immigrant population was not subject to any constructive policy of inclusion, although it had become an obvious matter of fact. The migration historian Klaus Bade characterised this situation as follows: West Germany 'was not only an ambivalent de-facto immigration country with an inclusive welfare policy and an exclusive nationality law. Also, the foreign population, stemming from the former "guest-worker population", had in a way all of a sudden grown into an immigration status without any corresponding offers from the side of the stubborn immigration country' (Bade 2000: 338).

The necessity to revise the related paradigms in Germany became an issue of heated debate only in the late 1990s when the Social Democrats and Greens took office. Likewise, new options of labour immigration to Germany were discussed only after the 1998 change of Government. The lack of experts in certain fields such as information technology put the question on the political agenda of whether a sort of 'Green Card' should be introduced to attract skilled personnel from abroad. Before that, the dominant discourse on immigration had been motivated by aims of restriction rather than recruitment. This was related to the fact that after the events of 1989–1990, immigration rates increased considerably, though obviously not in the form of labour immigration. Asylum seekers and refugees from the separatist wars in former Yugoslavia as well as immigrants of German ancestry from the former USSR came to Germany. The latter enjoy a special status of nationality, because of historical residues of recognition and support during the Cold War. When the demolition of the Iron Curtain made these people's emigration easier, their privileged access became a matter of public debate in Germany, as it entailed a bundle of problems and ran counter to the declared norm of the no-immigration policy. The concept of German nationality was challenged and the modes of integrating immigrants became a contested issue.

## The German Nation Concept

The Federal Republic of Germany maintained a rather strict policy regarding nationality and naturalisation until 2000. Before the innovations of the year 2000, the politically unintended reality that the FRG had in fact become a host country for immigration was not thought to be an adequate reason for revising the nationality laws, which dated from the German Empire in 1913. Being mainly based on the *jus sanguinis*, German nationality was constructed in an exclusive fashion. It was tied to ancestry and consequently hard to acquire for immigrants of non-German descent. This does not mean that naturalisation of foreigners was impossible but it was rather exceptional until

1990, and immigrants were not encouraged to 'become Germans'. A law issued in 1990 gave immigrants the right to naturalisation after fifteen years of legal residence, where before it had been a matter of discretionary decision. Still, the ancestral principle was not yet given up, and the implication that 'being German' in the proper sense would not just refer to formal political citizenship but include a genealogical dimension of ethnic Germanness was kept alive. Foreigners with a different ethnic background had the possibility to join the German *demos* but this aspect was not brought to public attention with adequately clear regulations nor with any official initiative to foster acceptance of such 'other Germans' (Mecheril and Teo 1994; Mecheril 1997). The tendency was to equate the demotic and the ethnic dimensions of the nation and 'to attribute higher value to the *ethnos*' (Hoffmann 1996: 253) within this structure. Of course, ethnic membership can also be attained but it takes much longer than a model of nationality that operates on the basis of demotic inclusion such as the ethnically blind republican concept in France.[5] Within the ethno-national German understanding, 'becoming German' was also possible before the 2000 amendment of the nationality conditions, but it took generations of living in the country. The descendants of the nineteenth century Polish labour immigrants are for instance not exposed to any doubts about their Germanness any longer. But when the Poles immigrated 100 to 120 years ago, it was doubted whether they could ever become part of the German people due to their presumed otherness. A rhetoric flourished against the 'foreign infiltration' from the East that parallels in many aspects the culturalist discourses from the 1980s and 1990s about the otherness of the labour immigrants from the South (see Bade 1992; Budzinski 1999; Mannitz and Schiffauer 2004).

The 'exclusive nation' concept with its corresponding legislation to regulate nationality and the failure to recognise immigrant diversity had the effect of very low naturalisation rates in the FRG. Most of the former 'guestworkers', as well as their children and grandchildren, remained foreign nationals in Germany. The new law that took effect in 2000 introduced *jus soli* as an additional way to perceive German nationality. According to *jus soli*, the children of foreigners who are born in Germany and live in the country permanently acquire German nationality automatically, regardless of whether ancestral nationality is acquired through their parents or not. At the age of majority they must choose nationality, because dual nationality is only allowed under a few exceptional conditions. The terms of naturalisation were also altered in 2000, but were not necessarily made easier in all respects: people can now be naturalised after eight years of legal residence if they meet certain requirements, such as passing a German language test and being able to support themselves. The latter is, for example, not the case during times of unemployment and means a newly introduced obstacle.[6] On the whole, the amendments do, however, mark the attempt to introduce rational, civic criteria and loosen the exclusive ancestral principle in the construction of the nation. In order to get an idea of the important social implications one should take into account, it is worth focusing on the immigrants that became particularly significant in the 1990s, the so-called 'resettlers' (*Aussiedler*).

The ancestral concept of *jus sanguinis* was always understood to include people of German descent who lived elsewhere due to historical emigrations. Upon immigration to the Federal Republic they were immediately treated as German nationals with full citizenship rights. Most of the relevant populations that were concerned by this right to an 'ethnically privileged immigration' (Münz *et al.* 1997: 170), as well as by the potential desire to re-migrate to their ancestors' German homeland, lived behind the Iron Curtain and could not migrate easily before 1990; so they were received in the FRG without much discord as having escaped totalitarian regimes. The number of people who immigrated on this basis was not overwhelming. They made up a total of 1.6 million people between 1951 and 1988 (Bade 2000: 412). With the opening of borders in 1990 their numbers increased rapidly and reached a total of 3.6 million by 1996, meaning that 2 million *Aussiedler* immigrated in just six years (Münz *et al.* 1997: 170). Their immediate entitlement not only to a German passport inclusive of all civic rights, but also to a number of special welfare benefits and integration assistance meant aggravating circumstances in the economic depression that marked the 1990s in unified Germany. In order to reduce the rate of *Aussiedler* immigration, a number of requirements have meanwhile been imposed for obtaining permits from the German embassies in the sending countries. These restrictions were introduced not only for financial reasons, but also because of social problems: the *Aussiedler* had come to be perceived as fairly problematic immigrants (for details see Bade 2000: 413ff.).

Many of the ethnically privileged 'resettlers' who arrived in the 1990s belonged in fact to a generation that did not speak adequate German to cope with daily life in German society. Many adolescents had not even wanted to emigrate, but had been given no choice but to follow their parents. They were hence not enthusiastic to find themselves in a setting that devalued everything they had learnt thus far and demanded acquisition of different skills not only in terms of the language. Reluctance and experiences of alienation prevailed. Given the rather restrictive regulations that were applied to immigrants without German ancestry with regard to their options of national inclusion, the situation was clearly unbalanced and made tensions grow in the 1990s. The normative concept of accepting *Aussiedler* right away as fellow nationals thus created multiple problems. Last but not least, it became very obvious that German descent and a possible continuity of supposedly German cultural traditions (which was moreover understood to bear problematic connotations in itself) did not entail familiarity with the norms of societal life in the Federal Republic.[7] In other words, the assumption that some diffuse sameness underlies ethno-national conceptualisations was not borne out in reality. Yet while the idea of self-evident ethno-national cohesion appeared to become questionable in view of the 'resettlers', it constituted at the same time a topical issue in the attempts to create some sense of unity in post-unification Germany.

## 'Growing Together' in Germany since 1990

Since unification, the question of the so-called 'growing together' in Germany has become standard in public discourses. It was used first by Willy Brandt on the occasion of the Wall opening in November 1989 and the resulting possibility of unifying the two German Republics: 'What belongs together, grows together now' is what he said. As a motif this had also come to dominate the final demonstrations that contributed to the GDR breakdown: the demonstration slogan turned from 'we are the people' into 'we are *one* people' in November 1989, thereby also extending the target group, which was at once no longer just the GDR Government but a national public. In spite of this national rhetoric that had appeared suddenly in 1989, when the State unification took place one year later it bore a rather formal character and showed no signs of collective excitement. The setting was instead marked by the ambivalence and restraints that had been developed vis-à-vis all national issues in West Germany before 1989. The Federal Republic had, after all, projected its identity within the transnational context of an increasingly integrating Europe and had distanced itself from the national frame of reference in its political culture.[8] This was not suspended in 1989–1990 as is recognisable, for example, in the way the German unification is represented in school History textbooks which can be read as an intentional programme for political 'enculturation' (Jacobmeyer 1994; Meyer *et al.* 1992; Schiffauer and Sunier 2004; Bertilotti *et al.* 2005).

The 1990 unification is represented in textbooks without much emotional enthusiasm. In one widely used series, *Zeiten und Menschen* (Goerlitz and Immisch 1991), the breakdown of the GDR is explicitly located in the larger transnational context of revolutionary changes in the Eastern hemisphere. The State unification process itself is treated very briefly in an account of the course of events without any sentimental connotations. A second popular series, *Die Reise in die Vergangenheit* (Ebeling and Birkenfeld 1991), devotes one hundred pages to the German separation and its eventual solution. In spite of the supposedly national focus, strong emphasis within this unit is laid on post-war efforts of international reconciliation with former enemies. Regarding the events of 1989–1990 in Germany, the fact that the State unification took place in a much more 'reserved' way than the opening of the Berlin Wall is assessed as 'certainly quite good this way' (ibid. 112). And although the former separate existence of two German States is once called 'unnatural' in this book, thus assuming the nation-state was a natural condition or even necessity, it is also made very clear that the German nation became divided effectively by living in different States; descriptions of mutual indifference, disapproval and 'alienation' between East and West Germans occupy several pages (ibid. 152) and lead to the conclusion that this poses a historical challenge to overcome internal splitting.

Thus, the nation has certainly entered the normative discourse of German self-definition in a new way since unification: talk of the nation is no longer absent but rather taken for granted. The new 'normality' is, however, accompanied by a subcutaneous fear that nationalists could make too big an issue out of it and thus jeopardise Germany's standing in the world (Bertilotti, Mannitz and Soysal 2005). The message is hence ambivalent: while the international perspective persists, pupils in grade 10 – aged fifteen to seventeen – do also learn explicitly that they should see the 'growing together' in Germany as their historical task (Ebeling and Birkenfeld 1991: 157). Even though no clear idea is ever given as to how that could be achieved, the organic terminology itself is remarkable: it focuses more on an imagined living structure that is to be established between the people from East and West and less on procedures, methods or instrumental conditions of membership and participation. The status of residents with a different nationality is specially affected by the related focal shifts. Without any doubt, they are part of the population and participants in civil society, but they are not necessarily members of 'the people' or the citizenry[9] that is addressed in official appeals to 'grow together'. The following case analyses will cast some light on how adolescents from immigrant families acted in this field of contradictory forces and what meanings were reflected in their discursive practices with regard to the construction of collectivity and the related drawing of boundaries.

## Germans versus Foreigners? Constructing Collectivity: Case Analyses

The first situation to consider took place in a grade 9 history lesson that was concerned with the end of the German Empire on 9 November 1918.[10] The class was asked if they knew any more important German historical events that had occurred on a 9 November. Some pupils did know that the Wall fell on a 9 November but a few Turkish[11] girls wondered whether that was important. A classmate, a Turkish boy, told them: 'Well that's clear, for the Germans! Hey man, logically! They gained half of Germany in addition!'. The lesson went on with another pupil mentioning 9 November 1938, what the Nazis called *Reichskristallnacht* (Night of Broken Glass). Their teacher explained the term and its cynical dimension and was then asked by a Turkish pupil why the Jews had not fled from Germany in 1938. The teacher replied by questioning why the Turks did not flee from Germany today:

> *Kenan:* Why didn't the Jews flee from Germany then?
> *Teacher:* Well yes – why don't the Turks flee?
> *Kenan:* Why should the Turks flee?
> *Teacher:* Today there are murders, arson attacks and assaults on Turks – why don't the Turks flee? …
> *Kenan:* The attacks are not carried out by the State today. The people who do such things are not in power. …
> *Fatma:* We have much more security now.
> *Teacher:* … What if many people suddenly voted for Right-wing parties?
> *Fedor:* Things won't get *that* bad.
> *Teacher:* Exactly! That is what many Jews believed as well. And then you also have to consider what it means to go away: the Turks have, after all, property here – maybe a flat, a shop, money in the bank. If someone said 'You are only allowed to take with you what you can carry in two suitcases, and the rest belongs to Germany', who would want to leave then? It was just like that with the Jews at that time.

Although well intended pedagogically, the teacher's argument implies a double discrimination: the question of why Jews did not flee from Nazi Germany is not explained by their national status and self-evident identification as belonging to the German people but by material aspects that always make emigration difficult. Following the bias of ethnic and cultural difference, this treats Jewish Germans of 1938 as if they had been foreigners, and even reproduces the anti-semitic idea of their otherness. In that classroom, not only was a boundary drawn between Germans and Turks, but the historical comparison moreover implies an opposition between potential culprits and victims.

A similar sense of updated history came up in another lesson. One pupil asked, 'How was it possible for millions of people to be killed in Nazi Germany?' Again, the teacher's way of putting the topic sounded as if Jews had been a separate category of citizens, for he spoke of Jewish *Mitbürger* in contrast to 'the normal population in Germany'. The same term *Mitbürger* is a common word for today's foreign residents, used by politicians, trade unionists, the media etc. in Germany ('*ausländische Mitbürger*'). It means 'fellow citizen' but not citizen in the proper civic sense. This notional ascription was also used in teaching. Like the ethnic terminology which was likewise common in school, it distinguishes between Germans and other groups, e.g., *the* Turks or *the* foreigners, on the basis of presumed collective traits or a common societal allocation.

In the first quoted scene, it was the teacher who drew a line between Turks and Germans. However, the Turkish pupil who explained at the beginning of the lesson that the opening of the Wall meant an important success 'for the Germans' who 'gained half the country in addition' followed the same taxonomy. He stressed what the unification meant 'for the Germans' and thus withdrew from the affected collectivity. Yet, when one looks at it again, the way in which he phrased the fact that Germany has become bigger indicates as well his own socialisation in the former West, meaning he took over the perspective of the former FRG that *gained* five more Federal States. Although just a relatively small hint, this adoption of the Western view of the historical process indicates a subconscious identification with the 'old West' which refutes the assumption of clearly bounded collectivities consisting of Germans versus foreigners.

The general bafflement and lack of understanding of their teacher's idea that the Turks might have reasons to leave Germany after the rise in xenophobic attacks in the 1990s points into this direction, too: The Turkish pupils were familiar enough with post-war West Germany to declare the proposed parallel to the Nazi period as inadequate: 'Things won't get *that* bad' because hostilities against foreigners 'are not carried out by the State' was their estimation, and the political situation was judged to ensure 'much more security now'. These balanced comments reveal an informed confidence in the societal acceptance of plurality as well as in the stability of democracy and reflect a certain self-evidence that the speakers are part of German society. The impact of themselves being conceptually excluded from nationhood as 'foreigners' did not seem to worry these teenagers. By stressing (and trusting) civil society instead, they followed the priorities that had dominated the political agenda in post-war West Germany and that had moreover been the site of successful practical inclusion with respect to the labour immigrants before unification (see Thränhardt 2000).

## *Images of Otherness: West versus East*

In spite of the trust that German civil society would not exclude let alone persecute her foreign residents, the adolescents from immigrant families in the field of my research clearly noted that national issues had in fact taken on different meanings after unification. They observed the changes in and around Berlin with uneasy feelings and feared that societal solidarity could come under pressure. While German friends of mine from West Berlin were happy that Berlin had 'regained' the surrounding areas, so that it became possible to spend the weekend out in the country, or to commute from there to the workplace in Berlin, the scopes of action for the young people from immigrant families had become smaller. They felt restricted by surroundings that they associated with xenophobic East Germans,[12] and perceived of the former GDR and eastern Berlin as threatening no-go-areas. 'Be honest: it was a mistake to demolish the Wall, right?', I was once asked by a Lebanese seventeen-year-old when conducting fieldwork in his school in 1997. Together with his Turkish friend Ferhat he went on to explain this to me:

*Ferhat:* The Nazis, those baldies, they don't dare to come to our school or to Kreuzberg, because here there are so many foreigners around. They only dare to go where foreigners are less numerous .... It works out well here: At our school, there are no problems between foreigners and Germans.
*Kamil:* On the whole, it's only a problem since the Wall is no longer there. Every evening we go and try to rebuild the Wall but we can't manage, right Ferhat? [He laughs.] Formerly it was no problem. And we even went to throw bananas over the Wall so that they would have it better in the East! [I laugh.] You don't believe me, hey? We threw kiwi fruit over the Wall for them! But probably they thought they were hand grenades – now all the Nazis come here!

Unlike a widespread negative image amongst the German public that immediately associates a high rate of foreigners in schools with problems, and that in the same vein depicts boroughs like Kreuzberg or Neukölln as desperate ghettos, the foreigners' hegemony in these quarters of Berlin receives only positive evaluation in these accounts. Since 'the Nazis' supposedly avoid such places, the in-group of 'the foreigners' are ensured a safe haven. A counter-collectivity was mobilised along the lines of potential victimisation: where the structural minority is in terms of numbers a majority, the danger seems averted. Several adolescents from Turkish, Kurdish or Palestinian families expressed their view of the situation similarly. Since they were convinced that xenophobia was a problem originating from the former East, the opening of the Wall was interpreted as having caused a state of siege and danger for the foreigners in the West. Moreover, many of them reported that their parents had become more anxious since unification. They had introduced more restrictions on their children for going out in the evenings or for approaching areas close to the former State border. On the whole, the abolition of the Wall was experienced as having installed new borders of a different kind in their own social space.

In the quoted statement, the people from the former GDR appear as the stereotyped 'bad Germans'. The way in which the two young men construct this image deserves a closer examination. In fact, their view parallels the paternalistic construct of the so-called Third World according to which their families' countries of emigration are represented in the Geography teaching at school. One could paraphrase the related message as: 'The underprivileged need our help, but in return they should at least be grateful and try to meet our expectations'.[13] Kamil said that he threw kiwi fruit and bananas over the Wall, but instead of appreciating the good deeds by being grateful and nice, the Germans from the GDR caused only trouble. So, 'they' do not even share 'our' terms of trade and politeness – an argument that can be found in his Geography book to explain why German development aid is not as successful as it could be. The different cultures of the others are considered as obstructions to progress, as an aspect of and explanation for their backwardness, and hence close to acts of sabotage against the beneficial measures of developmental aid (e.g. Krauter and Rother 1988, analysed by Mannitz and Schiffauer 2004). Kamil and Ferhat made use of this causal chain and applied it to German society – claiming such a difference to run between former East and West. In this narration, pride and identification are expressed by the economic success of the former West: we *had* enough exotic fruit to throw them over the Wall. The two young men thus tried to establish a level of solidarity and agreement with me as somebody from the West by means of 'othering' (Abu-Lughod 1991) the Germans from the GDR; and they knew the situation well enough to hold this alliance for plausible, since Germans from East and West have in fact simply not 'grown together'. On both sides of the former border, mythical stories of the better past can be found, and this is exactly what Ferhat and Kamil appealed to – within our in-group as Westerners, that means.

The emphasis on 'our' economic superiority was not accidental in this context either. Political culture could no longer draw on national features to define a positive collective project after National Socialism. Economic success was used after 1945 to describe in positive terms 'what Germany stands for'. In reverse, a functioning economy is held to be a good remedy against Nazism, and a number of the school History lessons I observed put unemployment and a susceptibility to nationalist ideology into causal context. With the help of these argumentative patterns, the idealised image of the good old West with economic wealth and social peace was designed by Ferhat and Kamil. Moreover, the labour immigrants also participated in the making of the Federal Republic's economic success story. It constitutes thus an ideal site to express claims of belonging and was, not surprisingly, brought into play accordingly by many adolescents from immigrant families.

### *Cross-Cutting Space In Between*

After leaving school in former West Berlin, my interview partners inevitably came into closer contact with people from the former GDR, as job training centres and universities now cover the whole of Berlin. For all of them, this had meant confrontations of a new kind, which dominated the interviews in 2000–2001. It had also, however, effected discoveries of space in between the conventional categories. The following statement about the people from former East Berlin was made by a young Palestinian woman in 2000. She was twenty years old at the time:

> They have a much more aggressive attitude towards foreigners than a normal German. I do not want to lump them all together, but the people from the West, who have had a lot of contact with foreigners already in school, and who have found many good friends among foreigners, behave completely different and will do so for the rest of

their lives. But those, they have always been isolated and have never been in contact with anybody else; now when they meet somebody with a headscarf – that's just a big question mark for them. ... The problem is that they have not grown up together with foreigners like the people in the West – here it has never been a problem.

Her judgement is typical in many respects; she glorifies the pre-unification West and depicts the GDR as representing a state of isolation and pre-civility, which was, according to her version, overcome in the FRG *with the help of the immigrants*. The 'normal Germans' are constructed on this ground as to differ from the people in the East who are denied the crucial experience of having learnt to live with foreigners. The latter thus represent the danger of falling back to the stage of nationalism and xenophobia. If Elias and Scotson (1990) are right to assume that the power to define normality in society is a resource of the established, this construction is a remarkable sign of engagement with German society, and it entails clear claims for recognition. In addressing the people from the West, the relation is defined by indebtedness in this view; the FRG Germans were able to develop their liberal democratic competence and become 'normal' because they 'had a lot of contact with foreigners', which had consequences 'for the rest of their lives'. Addressing the people from the East, the assessment – which was undisputed among my interview partners – that 'Easterners' lacked the crucial experience of handling plurality in society implied a need to catch up. One should add here that the 'foreigners' from West Berlin have obviously also assimilated the paternalistic gesture that was caricatured as Western bossiness by many East Germans after unification.

This assumption suggests an important role for the young foreigners in the context of 'growing together'; as very visible representatives of societal plurality theirs would be a catalyst's role in the process of civilising – in this case, de-nationalising – the collective German self-projection after unification. Some of them also went a step further to adopt this role in a more committed way by expressing their own feelings of responsibility for the process of creating an open post-national society in Germany. The following statement of a young woman, aged twenty-one, who shares the opinion about the 'narrow-minded' people from the East illustrates this approach very well. She would want to take part in promoting plurality and puts this into a wider context of creating a social cohesion that transcends national borders:

When I was still a schoolgirl in grade 8 or 9 [= ca. 1993/1994, she was fourteen then] we had a kind of workshop in East Berlin. All the children over there looked at us in such a strange way, and they called us some dirty swearwords; but somehow they were also intimidated, because we were so many [with an ironically lowered voice:] Turks and Arabs, you know – I found that quite funny! ... At the moment, I do *unfortunately* not have any contacts with Germans from the East, apart from one friend I have from Saxony. I read an article once which said that most East Germans do not like any foreigners. But it is also a region where very few foreigners live. That made me think... The prejudices people from the East have against foreigners – or one should rather say against people who hold different opinions – can be dispelled in personal contact! In the circles I move in, people of my age are really cosmopolitan. They have travelled and everything, and that has really affected their development. I believe that my generation will not accept borders any more but see the world as *one*, as *our* world, and see the interconnections. That is a change which I appreciate very much, and I want to encourage that as well.

Apart from this discovery of their own potential role in the space in between if not beyond East and West, some of the young 'foreigners' had developed a perspective for cross-cutting similarities in their intensified encounters with peers from the former GDR. They saw themselves placed in a structurally comparable situation with the so-called Easterners. In an interview with two young women from immigrant families in spring 2000, when they were twenty years old, one said: 'The people from the East say "the foreigners take all the jobs", but the foreigners say "because of the people from the East we have lost our workplaces". It really is like that! The Wall is no longer there, and *everything* has changed.'

The observation of parallels was not restricted to complaints about a worsened job market. Furthermore, the young 'foreigners' from West Berlin discovered that they shared (rather unexpectedly) with some of the 'Easterners' the ironically phrased desire to 'undo' history. With amusement as well as some bewilderment they recounted alliances in their vocational training classes when foreigners and their classmates from East Berlin regularly agreed that one should erect the Wall anew. They had in fact established joking relationships on this common ground, as a means of coping with otherwise ambivalent and tense relations, and thus they could bridge the gap with humour.[14]

## Conclusion

The demolition of the Berlin Wall, as of the Iron Curtain in general, has not simply washed away conceptual boundaries but triggered off the possibility for their redefinition and transformation. The projections of collective identities that had marked the Cold War period were rendered invalid, and the question was at once open again of how to define 'us' and 'them'. In unified Germany, the related shifts of belonging and exclusion seem unambiguous at first sight: having regained national sovereignty in the frame of a unified nation-state, the priority appears to lie in the creation of a collective self-image that allows for reconciling the former disjunctions of East versus West. Stressing national integration is one way to cope with forms of diversity that might endanger social peace, and the fact that school textbooks continue to stress the need for a 'growing together' in Germany sustains such a tendency. Yet the very appeal also indicates that ethno-national cohesion is an artefact that needs to be taught as being significant over and above commitment to other social groups. In the particular setting of unified Germany however, any endeavour at creating State nationalism entails particular problems. Given its dreadful nationalist past, there is no straightforward vision of a German national identity that one could want to celebrate. The solution to this dilemma is to see the nation principally in relative terms of an internationalised setting. The characteristic ambivalence which had come to dominate political culture in the FRG by the time the Wall disappeared allowed for cross-cutting processes of identification as became visible in the analysed discursive practices.

For the quoted youths from labour immigrant families, the German unification did apparently stimulate awareness of their own identifications, however not with unified Germany nor with Germanness itself but with the pre-1989 West. Seen from the angle of the young foreigners, the unification represents a social step backwards; they construct the GDR Germans in a stereotyped way as embodying a relapse into times before civility. Against that image, the past is glorified as a time of harmony without *any* problems. My interview partners displaced otherness in their narratives; being customarily others for the Germans, they applied the dichotomising concept to frictions within the ethno-national collective. This way of arguing relativises potential oppositions of Germans versus foreigners by its emphasis on the insinuated watershed between East and West. It supports the implicit diagnosis of a persisting divide, which can be found in textbooks and other mass media as posing one of the crucial challenges for the future. Even more so, the myth of the grand old West also points to the possible role of the immigrant population in the process of 'growing together' and defining collectivity.

Referring to a common past, the glorification of West German society before 1989 symbolises a form of membership that does not require identification with the ethno-national concept of Germanness for the creation of social peace; 'There was also more acceptance formerly', said one of my interview partners when she recollected the pre-1989 West. Although arguing with the past, the mythical memorising of the time before unification can therefore be seen as an attempt to invest a particular strand of experiences into the emerging stock of memories in unified Germany and to (re)gain acceptance. The fact that the quoted adolescents and young adults all continued to label 'Germans' vis-à-vis 'foreigners' in their emic taxonomy does not contradict this sense of belonging but can in itself be taken as an example of the enculturation process they have undergone in West Berlin: they have assimilated the exclusionist notion as well as the negative connotations of Germanness and have thus distanced themselves somewhat from it. Likewise, their inclination to handle the East–West discourse with irony and joking reveals a mélange of emotional affiliation and experiences of distance at the same time. Because of this ambivalence, identification can only address fragments, e.g., the good, non-nationalist, 'normal' Germans, or economic success that was achieved together with the labour immigrants. The myth of the grand old West before unification combines both aspects; It emphasises economy and civil society as the sites that allowed foreigners' participation and inclusion at times when their national integration was not yet foreseen, and also approves of an integration model that leaves ethnic origin or cultural peculiarity aside whilst attributing high value to plurality itself. If understood in this sense, unified Germany can 'grow together' without opposing ethnic minorities vis-à-vis the German majority and thus avoid relapses into nationalist simplification.

Given the tradition of construing German nationality ethnotropically, ethnic and cultural diversity is far from being a self-evident element. The boundary between Germans and foreigners allowed no easy blurring or shifting in the past but was lifted only over a span of generations. The legal amendments of 2000 have created a new normative project that enables a more rational way of constructing nationhood and eases civic inclusion. Its effects on the notion of 'being German' will nevertheless take time to be clearly seen and will be subject to public debate. Whether and how the immigrants will become a part of the national imagery at long last will also depend on their commitment in this matter.

## NOTES

1. My study in Berlin was part of the international research project *State, School, and Ethnicity*. We investigated the interrelations of identity articulation among immigrants' children and dominant discourses of their residential societies in four West-European countries (Schiffauer *et al.* 2004).
2. There was also migration in the opposite direction, but it was much less significant in terms of numbers. This can be taken as an expression of the 'different appeals of the two German states' in the 1950s, 'not only in terms of economics but also in terms of the political institutions' (Münz *et al.* 1997: 29–30). Detailed reports of the different immigration phases as well as all the corresponding figures for key years are given in both Bade (2000) and Münz *et al.* (1997).
3. For more details see Potts (1988: 175–82) as well as Münz *et al.* (1997: 37ff).
4. Bade (2000) gives a thorough account. For the time in between 1961 and 1989 see Bade (331–40).
5. The different nation concepts of Germany and France have most prominently been analysed by Rogers Brubaker (1992). Castles and Miller, whose classification scheme differentiates an 'exclusive model' from an 'assimilationist model' and a 'multicultural model' of citizenship, have confirmed Brubaker's findings (Castles and Miller 1993: 244–50), but the legal reforms that took place in both countries in the 1990s blurred the distinctions to some extent (see Bade 2000: 340–48). Nevertheless, different traditions of citizenhip and nationality mark each case and still have an important impact on the respective 'imagined communities' (Anderson 1991).

6. Conditions of the new nationality law can be studied at http://www.einbuergerung.de.
7. One should add that German descent was not understood simply to mean a German ancestor from the past. The 'resettlers' who came to the FRG from the 1950s onwards had to prove their conversion to Germanness, e.g. by their use of the German language or by being classified as of German nationality in their personal documents (as was possible in the USSR). Declaring oneself German before the competent embassy of the FRG was not sufficient.
8. In her survey about national identity in West Germany, Sigrid Rossteutscher stresses that 'if there is something special about Germany it is not its frequently discussed lack of national identity, but the strong push in the negative direction' (Rossteutscher 1997: 624).
9. Citizenship in the meaning of citizenship practice applies in fact to many immigrants who do not hold the formal status of nationality but nevertheless do participate in crucial institutions and basic structures of civil society in an active fashion. They thereby exert what Thomas Marshall called 'social citizenship' (1965) and earn a large part of the social capital in democracy.
10. In German grade 9 the pupils are fourteen to sixteen years old. Primary school starts at age six, but depending on the month of their birthday and their personal maturity children may also be enrolled at the age of five or seven years.
11. For the simple reason of comprehensibility I make use of this otherwise debatable vocabulary and call, e.g., the children from Turkish families Turks. Most of them did indeed have their parents' foreign nationalities and made use of this terminology themselves. In their own use it comprised a variety of meanings – ethnic, cultural, national – depending on the circumstances of articulation.
12. This refers to a public controversy: the West German criminologist Christian Pfeiffer argued that xenophobia is more widespread in the former GDR because of repressive education norms that were inculcated in the State-run childcare institutions. His hypothesis came under heavy attack and provoked strong reactions among education experts from the former GDR who perceived it as typical Western arrogance. Later, Pfeiffer was however supported by the East German researcher Annemarie Karutz: according to her, neither children nor nursery school personnel had ever learnt to handle conflicts in the GDR because they were denied to exist in socialist society. Subordination being the highest aim, any deviation would have been ousted. Karutz sees the resulting education as still effective in the shape of bi-polarised concepts of good adapted vs evil deviants (see the report on the conference 'Socialisation and Prejudice', held in July 1999 at the Technical University, Berlin, in: *die Tageszeitung* 12 July 1999).
13. For an analysis of the relevant discourse in school see Mannitz and Schiffauer (2004).
14. 'The joking relationship is a peculiar combination of friendliness and antagonism. ... Any serious hostility is prevented by the playful antagonism of teasing, and this in its regular repetition is a constant expression or reminder of that social disjunction which is one of the essential components of the relation, while the social conjunction is maintained by the friendliness that takes no offence at insults.' (Radcliffe-Brown 1952: 91–92).

## References

Abu-Lughod, L. 1991. 'Writing against culture'. In *Recapturing Anthropology: Working in the Present*, ed. R. Fox. Santa Fé, School of American Research Press.

Anderson, B. 1991. *Imagined Communities: Reflections on the Origin and Spread of Nationalism.* London, Verso.

Bade, K. ed. 1992. *Deutsche im Ausland, Fremde in Deutschland: Migration in Geschichte und Gegenwart.* Munich, C.H. Beck.

Bade, K. 2000. *Europa in Bewegung. Migration vom späten 18. Jahrhundert bis zur Gegenwart.* Munich, C.H. Beck.

Bertilotti, T., S. Mannitz and Y. Soysal. 2005. 'Rethinking the nation-state: Projections of identity in French and German history and civics textbooks'. In *The Nation, Europe, and the World: Textbooks and Curricula in Transition,* eds H. Schissler and Y. Soysal. Oxford, Berghahn.

Brubaker, R. 1992. *Citizenship and Nationhood in France and Germany.* Cambridge, MA, Harvard University Press.

Budzinski, M. 1999. *Die multikulturelle Realität: Mehrheitsherrschaft und Minderheitenrechte.* Göttingen, Lamuv.

Castles, S. and M.J. Miller. 1993. *The Age of Migration: International Population Movements in the Modern World.* Houndmills, Macmillan.

Ebeling, H. and W. Birkenfeld. 1991. *Die Reise in die Vergangenheit,* vol. 6. Braunschweig, Westermann.

Elias, N. and J.L. Scotson. 1990. *Etablierte und Außenseiter.* Frankfurt/Main, Suhrkamp.

Frantzioch, M. 1987. *Die Vertriebenen: Hemmnisse, Antriebskräfte und Wege ihrer Integration in der Bundesrepublik Deutschland.* Berlin, Reimer.

Goerlitz, E. and J. Immisch eds. 1991. *Zeiten und Menschen,* vol. 4. Paderborn, Schöningh.

Hoffmann, L. 1996. 'Der Einfluss völkischer Integrationsvorstellungen auf die Identitätsentwürfe von Zuwanderern'. In *Die bedrängte Toleranz: Ethnisch-religiöse Konflikte, religiöse Differenzen und die Gefahren politischer Gewalt,* eds W. Heitmeyer and R. Dollase. Frankfurt/Main, Suhrkamp.

Jacobmeyer, W. 1994. 'Konditionierung von Geschichtsbewusstsein'. In *Historisches Bewusstsein und politisches Handeln in der Geschichte,* ed. J. Topolski. Poznań, Adama Minkiewicza Uniwersytet.

Katzenstein, P.J. 1997. *The Culture of National Security: Norms and Identity in World Politics.* New York, Columbia University Press.

Krauter, K.-G. and L. Rother eds. 1988. *Terra – Erdkunde* (edition for Berlin, vol. 8). Stuttgart, Düsseldorf, Berlin and Leipzig, Klett.

Mannitz, S. and W. Schiffauer. 2004. 'Taxonomies of cultural difference: Constructions of otherness'. In *Civil Enculturation: Nation-State, School and Ethnic Difference in The Netherlands, Britain, Germany, and France,* ed. W. Schiffauer et al. Oxford, Berghahn.

Marshall, T.H. 1965. *Class, Citizenship, and Social Development.* Garden City, NY, Doubleday.

Mecheril, P. 1997. 'Zugehörigkeitserfahrungen von Anderen Deutschen. Eine empirische Modellierung'. In *Transnationale Migration,* ed. L. Pries. Baden-Baden, Nomos.

Mecheril, P. and T. Teo eds. 1994. *Andere Deutsche: Zur Lebenssituation von Menschen multiethnischer und multikultureller Herkunft.* Berlin, Dietz.

Meyer, J.W., D. Kamens and A. Benavot. 1992. *School Knowledge for the Masses: World Models and National Primary Curricular Categories in the 20th Century.* Washington DC, Falmer Press.

Münz, R., W. Seifert and R. Ulrich. 1997. *Zuwanderung nach Deutschland: Strukturen, Wirkungen, Perspektiven.* Frankfurt/Main, Campus.

Potts, L. 1988. *Weltmarkt für Arbeitskraft: Von der Kolonisation Amerikas bis zu den Migrationen der Gegenwart.* Hamburg, Junius.

Radcliffe-Brown, A.R. 1952. 'On Joking relationships'. In *Structure and Function in Primitive Society. Essays and Addresses*. London, Cohen & West.

Rossteutscher, S. 1997. 'Between normality and particularity – national identity in West Germany'. *Nations and Nationalism* 3, no. 4: 607–30.

Schiffauer, W., G. Baumann, R. Kastoryano and S. Vertovec eds. 2004. *Civil Enculturation: Nation-State, School and Ethnic Difference in The Netherlands, Britain, Germany, and France*. Oxford, Berghahn.

Schiffauer, W. and T. Sunier. 2004. 'Representing the Nation in History Textbooks'. In *Civil Enculturation: Nation-State, School and Ethnic Difference in The Netherlands, Britain, Germany, and France*, eds W. Schiffauer *et al*. Oxford, Berghahn.

Thränhardt, D. 2000. 'Conflict, consensus, and policy outcomes: Immigration and integration in Germany and The Netherlands'. In *Challenging Immigration and Ethnic Relation Politics*, eds R. Koopmans and P. Statham. Oxford, Oxford University Press.

Wiener, A. 1998. *'European' Citizenship Practice: Building Institutions of a Non-State*. Boulder, CO, Westview Press.

# Chapter 6
# Invisible Community: Russians in London and Amsterdam

Helen Kopnina

### Introduction

Crossing boundaries in the context of migration is often associated with border crossings, where boundaries are seen merely as demarcating nation states. Yet, migration, like other global phenomena, has become more complex than just leaving one nation-state for another. Recent literature on migration speaks of migrants as constantly moving, crossing national borders not only to settle in the host country, but in order to carry out business or to visit relatives abroad, forming transient transnational communities (Gardner 1995; Raj 1997; Kroes 2000; Rouse 2002; Rex 2003).

Migrants from Eastern Europe are particularly notorious for relatively unobstructed border-crossings, as thousands of (mostly illegal) East European citizens are known to work and live in Western Europe. This border penetrability challenges the very idea of 'fortress Europe' (Mandel 1994; Goverde 2000), as well questioning the very notion of immovable boundaries (Pratt and Brown 2000; Johnston *et al.* 2002).

The *Economist* article entitled 'The coming hordes: Fears of migration from east to west' speaks of Eurosceptics, trade unions and some governments that fear that enlargement of the European union will bring a stream of migrants from Eastern Europe chasing jobs and social security benefits (*The Economist* 2004: 25). On the other hand, benefits of such migration are being praised as migrant workers could be seen as economic and political as well as cultural assets to the host countries. Such movements from east to west, either feared or desired, are at the forefront of the social and political agendas of most West European countries.

Russian migrants, whose communities in London and Amsterdam I studied between 1998 and 2004 (intermittently), are an example of a group that engages in boundary and border crossings, presenting a good case for studying 'transnational migrant communities'. In the process of my research I have, however, discovered that the term 'community' is being disputed, negotiated and in some cases even denied by the migrants themselves.

Although I have primarily concentrated on the 'new' Russian migrants, a quick look at the history of Russian migration to Western Europe should provide a context against which discussion of community may be placed. Twentieth century 'waves' of Russian migrants consisted mostly of intelligentsia and politically or ideologically motivated individuals. These 'waves', which spread massively into America, Canada, France, Germany, Israel and other countries, may be broken into a few phases. Only a few hundreds of Russians went to Britain and The Netherlands throughout the first three-quarters of the century.

The first wave was in the period just before and after the Russian Revolution of 1917. The first wave included famous revolutionaries like Lenin, who continued activities for which they were persecuted in Russia abroad. These were mostly political exiles, wishing to return to Russia if circumstances allowed, although some of these revolutionaries and intellectuals remained abroad till their death. The second wave originated after the Second World War and involved predominantly ethnic Germans as well as few Russians taken to work in Germany during the war and fearing return to their motherland (the latter group was mostly present in The Netherlands). According to Codagnone (1998), the third wave originated in the 1950s and intermittently ran until the 1980s. It consisted of ethnic Jews, Germans, Poles and Greeks. Some moved from other European countries to London and Amsterdam (notably from Germany in the latter case). Codagnone (1998) attributes this wave to the Western diplomatic pressure that relaxed Soviet controls, enabling some 340,000 individuals to leave Russia. This migration is characterised by those who disagreed with the Soviet system and were highly educated (Snel *et al.* 2000: 61). The fourth wave occurred in the late eighties during *perestroika*, when more Jews and ethnic Germans, as well as Greeks and Armenians, departed for their respective motherlands (Siegel 1998).

To sum up, the earlier waves of Russian migrants had 'common themes', either ethnic, religious or political, that kept them together: 'One very striking feature of all three waves – inevitably, of the first more than the others – the way in which the immigrants have kept together. There is now a kind of émigré international that will look after you in any city in non-communist world' (Glenny and Stone 1990: xvii–xviii).

The last wave, which my research is devoted to, occurred in the nineties, right after the break-up of the Soviet Union. The 'new' migrants are very diverse ethnically, representing groups such as Armenians from Azerbaijan, Jews from Siberia, or Russians from Estonia. Most legal Russian migrants who entered London and Amsterdam since the 1990s, appear to be constantly on the move. The geographical proximity of Russia, relatively high incomes of the migrants, and lack of strict legal regulations prohibiting travel all facilitate a commute between the host country and the country of origin. While earlier waves of the Russian migrants (pre-1990s) could rarely dream of seeing their home country after 'deserting' it (mostly due to the strictness of migration and transit policies), most recent migrants enjoy greater openness and freedom of movement. Borders that used to separate the migrant's country of the past from his present country of residence became more permeable. Does this mean that the concept of the migrant community has changed?

The lack of statistical data on Russians immigrants is striking in the light of the fact that the number of Russians could, by unofficial estimates, add up to hundreds of thousands in Britain and tens of thousands in The Netherlands. Amsterdam and London host the largest number of these migrants. But can we assert that there is a Russian 'community' in London and/or Amsterdam? Why is there so little known about it through Dutch and English academic journals or through the media? Is it true that since the population of Russians at present (and as opposed to the earlier waves who represented particular social classes) is so heterogeneous that we cannot speak of an original community in the first place? Does social fragmentation prevent Russians from forming a unified community or becoming visible to its members?

## What is 'Community'?

'Community' can be perceived as an abstraction, employed for practical purposes by the researcher; a geographically or socially defined entity; a symbolic means of expressing group's identity; a feeling of affinity with a group that shares common characteristics; or even a useless and potentially confusing concept altogether. Thus, the 'measure of migration is,.. complicated in a given population by the inadequacy of conceptualisation of "community" or society' (Jackson 1969: 5).

The use of the term 'community' ranges from practical, as in the case of a group collecting joint benefits; to ideological, as in the case of asserting a group's solidarity and ideological unity against other groups. From Benedict Anderson's 'imagined communities' (1991, orig. 1983) to Anthony Cohen's 'symbolic communities' (1985), social scientists suggest different ways of conceptualising 'community' without the limitations of the old dogmas like 'geographical proximity' or 'common heritage'.

Criticism of a 'community' as a closed, self-contained, static system has been widely spread in the 1990s (Boissevain 1994; Al-Rasheed 1995; Baumann and Sunier 1995; Glazer and Moynihan 1996; Smith 1996). Alternatives to 'traditional' community (seen as closed and territorially ascribed and often ethnicity- or nationality-based), such as 'international' (Rex 2003) or 'transnational' (Rouse 2002; Vertovec 2003) communities, have been offered. Rouse, in his discussion of Mexican migrants in the United States, describes territorially unbound communities connected to the 'transnational migrant circuit' and occupying no single national space (Rouse 2002: 171).

## Establishing Invisibility

I have arrived at the realisation of the invisibility of the Russians in Britain and The Netherlands through my conversations with the British and the Dutch as well as through the media analysis. In most cases, only partial awareness of the Russian presence was admitted. Very few sources claimed to have information on the numbers of the Russians present or characteristics of the supposed Russian 'community'. Russian invisibility was admitted both by the Russians and by members of the host society.

My Dutch informant interested in 'everything Russian' and one of the founders of an Internet site for Russians in The Netherlands (Rusland.net) was surprised when I told him that there are 'more than a handful' of Russians in Amsterdam. A British co-owner of a Russian café in London told me that he knew about the existence of other Russian cafés and restaurants but had no idea who owned them or who their clientele was (most of the owners and clients were in fact, Russian). A Russian organiser of the Russian theme nights and discos in one of London's night clubs said that although he thought there were 'hundreds of thousands' of Russians in London, 'most of them were old and didn't like disco' (Garik). He thought that his clients were the children of the older émigrés (from previous 'waves') and was surprised when I told him that on the basis of my interviews most of his clientele were independent new arrivals.

While some of my informants expressed amazement at seeing 'so many Russians' at a party of twenty people and were even more surprised to hear that other guests knew more Russians, others asserted that there are hundreds of thousands of Russians living in London or Amsterdam alone. Some of the Russians who supposed that there were thousands of their compatriots in London or Amsterdam personally knew only a few of them; while others, knowing tens of Russians, assumed these were the only Russians present.

The most common acknowledgement of communal unity is the self-definition as a 'Russian' and an acknowledgement that other 'Russians' are present in London or in Amsterdam. Generalisations such as 'We have a hard time adjusting to local culture', or 'The Dutch/the English don't understand us' suggest that these Russians see themselves as part of a distinct group, contrasting with other groups. Yet, when asked directly whether they feel part of a community, their answers are ambiguous. Inna, a housewife from London, reflected: 'On the one hand, I'm Russian, I guess I'm part of Russian community. On the other hand, I don't really have much contact with these people, I don't know who they are – I have my family and my interests, and that's my world, I don't know about theirs …' (Inna).

## Russians' Perception of 'Community'

For an anthropologist, the most interesting aspect of a 'community' is the social actors' definition of it. But how do people in everyday lives think and act 'community', and what are the characteristics of the social relationships that, according to them, make up their communities, or have nothing to do with communities whatsoever? While academics were de-essentialising and de-reifying 'community', it seemed to have prospered in the minds of people who thought they belonged to a 'community' and those who defined them as such. It has been argued that instead of being diffused in the postmodern world of shifting identities and continuously re-negotiated boundaries, 'community', as well as 'culture' and 'ethnicity' remained and even solidified in popular institutional discourse (Eriksen 1993; Chapman 1994; Baumann 1996; Verkuyten *et al.* 1999).

From the inside, the Russians express diverse opinions about their own 'community'. The word for a 'community', *obshina*, has similar connotations to the English term. The grammatical stem is shared by words like *obshiy* (common), *obshnost* (commonness), *obshestvo* (society), *obshestvenniy* (public), *obshenie* (social intercourse) etc. Yet, the strict meaning of obshina has a more limited connotation than in English and implies a commune, a group, a tribe, a ghetto, a social enclave. *Obshina* is usually used to describe concrete social groups and cannot be generalised as a 'community of people', for example. *Obshina* is often used to describe a group of outsiders that hold common beliefs or possess common values; people rarely refer to themselves as belonging to *obshina*. Consequently, Russians in Amsterdam never use the term obshina literally but imply it in relation to their affiliations. Churchgoers, for example, refer to themselves as *prihozhane* (congregation) or *veruyushie* (believers). In Amsterdam, café habitués of the *Oblomov* sometimes referred to themselves as Oblomovtsy.[1]

Russians were mostly sceptical about their 'community': 'I feel like an island in the sea'. Sveta, my key informant in Amsterdam, told me: 'Others are also just floating, alone or with their families and friends'. Another informant refers to himself and his family as an 'outpost', or on another occasion as a 'hard-working guy for the Russians and hard-working Russian for the Dutch'. These statements suggest that although at times Russians describe themselves collectively as a 'community', it is usually done along very general principles (such as the country of origin) and in opposition to the host society. Aside from this broad assignment (which does show, nonetheless, the importance of the concept of 'community' for the Russians), few concrete bounding features or conspicuous markers were identified, making such a mega-community rather vague and elusive.

From 'Maybe elsewhere, but not here' to 'They must be talking about Indians (Turks)', Russians implicitly suggest that they understand what a 'real community' should be like while denying its existence at present and in the place they live. They suggest that 'communities' exist elsewhere or at other times. If many Russians felt that a 'Russian community' in their city existed, they did not feel part of it. Russians gave examples of what they thought communities were, such as the Jewish 'community' that congregates around synagogues and cultural issues, or the Russian communities in Germany or France.

Natalya Shuvaeva, a major Russian newspaper editor and Alexander Fostiropoulos, an Orthodox priest in London, testified to personally knowing 'hundreds of Russians' by virtue of their profession, and while approximating that there were 'tens to hundreds of thousands' of Russians in London, neither of them could describe these migrants as a unified community. Natalya Shuvaeva, however, refers to her newspaper's readership as a podium for a kind of 'community'.[2] Alexander Fostiropoulos also referred to his congregation as a kind of community, but one that is based on religious principles and includes many non-Russians:

> I wouldn't speak of the Russians here as a community. Community in this case can be used only as a collective term. Church membership doesn't make Russians into a community, as the church embraces all Orthodoxes, such as Greeks, Serbians, British. Our goal at the Church is not to bind Russian-speakers together but to bring forth a greater awareness of Orthodox unity for all nations. Even if sometimes the church fosters a sense of community, this is not its major goal. At the end of the twentieth century the church became less of a religious institution, it seems, a condition that we attempt to rectify. We allow people to be themselves and interact with others, but we don't foster a sense of ethnic identity. One doesn't need to be an Orthodox Christian to be Russian. We can therefore speak only of a community of believers, and different factors make believers into a community. As soon as you try to draw a line around the people, they slip out one by one. It's easy to force the issue of community... But I would speak of the Russians in London and Russians who come to church, not of Russian community.' (A. Fostiropoulos)[3]

Father Alexander referred to the 'old community of believers', noting that the previous waves of migrants did perceive the church as a 'community centre'. Thus, the newspaper editor and the Orthodox priest speak of 'communities' that are not encompassing of all the Russians but only those that join in certain activities (reading a Russian newspaper, participating in worship) or belong to certain institutions. By contrast, another example of such 'communities' comes from Sasha Kolot, the former owner of the only Russian café in Amsterdam, who referred to his café's habitués as a 'community'. Anton, the organiser of cultural events in London, also spoke of a 'community' of Russians that assembles during events and cultural festivals.

Russians showed only partial awareness of the Russian institutions and very selective participation in Russian events. Only very few socially active individuals managed to attend many diverse parties and events. Younger informants tended to explain their lack of interest by the presence of other cultural attractions offered by London or Amsterdam city agendas. A teenage hard rock musician from Amsterdam asks: 'Why would I go to *Sputnik* concert if there's always new and hot stuff at the [Dutch] clubs? If I wanted a Russian disco or music I could get it in Russia – that's not what I'm here for' (Vadim). Older informants give broader reasons, such as busy work schedules, or fatigue, as a retired doctor from London testifies: 'I feel like I left my active life back home. Here I'm just floating. I'm too tired to bother about all these events, singing, talking. I just don't have the energy' (Vasya). Many immigrants find themselves detached, and worried about practical issues, such as obtaining legal documentation and finding work. It could be that Russian cultural events are not attractive or popular enough to forge a sense of 'community', as Sergei, a theatre director from London, suggests:

> I remember my first visit to the St Luke's Anglican church in London where masses were held in Russian. Although the congregation numbered less than thirty, and the Russian priest and his family's band were singing inspiring carols in Russian to which everybody clapped and cheered, there was a sense of fragmentation. Russians were scattered throughout the building, in small groups or alone. After the sermon, tea and biscuits were served which brought the Russians in closer physical proximity, but I have noticed that most groups – consisting of families and friends – stayed intact, and although I later found out that most people knew the names or even stories of other members of the congregation, few open contacts were made. I had to be rather forceful to introduce myself and to enter small group discussions, sensing surprise and suspicion produced by my intrusion.

Events and participation in communal activities is an important topic of Raj's work on Hindu Punjabis in London. She views a 'community' as a processual and contextually defined entity. When Hindu Punjabis participate in religious or cultural events in London, they view themselves as belonging to a 'community': 'The Hindu Punjabi temple involves an understanding of a spatially bounded place temporarily coherent with a specific organisation and structure. As such, it is a community. It is a community which is spatially defined and comes together at certain moments' (Raj 1997: 109).

Feelings of 'belonging' or 'being excluded' are often associated with temple attendance. Raj asks whether this 'community' membership extends beyond the physical compounds of a temple. Raj notices that the Hindu Punjabis form 'smaller social groups, cliques or "circles of friends" whose existence challenges a view of the temple community as a "unified" group' (Raj 1997: 109). Despite internal stratification 'individuals may see themselves as nominally part of a Hindu "community" when they are not physically present "in" the temple. Exploring ethnic and community identity begins with the realisation that there is no Hindu Punjabi "community", in a sense of a whole, but only moments when community occurs, when people gather as a whole, because of a certain criterion of identification' (Raj 1997: 110). Punjabi temple attendance also has a strong social component, which 'leads us to understand the temple, not as a site where "community" meets ..., but a place where friends can be found' (Raj 1997: 110).

As in the case of Hindu Punjabis, Russians may sometimes be referred to as a 'community' by the virtue of their membership of certain institutions or participation in certain events. This 'community' is neither unitary nor stable, and its definition depends on the institution or event that claims to assemble such a community.[4]

## Reasons for Invisibility

### *Outsiders' Perspectives*

The primary reason for Russian invisibility may lie in the simple fact that Russians are still relatively few in London and Amsterdam. Far fewer than 'traditional' groups of migrants in Britain and The Netherlands, Russians are less conspicuous for the members of the host society and for each other. Low critical mass may effect the cultural unity of the group – the more fragmented the groups of migrants, the less chance they have of sharing common cultural features or participating in the joint maintenance of what Bourdieu (1977) calls 'cultural capital'.

Another likely explanation for Russian 'invisibility' is a matter of superficial physical similarity with the resident population. Migration studies in Britain and The Netherlands often mention 'race' as an important aspect of relations between the receiving society and the migrants (Castles *et al.* 1984; Baumann 1996; Bryant 1997; *Economist* 2002). Russians, however, are not conspicuously different in terms of skin colour or dress. Indeed, when I asked my British acquaintance whether he met any Russians in London, he replied that he 'Wouldn't know them from the British if he met them on the street'. He also admitted to automatically 'spotting an Indian, even if they are as British [nationality-wise] as I am'. Unless a Russian talks loudly on the street or seeks to attract attention in public places as some 'new Russians' do in expensive shops in London and Amsterdam, he can easily be mistaken for a local or any other European tourist.[5]

Thus, I have isolated a number of possible explanations for the Russian invisibility in Britain and The Netherlands: low critical mass in comparison to other migrant groups; an inconspicuous way of entry that discourages statistical monitoring; and the lack of specific problems (except for growing concerns with Russian crime, which will be discussed later) associated with their presence. Another significant explanation for Russian invisibility is novelty of their presence in Britain and The Netherlands and the lack of established communities. Members of the host societies are not used to the 'Russians coming' (de Lange, 1997) as there is no acknowledged history of hosting this group of migrants. However, awareness of the Russian presence is currently growing; images of male criminals and female prostitutes and mail-order brides abound.

## Insiders' Perspectives

One obvious reason why Russians are invisible to the outsiders as well as to each other is the fact that most of them are not 'registered' migrants but temporary, commuting, 'tourist', or illegal. Most are not interested in making themselves visible to the authorities. It is not in the Russians' interest to present themselves as a 'community' in order to remain inconspicuous. Furthermore, these 'unregistered' migrants often pursue individual rather than collective objectives and often come into contact with each other through competition (for black jobs, sublet housing, etc.) rather than cooperation (as larger migrant groups might, lobbying for their collective rights, etc.). Migrants often choose individual rather than collective survival strategies because of either the precariousness of their situation, or uncertainty of their legal status and future, or lack of common aims, or practical need of remaining individually aloof to avoid authorities' attention.[6] 'We may speak of a great degree of differentiation of migrants from ... the former Soviet Union. We are talking about people who in their everyday life here in The Netherlands, despite the fact that they come from the same country, do not come into contact with each other' (Snel *et al.* 2000: 71).

Another reason for not wanting to identify with the 'Russian community' could be the negative imaging of Russians as criminals. The previously mentioned article in The Observer quotes an anonymous Russian source lamenting the negative image of the Russian community:

The wide reach of his criminal empire and the fear he generates among one of the UK's fastest-growing ethnic communities mean few people are willing to talk, and those who do ask not to be named. 'There are increasing numbers of Russian businesses over here, and many people are doing very well,' says one community member. 'In Russia it is normal to pay for protection, and working here it is often no different. Men like Karelin are a thorn in the side of the community here. For the most part people are here to work hard and make a good life for themselves. The few criminals among us means everyone gets tarred with a bad brush. (Thomson, *The Observer*, 2001)

The reason some Russians felt they did not belong to a 'community' was that they did not have enough in common (*nedostatochno obshego*) with the other 'community' members. 'I have my interests, they are work interests. Others have their own work interests,' explains a Russian computer scientist from Amsterdam. 'Outside work, I like to go bowling, I like playing chess – I don't know of many Russians who share my hobbies, so I play with whoever enjoys it' (Kirill). A housewife from London adds: 'I don't think other Russians are interested in my life, it's rather boring. We exchange recipes and talk about soap operas with my friends, but actually I'd rather read a book or take some professional course – others don't seem to be as interested in improving themselves' (Marina). A presently unemployed doctor living in Amsterdam feels that contact with the 'Russians' holds him 'back from the future': 'We can talk endlessly about old Russian films, old Russian music, old Russian dachas. I feel empty after these reminiscences because there's nothing new. I'd rather talk about the future' (Lev).

Alienation from one's fellow citizens may have positive connotations, as a poet from Amsterdam reflected, as this isolation implies independence and self-sufficiency: 'I don't want to belong to a herd where others instruct my conduct or check my life' (Margarita). It is interesting to note that some of the more negative definitions of *obshina* imply a herd, a group with archaic morals, which suppresses individuals and is narrow-minded and closed. Margarita explains why Russians are reluctant to see themselves as a whole group: 'We had enough of it in Russia. The good thing about being here is that nobody can tell you who you are… [From the outside] they do say who you are, but you can still lead your own life.' Grisha, a biologist from London confirms: 'Here, I don't need to be part of the group; here I'm just a specialist.'

These statements lead us to the following section about a widespread mutual antagonism among the Russians – a phenomenon not unknown among other migrant groups. As the following section suggests, antagonism can take particularly 'Russian' overtones since its roots may lie in Soviet and post-Soviet social history.

## Antagonism

Animosity between groups of Russians or individuals is a mysterious phenomenon since we have established that the Russians are geographically dispersed and usually content not to have too close contact with each other. Antagonism towards each other seems to be both the cause and the effect of the weakness of communal consciousness among the Russians.

Generally, there is a multitude of factors responsible for creating conflict within any, not just Russian, migrant group:

> Conflicts within a group can stem from a number of sources. Some are closely related to economic and social stratification and the inequitable distribution of wealth, prestige and power. Others reflect traditional rivalries between regions or localities in the former country or opposing political ideologies that relate more to conditions in the sending rather than the receiving country ... Such conflicts frequently coincide with generational differences and are aggravated by them. They necessarily involve some consideration of the processes of social mobility and adjustment experienced by migrants and the ways in which these influence the degree of identification with the new country. (Richmond 1969: 264)

Even though we have mentioned the lack of established communities, antagonism arises even among the few members of 'older' and 'newer' waves who come into contact with each other. Esman argues that 'even within the same ethnic group mutual support and solidarity may be strained by tensions and conflicts between earlier and later arrivals' (Esman 1996: 317). I have observed that the 'old' generation, mostly political dissidents or cultural exiles, expresses discontent with the 'new' generation, which, they feel, lacks political commitment, spirituality and 'what's worse – stain Russian names' in the receiving country (Glazer and Moynihan 1996: 135). Antagonism between the Russians also existed in the supposedly more unified pre-1990s communities. The post-revolutionary 'wave', superficially united in their anti-Soviet views, consisted of

> individuals displaced by a deluge [who] always kept a weather eye on the country to which many at first anticipated returning in a matter of months, the size of the population movement, and the very diverse forces that it involved, meant that internal differences and disputes soon became nearly as important as polemics with the common enemy, the new, Communist Russia ... Inevitably, the cultural life of the Russian emigration was subject to much same fragmentation and contention as its political existence: here again attitudes to the Soviet Union were crucial. (Kelly 1998: 299)

Among the recent arrivals, I heard the statement 'I want to have nothing to do with these Russians' from people of different occupation groups and social strata as well as different ethnic denominations (Russian, Jewish, Georgian etc.). The explanations for this antagonism, however, varied. Some migrants complained of how dishonest, unreliable and greedy their 'Russian' neighbours and friends were. Others explained their desire to stay aloof from their 'own' group by their wish to 'mix' with citizens of their 'new' country, making statements such as: 'Since we live in this country, we might as well be friends with its people.' Some others said that they 'did not wish to belong to a ghetto', or brushed my question off with 'We are not on a group tour'. Finally, some say that they do not avoid other Russians intentionally, 'it just happens'.

Some Russians, even those from common ethnic or social backgrounds, found their compatriots' behaviour embarrassing, backward, or irritating. In the interview with Hubert Smeets, a former Russia correspondent in The Netherlands, he mentioned that his Russian wife did not share his enthusiasm for visiting Russia and entertaining Russian friends, explaining it by the fact that she is tired of the culture of complaints: 'In the beginning my husband often invited Russians for our parties. Some of them lived in The Netherlands for five years but didn't speak a word of Dutch. But they did complain about everything; food was bad, education was bad. Then I'd say: "So, you have to go back." This would almost turn into an argument.' (Frantova, 6 August 1999)[7]

Natalya Shuvaeva, the Russian newspaper editor in London, reflected: 'Russians like to complain a lot, and the most popular subjects of criticism are the health and education systems. They say that the primary education here is so awful, they wish their children could still study in Russia. Private education is desirable, especially for new Russians. Russians also complain about the useless GPs, their lack of attention. Still, when it comes to serious surgeries, Russians try to bring their family members here to have an operation.' (Natalya Shuvaeva, June 1999).

But while a 'culture of complaints' breeds familiarity and boredom among the Russians, other cultural experiences have taught Russians to treat each other as strangers. Recalling Hardwick's (1993) discussion of 'cultural baggage' earlier in this article, part of this 'baggage' is the Soviet inheritance of fear. As one of the older émigrés stated, one reason for keeping aloof from each other is mistrust.

> For a long time we held aloof from the Russian colony in London. Those who have not lived under the Soviet regime must find it hard to imagine the psychology of persons who left that paradise during the first decade of the new order. I don't know how it may be today but, at that time, nobody who had previously belonged to the old Russia could be sure of his life and well-being, right down to the last minute of his existence. A careless word spoken in the street might give rise to a denunciation, arrest and imprisonment ... Even when we had spent some time in London, under the protection of English laws, in complete confidence that we were beyond the reach of the Soviet system, we could not shake off our instinctive reactions of fear.

My elderly informant in Amsterdam reported that although he left Russia during perestroika and realises that the 'spectre of Communism' has diffused, he is still haunted by the idea that the friendlier his compatriot, the more suspicious he is. The mutual antagonism among the Russians could also be seen in terms of old ethnic and class rivalries suddenly brought to the fore by relative geographical proximity (having come from different countries of C.I.S. and settled in the same city) of the migratory groups, whose only common desire might have been 'to go from one country to another. This exhausts whatever their minds can really have in common.' (Halbwachs 1960: 115).

Unlike the geographically proximate communities, such as Turks in The Netherlands (Staring 1999) or Indians in Britain (Baumann 1996), when whole neighbourhoods are occupied by houses, shops and cultural institutions of one migrant group, Russians in London and Amsterdam avoid such clustering. By contrast, Doomernik (1997) and Darieva (1998) report that Russians do cluster elsewhere, finding geographically proximate cultural institutions in Berlin.[8] The same phenomenon is found in Canada (Hardwick 1993), Israel (Siegel 1998) and other countries with large Russian populations. This brings us back to the question of critical mass and makes us suspect that for some ironic reason the fewer the Russians the less they like each other.

Finally, it must be noted that Russians actually do come from different ethnic, cultural and linguistic backgrounds. Soviet-style hierarchy of ethnic groups (with ethnic Russians presiding at the top of it) and other forms of State-condoned antagonism between social groups may account for the fact that Russian-speakers coming from different countries of the C.I.S. or different ethnic backgrounds do not want to be seen as part of a group of generalised Russians. Feelings of inferiority or superiority were indeed present among ethnically diverse groups of Russian-speakers present in London and Amsterdam. Angela, an ethnic Lithuanian from Lithuania, an asylum seeker in London, referred to the ethnic Russians living in her country and seeking asylum in Britain as 'fakers' – 'They are blaming Lithuanians for their misfortunes in order to get an asylum here'. Michael, a Jewish sociologist, now living on a pension in London, felt that the ethnic Russians in Russia did not consider him to be 'one of them' and he did not see the reason why Russians in London should suddenly shed off their anti-Semitic tendencies. Vadim, an ethnic Russian teenage rock musician from Amsterdam, referred to Georgians and Armenians living in Amsterdam as 'non-Russian'. Vadim did not see the reason why outsiders would group them together with ethnic Russians. Thus, 'community' appears to be ethnically divided if acknowledged at all.

Soviet communitarianism might also cause a pendulum effect of rejecting the State-imposed 'spirit of ethnic equality'. Since the sense of the Soviet 'community' was artificially fostered in the Russians for many years, their freedom from imposed identification with their fellow citizens may have led to the rejection of such 'community' spirit altogether. The Soviet propaganda of brotherhood of all Soviet peoples irrespective of social class, ethnicity, religion or personal beliefs could have created resentment and cynicism in those striving towards individual freedom and achievement.

How is this antagonism expressed? One expression of social distancing could be gossip, the subject which de Vries investigates in her article on Turkish girls in The Netherlands. Inter-group gossip restricts individuals' freedom. Girls' objections to gossip 'may result in an internal self-differentiation from their gossiping compatriots, but this never implies any desire to cease to be Turkish or to embrace "Dutchification" (*vernederlandsing*)' (de Vries 1995: 51). Russians from different backgrounds seem to engage in gossip about their close friends as well as more distant acquaintances. Gossip usually involves discussion of personal morals or material inequalities with disapproving undertones. Unlike the case of the Turkish girls, Russian gossip seems to be manifestly negative and may serve to increase social distance between the Russians. However, we need to note that social exclusion and even open confrontations and expressions of hostility are not uncommon among the Russians.

## Challenging Boundaries: Conclusion

As a group of people originating from the C.I.S. and residing in the same city (sometimes reading the same newspaper or going to the same Russian church, café or club), Russians in London and Amsterdam present an odd case of factual existence without external recognition or internal awareness. Russian 'community' may be granted its existence conditional on the flexibility of the Russians' and the outsiders' definition of the term.

Thus, the Russian presence in London and Amsterdam serves as an example of the problem of drawing clear boundaries to demarcate communities. European migrants, just as European States themselves, are actively manufacturing and adapting their identities, even though their actual presence can be described as 'invisible'. The boundaries involved in creation of the Russian migrant identity are created in response to larger political, social and cultural contexts and are sensitive to the larger entity called Europe and, indeed, the 'West'. The challenge of studying new migrant groups in Western Europe is related to the process of European identity formation as a whole.

### NOTES

1. At present, the new Russian café *Kalinka*, founded by a group of Armenians, is collecting a more ethnically homogenous crowd, thereby making non-Armenians feel excluded from this 'not quite Russian' café.
2. After Shuvaeva's talk in Oxford in June 1999, the following exchange occurred during the questions session:

Q5: It looks like there's no real 'community' whatsoever: no one church, or café like with the Poles ...

N.S.: Most Russians don't want to assimilate or form 'villages', they rather stay aloof from each other. But *LC* does serve as a kind of focal point through announcements of large common events, like opening of a church for Easter ... Readers' letters also form a kind of podium for a community ...

Q5: So they are like floating communities, scattered throughout London.

N. S.: There are certain areas where Russian live, like Highgate, Finchley, Docklands (where Russian life 'evolves around a certain pub'); Queensway ... but indeed, it's hard to pin them down to one area'.

3. A. Fostiropoulos makes more interesting observations about the 'community' and anthropology: 'I understand community as both geographically proximate and bound by something in common. Polish immigrants used to settle close together at their arrival in the areas of South-West London and Wimbledon, but now they've also moved apart. Sharing only common language and history isn't enough.'

I do not think it is generally possible to use anthropological methods to understand the Church. It can be seen through theological method and understood through committed religious experience. However, anthropology can help disentangle casual distinctions, such as national identity forged through religion.

4. By contrast, the Indians in London and Turks in Amsterdam are often seen as stable 'communities' by the media and through common discourse. If this research could expand its scope to include other migrant groups we might be able to gain more insight into the process of creating a migrant community. Comparison between Russian Diasporas in different European countries or elsewhere as well as between the Russian and other Diasporas may provide a useful clue as to which factors are responsible for creating a Russian communal identity.

5. Culturally, however, the Russians may present an odd case for the receiving society. In discussing Russian migrants in the Pacific Rim, Hardwick notes the following patterns of settlement and interaction with the receiving society, which might account for intentional 'invisibility':

Russians also carry the stigma of belonging to a strange and relatively unknown variant of mainstream Christianity. Eastern orthodox dogma and ritual often seem uncomfortably 'pagan' to more fundamentalist Christians ... Experiences in their homeland left many with scars that have not healed, even in the more open environment of the United States and Canada. Their need to remain unobtrusive and geographically isolated has sometimes created 'invisible' ethnic landscapes of anonymity, where only trained eyes can tell they are in a Russian neighbourhood. (Hardwick 1993: 4–5)

6. As might be the case with some other minority groups, calling themselves a 'community' might have practical advantages to the group (Baumann 1995). Members of a minority 'community' may claim collective benefits from the receiving institutions, no matter how internally divided they are. Yet, the Russians do not appear to be interested in collective lobbying for their own interests. This may be because these interests are mostly individual – most of my informants are relatively self-sufficient, be it through employment, political status or marriage. Only very few would profit from attracting attention to themselves through collective claims.

7. From the Dutch newspaper *Trouw*, 'Die Russen klaagden altijd over alles' (August 1999).

8. However, there is contradictory evidence on community formation in Germany, where ethnic Russians are said to exhibit more avoidance behaviour than Russian Jews or Ukranians: 'There is little affinity found among the [ethnic] Russians. According to experts' opinion, Russians are either not seeking or barely seeking communion with each other, also stronger communal tendencies and formation of institutions are observed among the Jews and Ukrainians' (Fedorov 1998: 83).

## REFERENCES

Al-Rasheed, M. 1995. 'In search of ethnic visibility: Iraqi Assyrian Christians in London'. In *Post-Migration Ethnicity: Cohesion, Commitments, Comparison*, eds G. Baumann and T. Sunier. Amsterdam, Het Spinhuis.

Anderson, B. 1991. *Imagined Communities: Reflections on the Origin and Spread of Nationalism*. London, Verso.

Baumann, G. 1996. *Contesting Culture*. Cambridge, Cambridge University Press.

Baumann, G. and Sunier, T. 1995. 'Introduction'. In *Post-Migration Ethnicity: Cohesion, Commitments, Comparison*, eds G. Baumann and T. Sunier. Amsterdam, Het Spinhuis.

Boissevain, J. 1994. 'Towards an anthropology of European communities?' In *The Anthropology of Europe: Identities and Boundaries in Conflict*, eds V.A. Goddard *et al.* Oxford, Berg.

Bourdieu, P. 1977. *Outline of a Theory of Practice*. Cambridge, Cambridge University Press.

Bryant, C. 1997. 'Citizenship, national identity and the accommodation of difference: Reflections on the German, French, Dutch and British cases'. In *New Community* 23, no. 2.

Castles, S., Booth, H. and T. Wallace. 1984. *Here for Good: Western Europe's New Ethnic Minorities*. London, Pluto Press.

Chapman, M. 1994. 'The commercial realization of Community boundary'. In *The Anthropology of Europe: Identities and Boundaries in Conflict*, eds V.A. Goddard *et al.* Oxford, Berg.

Codagnone, C. 1998. *New Migration and Migration Politics in Post-Soviet Russia*. Ethnobarometer Programme Working Paper No. 2. Available at http://cemes.org/current/ethnobar/wp2/wp2_ind.htm

Cohen, A.P. 1985. *The Symbolic Construction of Community*. London, Routledge.

Darieva, T. 1998. *Making a Community Through the Media? Post-Sowjetische Zuwanderer in Berlin*. Unpublished paper delivered at the conference 'Grenzelose gesellschaft?' (14-18 September 1998) Freiburg in Breisgau, Albert-Ludwig Universität.

Doomernik, J. 1997. 'Adaptation strategies among Soviet Jewish immigrants in Berlin'. *New Community* 23, no. 1: 59–74.

*Economist* (The). 2002. 'Fortuynism without Fortuyn: immigrants in The Netherlands'. *The Economist* 28 November: 46.

*Economist* (The). 2004. 'The coming hordes: Migration in the European Union'. *The Economist* 17 January: 25–26.

Eriksen, T.H. 1993. *Ethnicity and Nationalism: Anthropological Perspectives*. London, Pluto Press.

Esman, M.J. 1996. 'Diasporas and international relations'. In *Ethnicity*, eds J. Hutchinson and A.D. Smith. Oxford, Oxford University Press.

Gardner, K. 1995. *Global Migrants, Local Lives: Travel and Transformation in Rural Bangladesh*. Oxford, Clarendon Press.

Glazer, N. and D.P. Moynihan. 1996. 'Beyond the Melting Pot'. In *Ethnicity*, eds J. Hutchinson and A.D. Smith. Oxford, Oxford University Press.

Glenny M. and N. Stone. 1990. *The Other Russia*. London, Faber and Faber.

Goverde, H. ed. 2000. *Global and European Polity? Organizations, Policies, Contexts*. Aldershot, Ashgate.

Halbwachs, M. 1960. *Population and Society: Introduction to Social Morphology*. Glencoe, The Free Press.
Hardwick, S.W. 1993. *Russian Refuge: Religion, Migration, and Settlement on the North American Pacific Rim*. Chicago, University of Chicago Press.
Jackson, J. 1969. *Migration*. Cambridge, Cambridge University Press.
Johnston, R.J., Taylor, P.J. and Watts, M.J. eds. 2002. *Geographies of Global Change: Remapping the World*. Oxford, Blackwell.
Kelly, C. 1998. 'Russian culture and emigration, 1921–1953'. In *Russian Cultural Studies*, eds C. Kelly and D. Sheherd. Oxford, Oxford University Press.
Kroes, R. 2000. *Them and Us: Questions of Citizenship in a Globalizing World*. Urbana, University of Illinois Press.
Lange, W. de 1997. 'Te groot, te wild, te anders en te dichtbij: hoort de Rus bij oost of bij west?' *Trouw* 26 July 1997: 10.
Mandel, R. 1994. '"Fortress Europe" and the foreigners within: Germany's Turks'. In *The Anthropology of Europe: Identities and Boundaries in Conflict*, eds V.A. Goddard *et al.* Oxford, Berg.
Pratt, M. and J.A. Brown eds. 2000. *Borderlands Under Stress*. The Hague, Kluwer International.
Raj, D. 1997. *Shifting Culture and the Global Terrain: Cultural Identity Constructions Amongst British Punjabi Hindus*. Unpublished Ph.D. dissertation, University of Cambridge.
Rex, J. 2003. 'The nature of ethnicity in the project of migration'. In *The Ethnicity: Nationalism, Multiculturalism, and Migration*, eds M. Gibernau and J. Rex. Cambridge, Polity.
Richmond, A.H. 1969. 'Migration in industrial societies'. In *Migration*, ed. J.A. Jackson. Cambridge, Cambridge University Press.
Rouse, R. 2002. 'Mexican migration and the social space of postmodernism'. In *The Anthropology of Globalization*, eds J. Xavier and R. Rosaldo. Oxford, Blackwell.
Siegel, D. 1998. *The Great Immigration: Russian Jews in Israel*. Oxford, Berghahn.
Smith, A.D. 1996. 'Chosen peoples'. In *Ethnicity*, eds J. Hutchinson and A.D. Smith. Oxford, Oxford University Press.
Snel, E., De Boom, J., Burgers, J. and G. Engbersen. 2000. *Migratie, Integratie en Criminaliteit: Migranted uit Voormalig Joegoslavië en de Voormalige Sovjet-Unie in Nederland*. Rotterdam, RISBO Contractresearch BV.
Staring, R. 1999. 'Migratiescenario's'. In *De Ongekende Stad 1: Overkomst en Verblijf van Illegale Vreemdelingen in Rotterdam*, eds J. Burgers and G. Engbersen Amsterdam, Boom.
Verkuyten, M., Calseijde, S. van de, and W. de Leur. 1999. 'Third generation South Moluccans in The Netherlands'. *Journal of Ethnic and Migration Studies* 25, no. 1: 66–80.
Vries, M. de 1995. 'The changing role of gossip: Towards a new identity? Turkish girls in The Netherlands'. In *Post-Migration Ethnicity: Cohesion, Commitments, Comparison*, eds G. Baumann and T. Sunier. Amsterdam, Het Spinhuis.
Vertovec, S. 2003. 'Migrant Transnationalism and Modes of Transformation'. Unpublished paper presented at the Meeting of the Social Science Research Council (Princeton University, 23–24 May 2003).

# Chapter 7
# Merging European Boundaries: A Stroll in Brussels

Christina Moutsou

### Introduction

This chapter focuses on the city of Brussels, and its role as a symbolic representative of Europe. It seeks to understand how the idea of 'unity in diversity' (McDonald 1996), actively promoted by the European Union's campaign throughout Europe, is actually experienced by the local inhabitants of the city that hosts the EU's premises, and has come to be seen by the wider international community as characterising 'European union'. It is suggested that Brussels has a history that by far exceeds the more recent history of the EU's establishment, and, in that sense, living in the city can both reflect a more complex urban reality, but also put into question the idea of fixed European boundaries.

It has been argued that the nation-state, as the uttermost institution of modernity, has attempted to impose a unified and homogenised view of people's identity (Anderson 1983; Gellner 1983). To some extent, it could be argued that schemas such as the European Union could be a postmodern attempt to rule the world by now incorporating the 'diversity' logo (McDonald 1996). However, as Herzfeld (1997: 6) poignantly argues, top-down theories about nationalism experience the same pitfall against which they argue, i.e., that people can be manipulated by nationalist ideology, as if they completely lack agency. Instead, Herzfeld proposes the concept of 'cultural intimacy', which, among its other functions, is a way of understanding larger political processes from the perspective of the locals. He points out that anthropologists seek cultural intimacy with their subjects of research, i.e., direct experience of their way of life, in order to make sense of social phenomena. The same, he claims, is the case with ordinary people's handling of large-scale political processes; people need to embed political concepts with indigenous meaning, in other words to appropriate them, and it is only then that large-scale politics become substantial at the local level.

'Cultural intimacy' is the primary aim of the present chapter. Brussels is a city that has largely been viewed from afar, more as an abstract concept than an actual inhabited space. This chapter aims to deconstruct top-down views of the city, by taking a stroll through Brussels' different neighbourhoods, from the immigrant quarters to the bureaucratic headquarters. In so doing it aims to highlight how different parts of the population have acquired 'intimacy' with widespread stereotypes about their urban space, and the extent to which the actual larger political processes that come from Brussels' headquarters affect their everyday living.

What follows is divided into three parts: first, I give a brief overview of the recent history of Brussels with reference to immigration and the city's place within Belgium. In the second part, I proceed to briefly examine how two significant ethnic communities within the city, the Greeks and the Turks, view themselves and are viewed in relation to the idea of European union.[1] The choice of the above communities is rather revealing in relation to the topic of inquiry. This is because the former are from an EU member-country and the latter are not, while they both have an ambivalent relationship to the concept of 'Europe'. In the third part, I refer to Brussels' population that forms part of an international elite, such as the EU employees and students. I conclude by discussing how the lived experience of Brussels as a city by different parties informs us about the concept of 'European union' and its shifting boundaries.

## A Place in the City: The Flows to Brussels

Two facts are well known about Brussels, one mostly discussed by 'outsiders', and one by people who are familiar with the place. Brussels is reputed to be the conceptual centre of Europe. The EU's administrative buildings have been located in Brussels, and most of the central decisions are taken there. The city has come to be associated with functionaries, bureaucracy and the idea of a united Europe. It is quite common for people coming from other parts of the world to know of Brussels, but to be unable to locate it in a nation-state; In other words, people often tend to view Brussels as a State by itself.

After living for a short period in Brussels, one comes to understand that the central concern in Belgium is not 'Europe', but the conflict between the two dominant groups, the Walloons and the Flemings, and the ways the State has attempted to mediate between them. Brussels is the most contested place. It is argued that historically and geographically it belongs to Flanders, but it is a predominantly French-speaking city (Martiniello 1997). It is perhaps an irony, then, that Brussels has come to be seen as a State in itself. In the constitutional revision of 1988, Brussels had a separate Government along with the Flemish, Walloon and national Government within the recently created Federal State (Vos 1993: 142–43).

Because of its geographical location in the centre of Western Europe, Brussels has, since the nineteenth century, accommodated a significant number of foreigners. Migration was not originally organised centrally, and foreigners tended to merge into Belgian society after a certain period. Morelli argues that unlike in the United States, where immigration constitutes a part of the official national history, immigrants' place within European nation-states has not been recognised. Contemporary Belgium is a mixture of people with various ethnic origins who frequently perceive themselves, and are perceived as Belgians (Morelli 1992). The following statement is a humorous example of this: 'I am a real Belgian. – Really, since when?' (Morelli 1992: 3).[2]

From the beginning of the century, employment in the coal mines attracted a more steady flow of foreigners.[3] Before the Second World War, Italians, Polish and North Africans (originally going to France) were hired by the mines in Wallonia, but comprised only 10 percent of the mine-workers (Lewin 1997: 14–17). It was after 1945 that migration began to be dealt with by the State. The State was in desperate need of labour for the coal mines, and attempted to increase the labour force by compelling war prisoners to work in the mines and releasing those who volunteered to work in the mines from military service. These policies failed to attract an adequate number of mine-workers. More than thirty thousand Italians were hired, but this proved a short-term solution. After the so-called *Catastrophe de Marcinelle* in 1956, where many mine workers (most of them Italians) died inside the mines, the Italian Government refused to send more workers (Morelli 1992). Therefore, a bilateral agreement was signed with Spain and subsequently with Greece in 1957 (Alexiou 1992).

After 1960, in a period of economic development, the Belgian Government decided to hire foreign workers not only for the mines, but also for heavy industry around the cities such as Brussels and Antwerp. In 1964, a bilateral agreement was signed with Turkey and Morocco (Lewin 1997: 22). The Moroccans and Turks who were hired worked mostly in the more recent coal mines in Flanders. Many of them were directed towards the industry in the suburbs of Brussels. In this way, immigration gradually became a more urban phenomenon.

'Foreign workers' were not accepted in Belgium solely through bilateral agreements with the Belgian Government. As a result of the economic growth of the 1960s, the Belgian government allowed many people to enter the country under the unofficial status of 'tourist'. These people came with a tourist visa and looked for employment in the large urban centres. Between 1964 and 1967, Belgium attempted to resolve the growing problem of low population by encouraging family reunions (Martiniello and Rea 1997). In 1974 legal and 'informal' immigration was officially stopped in Belgium as in many other European countries.

After many attempts by the trade unions to acquire more civil rights for the 'immigrants', the status of 'immigrants' was finally settled by law in 1984. The law was passed as a part of Belgian 'politics of integration'. According to this law, 'immigrants' could only obtain political rights by naturalisation, i.e., acquiring Belgian nationality. Belgian nationality was given to people who showed a 'strong will to integrate into Belgian society'. Naturalisation became automatic for second generation immigrants and for spouses and children of mixed marriages with a Belgian (Rea 1997).

According to recent statistics, in 1989 there were 20,613 Greeks in Belgium, 50 percent of whom lived in Brussels (Alexiou 1992: 274), and in 1996 there were 81,744 Turks in Belgium, 26 percent of whom lived in Brussels (Kesteloot *et al.* 1997: 29). It seems that Brussels has attracted a significantly larger percentage of Greeks than Turks. One reason for this is that many Greeks, having come to Belgium earlier than the Turks, have worked in mines in French-speaking areas, and have consequently chosen to move to Brussels, which is predominantly French-speaking. According to the same statistics 50 percent of Turks live in Flanders (Kesteloot *et al.* 1997: 29), particularly in Antwerp and Gent, which are Flanders's larger urban centres. One reason for this is that Turks arrived in a later wave of migration, at a time when workers were hired in Flemish-speaking areas. As a result, a smaller percentage of Turks than Greeks decided to move to Brussels.

The flow of foreign workers of all nationalities into Brussels has had a significant impact on the city. The newly arrived tended to settle in the nineteenth century working-class neighbourhoods, where accommodation was poor and cheap (Kesteloot *et al.* 1997: 35–39). These neighbourhoods are among the most central of the city. Gradually, the population of the centre came to be predominantly non-Belgian. This in turn had the effect of leading Belgians to look for accommodation in the suburbs.

As in many Western cities, the neighbourhood in which one lives in Brussels has significant implications for one's social status, and is a common topic of conversation. Belgian and Greek friends often criticised me for living in a 'dangerous neighbourhood'. They were concerned about my personal safety in an 'immigrant neighbourhood'. When they visited my home, they frequently commented on the ghetto-like nature of the surrounding streets, which they perceived as principally occupied by people belonging to Muslim minorities having informal gatherings in public spaces. Despite Brussels' multicultural character, the foreign workers who moved to the city in the 1970s have not been accepted willingly or integrated harmoniously.

From the above data one can extract very interesting information about the position of foreign workers in Belgian society. Most of them came originally to work in the coal mines. For many Belgians this was highly undesirable and marginal labour. The fact that the ostracised Second World War prisoners were made to work there reflects the low status of the work. Work in the mines was extremely dangerous. The Belgian State attempted to keep foreign workers in the job by compelling them to enter a five-year contract. For the miners themselves, the disadvantages of the job were balanced by the salaries and social and health benefits they were offered, as well as the opportunity to work elsewhere in Belgium after the end of the contract. Despite these incentives, my informants' accounts suggest that many workers did not manage to stay for the duration of their contract.

When the urgent need for foreign workers ended, they came to be seen by many as threatening the prosperity of Belgians (Kesteloot *et al.* 1997). However, unlike other European countries such as Germany, where citizenship is refused to non-Germans and their children (see Horrocks and Kolinsky 1996: x–xxvi), the foreign workers in Belgium were called 'immigrants', a title which implied their right to stay permanently. It is not coincidental, however, that tension has arisen since a significant number of these workers moved to Brussels, a place which also attracts more privileged groups.[4]

As noted at the beginning of this section, Brussels is internationally known as the home of the headquarters of the European Union and is also one of the most contested points of the conflict between the Flemings and Walloons. Both these facts have had an impact on the position of foreign communities in Brussels. The European Union has certainly contributed to the city's prosperity, providing job opportunities and attracting people able and willing to spend money there. Surprisingly, however, the role of Brussels as home of the EU has not been well received by the majority of its inhabitants.[5] The EU requires a city that can accommodate a large international elite, and Brussels has been internationally represented as a cosmopolitan luxurious urban centre. From this perspective, the presence of a significant number of foreign workers living in 'ghettos' can only be seen as a problem. Interestingly, the EU's elegant headquarters are situated in close proximity to immigrant (predominantly Muslim) neighbourhoods. The contradictory character of Brussels is easily sensed as one travels around the city.

The language problem within Belgium has led to Turks and Greeks settling in either the Flemish or the Walloon side. In the conflict between the Walloons and the Flemings, the position of Brussels was one of the most important issues. Many surveys were undertaken by the Flemings to prove that there is a significant Dutch-speaking population living in the city. The large percentage of Brussels' population that was foreign and largely French-speaking significantly affected the ratio of French to Dutch speakers, further swelling the French-speaking majority. In Brussels, there are both French- and

Dutch-oriented schools,[6] and parents thinking about their children's future must 'choose side'.[7] The position of 'immigrants' is even more ambiguous in a country where people's identities are contested and in conflict (Morelli and Schreiber 1994: 62–6). As Morelli and Schreiber (1994) argue, although this ambiguity has initially provided a cosmopolitan and accepting context for non-Belgians, the newly-born nationalisms of the two sides have recently acted as an additional factor for the isolation and exclusion of foreigners.

While Brussels is widely reputed to be cosmopolitan, the accommodation of difference within the city is often problematic. Brussels is a highly complex and frequently contradictory city and, in this respect, it conforms with Hannerz's description of the metropolis as a place where contrast and hybridity dominate (1996: 133–35). The contradictions of Brussels create many possibilities for shifting identities within the Turkish and Greek communities.

## Windows of Ethnic Presence

When I first arrived in Brussels I had with me a few local addresses and phone numbers, which might prove useful for my fieldwork. I also thought it would be interesting to see what information (if any) the Belgian authorities had on the Greek and Turkish communities in Brussels. I visited the Tourist Information Office, which holds detailed information on different aspects of the city's life, and asked whether there were any formal representatives of Greek and Turkish communities in Brussels.

The employee was particularly enthusiastic in helping me with the Greek case. She said that there were on file endless lists of Greek associations and strongly suggested that I contacted the Hellenic Community, as this was the formal representative agency of the Greeks. In contrast, she told me with no hesitation that she had absolutely no information on the Turks and there was no Turkish association mentioned in the files. After I expressed surprise, wondering how this was possible when there are so many more Turks than Greeks in Brussels, she rather reluctantly suggested I contacted the Turkish Embassy.[8]

The above vignette offers a glimpse of how the presence of Turks and Greeks in Brussels makes its way outside the conceptual boundaries of their communities. It also pinpoints the agencies that have come to formally represent them. At a much later stage of the fieldwork, thinking back to this short conversation, another striking element occurred to me. In addition to the lack of information on the Turks, there was no mention of religious agencies in either case. Religious agencies often have the role of formally representing Turks and Greeks of the Diaspora. It seems that what has come to be thought as central or formal representation inside and outside of the Greek and Turkish communities are not always in agreement.

The Hellenic Community[9] and the Greek Orthodox Church for the Greeks, and the Turkish Embassy and various religious agencies for the Turks, are the agencies which are seen as formally representing the Greek and Turkish communities. It seems that these central representative agencies are connected with the history of the Greeks' and Turks' establishment in Brussels, which is, in its turn, linked to the contemporary history of Turkish and Greek nation-states. Therefore, nationalism and 'history' are strongly reflected in the roles adopted by Greek and Turkish representatives.

I visited the Hellenic Community frequently during the course of my fieldwork. I also had access to its archives, which reflect its history and that of the Greek establishment in Brussels. The Turkish community on the contrary stands out by the lack of an appropriate establishment to represent the Turks. I suggest that this lies in the history of the Turks' establishment in Brussels, as well as the contemporary form of the Turkish community.

Religious agencies play an important part in formally representing the Turks and Greeks of the diaspora. As demonstrated by my experience at the Tourism Office, religious agencies are largely known to members of the Greek and Turkish communities and their links with outsiders are minimal. I had no access to Turkish mosques, but I discussed their function with many Turks. I had an easy access to the Greek Orthodox Church, but although I was present at a number of religious events my contacts were more irregular than those I had with the Hellenic Community. As Strathern notes, we always establish deeper connections with certain parts of the social reality during fieldwork (Strathern 1991).

I suggest that the term 'community', which is extensively used by central representative associations refers to a rather 'imagined' than de facto unity. An 'imagined community' brings to mind Anderson's (1991) famous definition of the nation in his discussion of nationalism. However, Greek and Turkish communities in Brussels should be seen within the context of the diaspora (Brah 1996). As Wicker (1997) observes, ethnic movements and nationalism are increasingly intermingled, with the effect that it has become impossible to talk about one without referring to the other. Both draw upon essentialising and homogenising social groups (Wicker 1997).

Interestingly, questions of central representation among Greeks and Turks in Brussels are also constructed by reducing and even denying the heterogeneity of Turkish and Greek migration, and by assuming that certain selected features constitute the essence of Greekness and Turkishness. In the Greek case (as my repeated visits to the Hellenic Community clearly led me to understand), the Greek community is thought to be composed of mineworkers and their families, that is, quintessential 'immigrants'. In the Turkish case, the assumed 'immigrant' lives in Schaerbeek (Figure 7.1) and comes from Emirdag. Not fulfilling these criteria is for many Turks equivalent to not being

Figure 7.1 The nineteen boroughs of the city of Brussels.

a 'Turkish immigrant'. In reality, those who fit into these models are far outnumbered by those who do not.

Not surprisingly, the people who have taken on leading roles within these imagined communities and have contributed to the construction of the above reductionist models rarely view themselves as 'immigrants'. All speakers in the Hellenic Community's fiftieth anniversary commemorative events were highly educated professionals who often had stronger bonds with political centres in Greece than with Greeks in Belgium. In the Turkish case, central representation is mainly accomplished through the Embassy, which is staffed by educated Turkish officials coming from urban areas in Turkey. There is a paradox in both Greek and Turkish cases: their central representatives are Greeks and Turks living in the Diaspora, who do not conform to the constructed images of those diaspora communities.

Most of the Greek and Turkish activists though feel excluded by the prestige which EU institutions bring. However, the employment of some Turks and Greeks by the EU-related institutions has significantly affected the dynamics within the Turkish and Greek communities in Brussels, as will be seen in the following section. The crucial difference between the Greek and Turkish communities is that while Greeks, with access to power centres, are prone to participating in the construction of a 'Greek community', many Turkish intellectuals have chosen to stand at a critical distance. Most Turkish intellectuals are political refugees who try to escape both the Turkish State and their past lives in Turkey. Moreover, the position of the Turkish and Greek States within power discourses in Europe and the EU seem directly relevant to the differences in representation between Greeks and Turks. Consequently, there have been fewer successful attempts to centrally represent the Turkish community in Brussels.

The character of the 'Hellenic Community', the lack of a 'Turkish Community' and the central role of the Turkish Embassy depend heavily on the recent political history of Greece and Turkey. When it comes to central representation, Turkish and Greek communities often appear as subsidiaries of the Turkish and Greek State. As Papadakis (1994) demonstrates through the comparison of the Greek-Cypriot and Turkish-Cypriot national struggle museums, nationalism is not based solely on the imagining of a homogeneous community, but also depends on the assumption that the State is the central actor in a series of events (Papadakis 1994). In the case of Turks and Greeks living in the Diaspora the centrality of the homelands' states in their lives stands as a striking paradox. The Turkish Embassy as the state representative per se attempts to control what is seen as the Turkish community, while the apparently independent 'Hellenic Community' has increasingly depended on the Greek State and reflects the dominant political segmentations in Greece.

The central representation of Greeks and Turks in Brussels is therefore linked to nationalism and the history of the Greek and Turkish States. This history is often viewed by the representatives as a linear series of strictly selected events. Modern nation-states have been built on this version of history (Hastrup 1992); it should not be forgotten that people choose to stress certain events and to ignore others in order to justify the present through the past (Papadakis 1993). The debates about the role of the Church in the Greek case, and about Islam in the Turkish case, as presented by Left-wing Greeks and Turks, are good examples of a highly selective and politically biased presentation of history. Anthropology has recently become concerned with history in order to make sense of the ethnographic present. However, as Blok (1992) has argued, anthropology, unlike the actors themselves, should see the past in terms of relationships and of the contradictory versions presented by different parties.

As stated above, religion is presented as a highly contested issue by different actors within the Greek and Turkish communities. Religious celebrations may be seen as belonging to the repetitive past. In other words, religious events are often fixed and repeated each year and in this sense they remind Turks and Greeks of their origins and bonds (Zonabend 1984). Although for some Turks and Greeks religious beliefs and participation provide a refuge, the role of religious authorities is often inseparable from the political histories of their countries. The Greek Orthodox Church in Brussels has been associated by Left-wing Greeks with extreme Right-wing ideology and has been used as a symbol of Greekness in the conservatives' political debates. However, for many Greeks abstaining from the community's leadership, Orthodox Christianity has a highly personal meaning. In the Turkish case, Islam has often been used as a blanket term by both Left-wing Turks and Belgians to construct the stereotype of the 'Muslim Turk'. However, the plurality of mosques highlights the complexity of religious affiliations within the Turkish community. It also demonstrates the direct role of religion in political debates about Turkishness.

Therefore, it seems that the central representative authorities of Greeks and Turks in Brussels resort to a highly constructed 'history' in order to present an image of a single or homogeneous Greek or Turkish community. It is not my intention to doubt the existence of Greek and Turkish presence in Brussels and the importance of their pasts. However, it seems to me that communities and their pasts are multi-faceted and dynamic. As Cohen (1985) observes, the only way to conceive of a community in a multi-ethnic environment is by viewing the ways in which people live in the larger world through symbolically belonging to a collectivity that is constantly shifted and redefined according to the changing boundaries that it comes across. From this point of view, Greek and Turkish communities in Brussels can only be seen as symbolic entities against which people constantly redefine their identities.

## Do Brussels' Inhabitants Speak Esperanto?

A significant part of Brussels' population are highly mobile international employees and students. Also, for some of the local population, composed of native Belgians and 'immigrants', finding employment within any international organisation is a highly aspired-to ideal. Of course, some Brussels inhabitants do work in EU-related establishments on a contractual or sessional basis, e.g., as translators or interpreters. It is a frequently heard joke in Brussels that the EU cleaners are much more favoured (in terms of payment and workload) than the local university lecturers. This reflects the locals' ambivalent position towards the EU within the city. The EU is seen by locals both as a source of local prosperity and as an institution detrimental to the local character of the city. The role of the EU within the city can also be understood by its influence on the way it is perceived by different parties within the Greek and Turkish communities living in Brussels.

In recent years, Greek employees of international organisations have been increasingly interested in the affairs of the Hellenic Community. The last two Presidents of the Community during my fieldwork were indeed employees of international organisations. Educated, well established Greeks have apparently been attracted to the Hellenic Community because of its close connections with Greek politics. The Socialist Party (PASOK), which has been the ruling party in Greece for most of the time since 1981, showed an active interest in Greek communities of the diaspora. This interest is explained by the fact that the majority of Greeks living abroad were Left-wing, and therefore potential supporters. Both the last Presidents of the Hellenic Community were active members of the Governing party in Greece.[10]

In my interviews with restaurant owners, the main reason they stated for not attending Community functions was the increasing participation of International employees in the Hellenic Community. There was a common feeling among Greeks who came to Belgium as workers that 'the Community that should belong to us and be our home has now been invaded by the "EUs". Despite the fact that the international employees who participate in the Hellenic Community are mostly Left-wing and often share the same political ideas as Greek workers, the latter still feel excluded from active participation in the Community.

The connections between the Embassy, the mosques and the State, and the power games that these institutions initiate were often mentioned by Turkish 'liberal' intellectuals.[11] The Embassy was seen as an obstacle to Turks' integration into Belgian society and as the reason for Turkey's 'failure' to become European. For many Turkish intellectuals living in Brussels, the exclusion of Turks from the EU's premises was particularly painful. It was often compared to Greece's inclusion, as for many Turks, cultural affinities of the two countries should ensure them the same fate with regards to Europe. It would make sense, then, that my Greek identity played an important role in influencing their comments on the EU, such as:

> I have lived and worked in Brussels for years, but I am still excluded from Europe. Turks in Brussels particularly, would really benefit if Turkey were an EU member ... Do you know what is Turkey's best connection to the EU? Our (Turkish) women who clean the Eurocrats' offices. Almost all cleaners in the EU premises are Turkish, that's our best connection![12]

As Shore (1993) argues, the recent attempt at the creation of a united Europe has created new boundaries of exclusion. EU member-states are often juxtaposed with non-members, 'the outsiders'. Minorities in Western Europe who do not originate from a member-country have therefore become foreigners in a double sense (Shore 1993). This double exclusion is particularly hard for educated Turks in Brussels, who often feel excluded both from Turkey and Belgium/Europe.

The 'Europeanisation' of Brussels has also been accused of distorting Brussels's rich tradition as a bohemian, entertainment metropolis. Such a tradition is difficult to miss if one takes the effort to visit Brussels and wander around the small cobblestone streets surrounding the *Grand Place*. As a matter of fact, however, many of the numerous central bars and restaurants are filled by international employees and students who can afford to frequent them on a regular basis. I have a personal, direct experience of how international employees and students tend to inhabit the urban space of Brussels by being myself a student and socialising with other students during fieldwork, and also by being an EU Research Fellow for two years.

Although there are significant differences between the students' and the EU employees' placement within Brussels, there are also some important similarities. Multilingualism is a common phenomenon in Brussels even among the least educated. The use of three languages (Flemish, French and English) is compulsory at school, and being fluent at both French and Flemish is a prerequisite to finding employment in the public sector. However, the use of language among EU employees and students during informal meetings and socialising might be highly revealing of the significant differences between them in relation to Brussels and the idea of Europe. Many EU employees speak more than three languages, and of course during work are able to switch from one language to another. However, in consistence with the logo of 'unity through diversity', EU policies about the treatment of its employees actively promote the recognition of national difference. EU employees come in a particular national distribution and representation. Many of the internal social events revolve around national origin, i.e., an Italian party, a Danish party etc. with food and entertainment to match. However, the effect that such policies seem to have on the everyday work environment is that of creating national groups within the EU, and the consequent predominant use of mother-tongue for communication between members of these groups within the EU premises. In fact what I was surprised to realise when I once spent an entire afternoon in a Greek employee's office observing him at work, was that I didn't hear him speak any other language than Greek once, during his numerous and lengthy telephone conversations with colleagues.

The social position of students within any particular context has been a largely absent topic in recent anthropological studies, quite possibly because being a student is 'too close to home' for a researcher anthropologist (Strathern 1991). And yet, students constitute a particular category of the population which has recently become highly mobile within Europe. It is not coincidental that many of the EU funds and projects aim at the domain of education and research, and attempt to promote mobility within Europe by funding people to study in countries other than their own. In fact, many of the students living in Brussels are directly linked with the EU, either by focusing their degrees on European studies or by being offered a base at the EU premises.[13] Therefore, students and EU employees in Brussels have occasionally been directly linked. Also, studying in Brussels is often a choice made by students who aspire to work in the EU for their future careers. In my experience during fieldwork, Greek students very often socialised with Greek EU employees.

However, there are some ways in which European students in Brussels are significantly different from EU employees. Students are the main part of the population taking advantage of the 'original bohemian character' which *Bruxellois* claim their city to have. It was indeed in Brussels where I experienced a particular social interaction that I never encountered in London or any other city. Groups of students of mixed nationalities would socialise in bars and cafés until late at night. These groups would often be very changeable in their composition and number of members, as the concentration of bars in Brussels's centre as well as the relatively small size of the city permitted acquaintances or even people from nearby tables to join the original group. In such encounters the use of the language of communication would be frequently shifted. English and French would be the most common lingua franca, but Flemish and other European languages would be frequently heard and speaking in one's mother tongue with somebody from another country who happened to speak it would not be unusual. It seems to me that the interesting fact about being a student is a potential openness to the world beyond nation-states. This is because 'being a student' is, at least in theory, a position of developing oneself and exploring the world beyond pre-established boundaries. A Greek student I got to know quite well during fieldwork used to boast that she was hardly ever excluded from conversations as a member of these groups of students, as she spoke six languages.

Therefore, it seems that among Brussels's different categories of population it is primarily among students where national difference is occasionally accommodated, and even under certain circumstances accepted as part of the lure of living in the city 'representing Europe'.

## Conclusion

In this chapter, I explored in passing the experience of living in Brussels for certain parts of its population, namely those who identify as Belgians, the Greek and Turkish communities, people directly linked through employment to the EU institutions, and international students. The history of Brussels within the Belgian State and the stages of population immigration to the city reveal that it is a much more complex urban space than how it is represented internationally. However, it also seems to be the case that dominant stereotypes about the affect of the EU establishment and its 'Europeanisation' of the city are perpetuated by different parts of its current population. Consistent with Herzfeld's definition of 'cultural intimacy', Brussels's inhabitants seem to often appropriate and reproduce the political agenda of a shifting of European boundaries and European identity through their understanding of such issues in their everyday lives.

However, it seems to be the case that, unlike what might be expected, national stereotyping and a fixed representation of what the EU stands for are reinforced by informal discourses among Brussels' inhabitants. McDonald (1993) points out that national and ethnic stereotyping are on the increase in Europe, despite a general expectation of the demolition of European boundaries. She observes that stereotyping is a universal process of differentiating between self and other and that anthropologists are not an exception to this process, as anthropological representation of a certain social group can further contribute to the stereotyping of this group. It has certainly been the case that anthropological studies of south and eastern Europe have seemed to reinforce the boundary between countries in those regions and the West.

Ironically, the same process seems to be taking place within the EU as national consciousness seems to be a predominant mode of distinction among its employees. In most tourist shops in Brussels one can find variations of a postcard (nowadays also seen in other European countries) with the circle of stars representing the EU and statements such as 'Hell is where the Germans are lovers, the British are cooks' etc. The national stereotyping connected with the EU might have something to do with this institution's connection and current alliance with the nation-state. In other words it reflects on the EU's origins and current connection to the political leadership of European nation-states.

McDonald (1996) poses the agonising question of whether 'unity in diversity' can be imposed from above. Having observed in detail the everyday life and institutional dynamics within the EU, she wonders whether 'Europe' as a meaningful concept has indeed entered the minds of its 'European' inhabitants. The present volume deals with the multiple ways through which European boundaries are crossed in people's everyday lives. This chapter raises the question of the sort of 'cultural intimacy' that is created when European boundaries are merged, as in the case of different populations co-existing in the symbolic and geographical centre of Europe. In informal gatherings in Brussels, such as those described among students, a more international picture seems to be formed. Such gatherings seem on the one hand to recognise national difference, but on the other seek to communicate and interconnect. Therefore, they might not deal with yet another shifting of European boundaries, but can demonstrate the creative potential of difference and diversity within Europe.

## NOTES

1. This chapter is based on doctoral research on Greek and Turkish representations of ethnicity in Brussels.
2. Morelli and Schreiber (1994) argue light-heartedly that because of the escalating friction between the Walloons and the Flemings, 'immigrants' have come to be the last 'real Belgians'.
3. Immigrants from Italy were by far the largest foreign population in Belgium in the 1960s and 1970s. There was a steady flow of immigrants from Greece. Immigration from Turkey and Morocco increased rapidly after 1974 while immigration from Italy and Greece decreased.
4. According to Kesteloot *et al.* (1997), problems about the use of urban space (related to the presence of foreign workers in Brussels) coincided with the economic crisis at the end of the 1970s. However, this seems to me only a partial reason for the anti-migrant feeling. Racism in the Media, particularly manifested through friction between the police and 'second generation' youth in 'migrant neighbourhoods', was frequently reported during my fieldwork.
5. There is a long debate about the role of the European Union in the city. Among the many accusations and complaints I heard were against its role in raising taxes and closing down small-scale enterprises as well as its destruction of the original 'bohemian' character of the city.
6. Both French and Dutch are compulsory at school, and people need to be fluent in both languages to find employment in the public sector. This is often an additional constraint to foreigners' 'integration'.
7. The financial and social power of Flemings has increased, I was repeatedly told by Turks and Greeks who aimed to raise the possibility of social mobility for their children by choosing to send them to Flemish schools.
8. Another very revealing incidence of the difference in public perception of which is the larger local population of the Greek and Turkish communities was when I lost my purse in a Moroccan café and went to a police station to declare it. The policeman loudly wondered why I chose to go to a Moroccan café rather than a 'nice little Greek restaurant'. Through his statements he was expressing the prevailing perception of the Muslim establishments in Brussels as dangerous. Greek restaurants were spread throughout Brussels and very popular during my fieldwork, while most Turkish restaurants were restricted in the Turkish neighbourhood and failed to attract middle-class Belgians.
9. I refer to Hellenic Community with a capital 'C', while community with a small 'c' will imply the conceptual entity of Greeks or Turks. The choice of the name 'Hellenic' instead of 'Greek' Community is not coincidental. The word 'Hellenic' is used by Greeks to refer to themselves, while 'Greek' is thought to have been imposed by the West. Moreover, 'Hellenic' implies a historical continuity between Ancient and Modern Greece, a version of history of which many Greeks are keen on (Herzfeld 1982).
10. I came to know that the President of the Hellenic Community had close connections with leading members of PASOK in Greece. His defeat in the elections was attributed by some to internal upheavals in PASOK. However, another possible reason stated by his opponents was his ambivalent ethics and alleged involvement in some 'not totally legal' financial affairs.
11. Another aspect of the power of the homeland over Turks in Brussels has been the recent success of ten Turkish television channels in Belgium. In the words of a Turkish political refugee: 'They don't even need to get out of their houses now. They have Turkey at home every day.' The increasing number of television channels in Turkey is directly connected with the role of the State and the evolution of Turkish society (Aksoy and Robins 1997).
12. Cleaning has become a common occupation for Turkish women in Brussels. Many cleaning companies have been set up by Turks, usually led by Turkish men.
13. This is often the case with *stagiaires*, students who are offered a six-month or longer period of being based on the EU premises and acquiring work experience within the institution as part of their degree.

## REFERENCES

Alexiou, A. 1992. 'L'immigration Grecque en Belgique'. In *L'Histoire d'Immigration en Belgique*, ed. A. Morelli. Brussels, Vie Ouvrière.
Anderson, B. 1991. *Imagined Communities: Reflections on the Origin and Spread of Nationalism.* London, Verso.
Blok, A. 1992. 'Reflections on "making history"'. In *Other Histories*, ed. K. Hastrup. London, Routledge.
Brah, A. 1996. *Cartographies of Diaspora.* London, Routledge.
Cohen, A.P. 1985. *The Symbolic Construction of Community.* London, Routledge.
Gellner, E. 1983. *Nations and Nationalism.* Oxford, Blackwell.
Hannerz, U. 1996. *Transnational Connections.* London, Routledge.
Hastrup, K. 1992. 'Introduction'. In *Other Histories*, ed. K. Hastrup. London, Routledge.
Herzfeld, M. 1982. *Ours Once More: Folklore, Ideology, and the Making of Modern Greece.* Austin, University of Texas Press.
Herzfeld, M. 1997. *Anthropology Through the Looking-Glass: Critical Ethnography in the Margins of Europe.* Cambridge, Cambridge University Press.
Herzfeld, M. 1997. *Cultural Intimacy: Social Poetics in the Nation-State.* London, Routledge.
Horrocks, D. and E. Kolinsky. 1996. 'Migrants or citizens? Turks in Germany between exclusion and acceptance'. In *Turkish Culture in German Society Today*, ed. D. Horrocks and E. Kolinsky. Oxford, Berghahn.
Kesteloot, C., Peleman, K. and T. Roesems. 1997. 'Terres d'exil en Belgique'. In *La Belgique et ses Immigrés*, ed. D.B. Université. Paris, De Boeck & Larcier.
Lewin, R. 1997. 'Balises pour l'avant 1974'. In *La Belgique et ses Immigrés*, ed. D.B. Université. Paris, De Boeck & Larcier.
McDonald, M. 1993. 'The construction of difference: An anthropological approach to stereotypes'. In *Inside European Identities*, ed. S. Macdonald. Oxford, Berg.
McDonald, M. 1996. '"Unity in diversity". Some tensions in the construction of Europe'. *Social Anthropology* 4, no. 1: 47–60.
Martiniello, M. 1997. 'The dilemma of separation versus union: The new dynamic of nationalist politics in Belgium'. In *Rethinking Nationalism and Ethnicity*, ed. H.R. Wicker. Oxford, Berg.
Martiniello, M. and A. Rea. 1997. 'Construction Européene et politique d'immigration'. In *La Belgique et ses Immigrés*, ed. D.B. Université. Paris, De Boeck & Larcier.
Morelli, A. 1992. 'Introduction'. In *L'Histoire de l'Immigration en Belgique*, ed. A. Morelli. Brussels, Vie Ouvriere.
Morelli, A. and J.P. Schreiber. 1994. 'De la difficulté de s' identifier à un pays sans identité'. In *L'Histoire de l'Immigration en Belgique*, ed. A. Morelli. Brussels, Vie Ouvriere.
Papadakis, Y. 1993. 'The Politics of memory and forgetting in Cyprus'. *Journal of Mediterranean Studies* 3, no. 1: 139–54.
Papadakis, Y. 1994. 'The National struggle museums of a divided city'. *Ethnic and Racial Studies* 17, no. 3: 400–19.
Rea, A. 1997. 'Movements sociaux, parties et intégration'. In *La Belgique et ses Immigrés*, ed. D.B. Université. Paris, De Boeck & Larcier.

Shore, C. 1993. 'Inventing the people's Europe: Critical approaches to European Community 'cultural policy''. *Man* 28, no. 4: 779–800.
Strathern, M. 1987. 'The limits of autoanthropology'. In *Anthropology at Home*, ed. A. Jackson. London, Tavistock.
Strathern, M. 1991. *Partial Connections*. Savage, Roman and Littlefield.
Volkan, V.D. and N. Itzkowitz. 1994. *Turks & Greeks: Neighbours in Conflict*. England, The Eothen Press.
Vos, L. 1993. 'Shifting nationalism: Belgians, Flemmings and Waloons'. In *The National Question in Europe in Historical Context*, ed. M. Teich and R. Porter. Cambridge, Cambridge University Press.
Wicker, H.R. 1997. 'Introduction: Theorizing ethnicity and nationalism'. In *Rethinking Nationalism and Ethnicity*, ed. H.R. Wicker. Oxford, Berg.
Zonabend, F. 1984. *The Enduring Memory*. Manchester, Manchester University Press.

# Chapter 8
# Bosnian Women in Mallorca: Migration as a Precarious Balancing Act

Jacqueline Waldren

### Introduction

In Mallorca, the terms 'refugee' and 'immigrant' are considered to reflect desperate, backward, dependent, poor, rural, uneducated, unskilled, disoriented, identity-less people who are 'all the same'. This generalisation has been a major problem especially since the 1990s when thousands of refugees from the former Yugoslavia poured into western Europe and shattered images of war-torn refugees as people from remote, far-away places.[1]

I have been following the resettlement process of thirty-three Bosnian refugees who came to Mallorca in 1992. In the absence of men (most of their husbands, brothers and sons were dead, unaccounted for or in the military), these women were forced to be the motors of contemporary social change as they struggled to overcome local values and stereotypes. They have fled from national and religious conflicts, traversed geographical, social and economic boundaries only to find they have been deprived of identity, conceptually lumped together not only with each other about whom they knew nothing prior to becoming refugees, but with 'strangers' as well. There are Latin American, Eastern European, Senegalese, Moroccan, Algerian and other refugees in Mallorca at the moment.[2]

Eight years after arrival, these women have gained legal status, made homes in Mallorca and reclaimed their Bosnian identity in exile.[3] 'At home' has a new meaning for many of these refugees who have chosen to remain in

Mallorca rather than return to Bosnia where they say 'the economy continues in crisis, housing, health care, education are inadequate and employment is scarce.' What this means in everyday life and for the future is not clear. However, it can reveal how symbolic and spatial boundaries take on new meanings as a result of war and migration, and how socio-cultural, ethnic, regional and national identities are formed and reformed against a backdrop of national and European economic and political conditions.

The movement of peoples whether by choice or forced migration brings together a number of overlapping issues which currently concern anthropology: How is identity formed and reformed in different circumstances and settings? How can gender differences in the experiences of migration and particularly the specificities that women bring to the migration process be built into policy and planning for the future? How does local activity relate to global politics and processes? How are global economic and social trends in migration carried out in local encounters? I hope to offer some insights into these questions based on this Mallorcan study. I agree that the refugee experience entails losses. However, while transformation and change are part of the experience, not all change is perceived as loss or defined as problematic or unwelcome by refugees themselves. If you have no future, no job, are a war exile or victim of war, anything is better than what you had 'at home'.

## Europe: Emigration and Immigration

In the modern system of nation-states as a conceptual order, in which the nation is perceived as the 'natural' place of belonging, identity and culture are secure and stable 'at home'. However, the concept of home is often circumstantial and as people out of place, refugees are an aberration of neat national categories, an anomaly in need of control as reflected in policies and planning. These 'natural' nation-states, constructed over time, are constraints on Europeanisation. However, caught between young nations, new borders, invented traditions, old customs, grand empires and the ever evolving European Union, Europeans are now struggling to comprehend their new identities.

For those who come from non-European countries the struggle to adapt to local expectations and fulfil their own hopes in new and unfamiliar surroundings is even more complex. Malika Abdel Aziz (2000), an Algerian journalist exiled in Spain believes that

> European is not a nationality for the inhabitants of the southern Mediterranean, it is rather a dynamic toward the citizenship that will liberate them from the legal marginality they suffer in their countries of origin. Europe feeds the consciences of the south with fantasies, causing an alienation and crisis of identity. Europe banalizes disequality, unequalness, makes light of the plight that many women face in their countries.

Europe is not aware of the strength of presence of the north over the south...Europe is not a place. It is a problem shrouded in myth and ideology. It offers false illusions and many future refugees only see the myth. No one tells them of the difficulties they will encounter. (Aziz 2000: 12 August)

Migration is a complex and diverse experience where mythical images of home or other lands are combined with socio-political ideologies to form new identities. Spain, along with the rest of the European countries, is having great difficulty adjusting to its new, late-twentieth century status as refugee destination. Legislation and administrative procedures must be brought in line with the changed and changing conditions they face. Formulating humane migration policies requires a precarious balancing act in liberal democracies. As a result, EU countries may well be inclined to give considerable leeway to the EC commission in designing migration policy for the community as a whole. The 1997 Treaty of Amsterdam introduced the concept of a European space '*sans frontiers*' where movement between nations was facilitated through a politic of cooperation of member-nations. However, Europe without frontiers is an enigma and does not exist for non-Europeans.

*El Ley de Estrangerias* (The Law for Foreigners) is the Spanish version of these community policies. The newly formed 'imagined community' of Europe based on common citizenship and currency has forced the re-definition of the status of immigrants in the member-nations of Europe. The massive presence of immigrants from eastern Europe and the Third World given residency through the new laws has provoked certain pre-occupations in some sectors of Spain. Refugees and immigrants are blamed for increased crime rates, mafia-type organisations, prostitution, drug trafficking etc. Gender analysis in migration becomes an important element for understanding globalisation process where not only goods but also human resources are involved.

People have forgotten that Spaniards were once immigrants who planted their roots in many distant places. Spaniards went to South America seeking work in the early 1900s and were much sought-after to fill the huge 'pull' by northern European countries for cheap labour after the Second World War. Some were 'pushed' out by poverty, family pressures or debts (see Gregory and Cazorola Perez 1985; Buechler and Buechler 1987). Migrant workers went seeking work when it was available and came 'home' when opportunities declined. Many houses in Soller, Deia and Valldemossa (north-west Mallorca coastal villages) were built with funds sent home from Venezuela and Uruguay by the first migration and from France and Germany by the second wave. Some of those who went to Uruguay were known to have opened bakeries and '*cambres foscas*' ('dark rooms', brothels well disguised behind the façade of warm bread and pastries!). Many were able to realise the economic freedoms they imagined using guile as well as hard work. Their economic contributions to their home country were important sources of survival during the rebuilding of Spain from the 1950s to the 1970s. 'Overseas migrants (Spaniards who went to northern Europe) may have been considered a "problem" when they left in 1950s and 1960s (the Spanish government encouraged unemployed men to take jobs in France and Germany to relieve the burden of unemployment in Spain) and a 'solution' in the 1970s and 1980s (when they were expected, as returnees, to contribute to development)' (Suárez-Navaz 2004: 32).

Migration from one area of the country to another, seasonal and permanent, within the countries referred to as 'the Mediterranean', has been common since the last century and increased greatly from 1960 to 1970 with tourism development (Waldren 1996). Interestingly, according to Sara Delamont, 'the number of people moving voluntarily in search of work since 1950 was much greater than the many millions of people who have been refugees in twentieth century Europe' (Delamont 1995: 69). In 1995 94.8 percent of newly registered residents on the island of Mallorca were Spaniards. By 2000, only 60 percent were Spanish nationals and the other 34 percent were from 'developing' countries.

## Immigrants/Refugees as a 'Problem'

I am working with Bosnian refugees who were brought to Mallorca by the Red Cross in conjunction with a group of Mallorcans in 1992 and have resettled in the northern town of Soller. I have been following their resettlement process and carrying out interviews. Most of the Bosnians in Soller are women, trained in business, banking, nursing, journalism and education. Through the Red Cross and local families they were provided with housing, a food allowance and menial jobs. Despite this support, some felt they were treated with disdain and seen as presumptuous if they criticised or complained (their hosts imagined themselves to be patrons providing an escape for victims of suffering and war and found the complaints most offensive).

The conditions and contradictory experiences that led to the migration of so many people from Bosnia are described by Amra Pandzo in his article 'War Time':

> The people are in the streets, going out, walking, getting ready for a new massacre. You ask me where they are going. To tell you the truth, they are going nowhere. They are all waiting for something – the end of the war, escape from Sarajevo, humanitarian aid, electricity. Moving is a way of survival. Physical motion is the only proof that one is still alive. Most people have lost everything but hope. One must lie to oneself and to others, pretending there is something more important than the elemental fear of death. (Pandzo 1993: 199)

In 1992, towns and villages were filled with refugees fleeing Serb advances. They slept rough on the streets in makeshift shelters and schoolyards. Letters of guarantee from western countries willing to sponsor the refugees were solicited by the Red Cross. Migration offered escape but to unknown places, surroundings and cultures. In the absence of men, many women were forced to form female-run and female-supported households. Since the Bosnian war, fundamental restructuring of societies is taking place and women are acquiring new skills and education to rebuild their lives and economies in Bosnia and in exile. Although not fully acknowledged as such, these women are forced to be the motors of contemporary social change as they struggle to overcome previously held values and stereotypes.

Thirty-three people were sent to Mallorca. Some had become refugees fleeing Sarajevo to avoid the oncoming war and were aided by the United Nations High Commission for Refugees (UNHCR) and then the Red Cross. The Red Cross organised families in Soller to take responsibility for housing, health, clothing and food provisions. Work was found which might lead to getting residence papers, which depended on having a work contract with an employer. A brief profile of one of the Bosnian women with whom I worked reveals the experiences, perceptions and frustrations that can occur as a refugee. Lidia is a Serbian from near Kosova. She married a Croatian architect from Sarajevo and moved to his paternal home. She lived with her in-laws for five years and described the difficulties involved: 'I walked for hours after work to avoid my mother-in-law's babbling'. She worked in a bank, and the couple soon bought an apartment of their own: 'A good job, friends, we had a full life.' In 1992 the fighting became too dangerous for her and her children (two girls). Her husband had been called to military service. She heard announcements on the radio and television for three hundred refugees to go to Spain. She said, 'it was not difficult to get on this first exodus as at departure only 290 had signed up.' She thinks that it was probably a lack of knowledge, ability to make contact, fill in forms etc. that prevented many from even being aware of the opportunity to depart, let alone doing so. Her pride in her education and resourcefulness was evident.

Lidia was given a job in Valldemossa (a village sixteen kilometres away) She left the house at 7:30 A.M. returned to Soller at 8:30 P.M., and worked washing dishes in the cellar kitchen of a restaurant run by South Americans who 'treated me like trash'. Her sponsoring family had to accompany her to the supermarket 'Syp', that provided food allowance for the refugees. She resented the control they asserted over what she purchased, the kinds of foods, amounts she could buy etc. Her daughters were under-nourished and needed meat while she was told her allowance only covered minimum amounts. She was housed with her cousin, Wilma, and Wilma's son and daughter. She had lived in a different part of the city in Bosnia and barely knew her cousin. She said: 'Six months sharing with her almost drove me mad.' Wilma was envious, reporting her to the Red Cross for taking advantage (e.g. buying more meat than her rations allowed, not sharing etc.). Their food allowance for six people was the same as that given to a single family of three or four. She also revealed resentment toward the other refugees: she felt some refugees received quite different treatment than others, depending on how needy they acted, causing sponsors or others (dentists, doctors) to give them advantages (free care) that others did not receive. She felt they played on the weak, needy stereotype of the refugee and she was unable (or too proud) to do the same.[4]

Others I interviewed from the same group found the provision of services by the Red Cross, the Government and the community at large – free housing, clothing, food supplies, medical and dental care (which they said were available to everyone) and aid in finding employment – to be the basis of their re-establishing their lives and new concepts of 'home' in Mallorca after a frightening escape from impending war and persecution. As Amit (2000) notes, for migrants (whether refugees, labourers, exiles etc.) spatial displacement and increased border crossings may not necessarily or easily engender new forms of imagined community if or when old notions of home lose their salience. Generational and gender relations can be quite different than they had been prior to the move.

The three Bosnian men who finally joined their wives in Soller found it extremely difficult to adapt to menial jobs. After their professional status in Bosnia, they felt they had lost their hold on their families, their finances and their manhood. One man's frustration vented itself in domestic violence and two of the three entered into affairs with foreign women residents. This has provided a different sort of identity for these men for whom sexuality had been confined to their marriage partner and traditional family values had been important enough to fight for by sending their wives and children away and fighting in the army against the Serbs, and then emigrating themselves. Through the intervention of their host families these men were re-united with their wives and children and offered different employment. Today, the town planner is a baker and the architect is working in a bottling factory. Neither has regained his self-esteem and both seem resigned to less than the ideal roles they once so fully experienced.[5]

Al-Ali also found that among Bosnians in the U.K., 'conflict and tensions were common and husband and wife relations deteriorated. Women in Britain felt homebound after having professional lives at home in Bosnia. Language held them back made them insecure away from family, friends, in strange physical and cultural surroundings.' She cites a Bosnian Muslim couple's description of life in the U.K. as 'living like a piece of wood – an inanimate state in which one is dependent on income support, has no regular employment or works in an unskilled job unrelated to what one had been trained for at home' (Al-Ali 2002: 103). Among those who came to Soller were

Muslims married to Serbs, Croats married to Muslims and Croats married to Serbs. In Bosnia they were part of a cosmopolitan society intermixed among Muslim, Croat and Serbian neighbours with whom they shared relations that respected one another's differences. They felt they had crossed the barriers of religion and migrated precisely because they feared persecution based on these cross-cultural/religious marriages.[6]

My informants' descriptions of life in Mallorca were very different from their countrywomen's in the U.K. Most of the women remarked on the support they received from the Soller families that 'fostered' them and what a difference that made to their feeling less isolated or traumatised. Their children were also important factors in their adjustment to place, routine and everyday activities. Employment, even when menial, gave them mobility, language contact and ultimately financial independence. Some have been able to have family members join them while others are endeavouring to adapt to having fewer family members nearby. Some of the young women have formed relationships and married foreign men they met on the island. Interestingly, at present, none have formed relationships with Mallorcan men. They describe themselves socially marginalised from the Mallorcans both by choice and circumstances. They find their Mallorcan neighbours closed and difficult to befriend. However this works to their advantage because they are not subject to social or cultural pressures to conform and have used their initiative to get ahead. Lidia has capitalised on her differences and language abilities (she speaks English, French and German as well as her native Serbo-Croat) by organising a group of Bosnian women that she hires out to clean foreigners' houses. She now perceives herself as 'better than' her Mallorcan hosts in that she has negated their stereotype of her as a refugee and is now a successful entrepreneur. Unlike many Eastern European and Latin American women immigrants who are employed mainly in private homes as carers, cooking, cleaning and/or caring for children, the sick or elderly, Lidia and some of her countrywomen have managed to create solutions to local domestic requirements for hourly help in maintaining other women's homes. They are self-employed, not domestics. The women in this group proved more resourceful than the few males and assumed financial, social and decision-making roles in their homes and outside.

Clearly, men and women are affected by exile in different ways. Doreen Indra noted that before 1980 little attention was given to gender issues and refugees were viewed in terms of 'genderless stereotypes' (Indra 1989). There has been a considerable increase in research on refugee women over the past two decades (see e.g. Callaway 1987, Afsar 1991, Buijs 1993 and Anthias and Lazaridis 2000). However, gender continues to be of peripheral interest in most studies and warrants continued research.

## Political Discourse

Lidia and the other Bosnian women's experiences make it clear that refugees are not passive victims simply going through the stages of adaptation or assimilation. The policies and practices of the receiving countries can aid in their adaptation or create a dependent group, forced to the margins of society and subject to the power and domination of the receiving society sanctioned by the new European laws for foreigners. Agents, employers, NGOs, lawyers and experts can reproduce unequal relations of power especially those based on class, ethnicity or nationality, reinforcing the dependence of immigrants on third parties. Women on their own may be refused loans to make down payments on housing, furnishings, businesses, goods etc. Provisions must bear these gender issues in mind to facilitate women making the contributions necessary to their families' survival and their own fulfilment in a new place and prevent them from becoming victims of loan sharks and other illicit actors.

As Liliana Suárez-Navaz (2004) points out: 'Experiences of citizens and refugees are constructed together, and they are fundamentally framed and shaped by the legal system'. Eastmond, writing about Bosnian Muslims in Sweden, found that:

> In the interaction of refugees and host societies there are various discourses affecting the incomers. Debates using refugees as a generalised term are part of the problem. The term 'refugee' is a very broad category, encompassing a population of varying legal status, length of residence, ethnic identification and social background, and tells us little about a person's degree of integration, personal ties or attachments. General rules cannot anticipate individual needs nor deal with them when informed. Assistance programs are still being planned without sufficient considerations of women's and other individuals' qualifications or needs. Some staff still believe that cultural traditions should take precedence over respect for human rights, even if these cultural practices are profoundly misogynist. (Eastmond 1998)[7]

One Senegalese migrant in Mallorca said that in his judgement, 'employers consider that Africans are savages, South Americans are dirty and violent and all of these stereotypes help them to rationalise exploitation of immigrants.' There are many trained people working in domestic service or construction due to this mythology which cannot conceive of immigrants being apt to undertake certain qualified jobs, despite having excellent training and papers from their countries. Ethnic and cultural distinctiveness can be a potential disadvantage in an increasingly restrictive host society and can encourage discriminatory practices. Beginning in January 2003, those who arrived in Spain at least two years before or anyone with a work contract could once again apply for residence.[8] However, thousands are being turned down. In contrast to the organised support of the Bosnians in Soller there are innumerable examples of the continued difficulties immigrants face on arriving in Mallorca. As Pere Salva, Professor of Geography at the University of the Balearic Islands (UIB) noted in a recent (January 2003) conference paper, 'Immigrants are sought after when needed to work, but when that is finished they are thrown out. The foreign worker is demonised to justify firing him.' However, expulsion (for lack of legal status) seldom succeeds, as it is a long process (at least two years).

Abdoulayi Konato came to Mallorca from Senegal sixteen years ago. He says 'it is difficult to rent an apartment or a room even when you have a job and your papers are in order. When you arrive in the Balearics your only choice is to sleep in a hostel or find refuge in the home of someone you know or have just met.' The Palma City Council has organised a rental and housing association but the results after six months in operation are quite distressing, with 95 percent of the requests by immigrants unmet. There is a thriving business, which takes advantage of immigrants by renting them flats that are uninhabitable (in ruins) at exhorbitant prices. A regular strategy used by the immigrant is to ask a Spaniard to intervene with the landlord and try to convince him/her to rent to a foreigner. There are many families where each member lives in a different place as they have been unable to secure a flat together. Owners are afraid that two people will rent an apartment and then move in eight or ten others. Many of the Latin Americans I have interviewed are living six to eight in one flat.

Most Mallorcans continue to perceive their own 'imagined community' of like-minded and historically connected members based on common heritage and citizenship in contrast to all these outsiders they find in their midst. However, citizenship has long been available to foreigners who reside for five years on the island or have Spanish parentage (Waldren 1996). The European Union's Foreigners' Law lumps all foreigners into a single group who may have little or nothing in common. Seemingly neutral migration laws contain implicit ethnic stereotyping and prevent the formation of new groupings based on shared experiences e.g., as workers in construction, domestic service or agriculture. However, advantages may be gained for a group by asserting their 'refugee status' or an 'ethnic identity', however tenuous.

The category of 'refugee' overlaps into every aspect of their lives in their new location: e.g. housing, access to employment, health care, legal documents, social life and schooling. However from the refugees' perspective, the major concern in their lives is rather the active reconstitution of 'normal life' which means recovering or gaining a sense of economic independence and control over their own lives. While differences in language, health status and culture are important considerations in the integration of refugees, the tendency is to simplify the very complex process of reconstituting viable lives. Increasing political restrictiveness, bureaucratic delays, limited access to accommodation, legal employment etc. helps to shape popular explanations of social marginality. This legitimates and perpetuates dependence rather than empowerment.

Research has revealed the difficulties created in refugee encounters with social, political and economic institutions. One finds that the effect of State policies on immigration, residency and citizenship as well as institutional policies on credit, equity and opportunity are gender-specific. Many comment that they were treated like children when they arrived. Contrary to this general image of refugees, we need to recognise that there are many types of people from different backgrounds with distinct needs and agendas as well as beliefs and values. Their perceptions and expectations of us and each other need to be understood.

## Conclusions

Eight years after arrival, the Bosnian women with whom I collaborated and was able to conduct this research have gained legal status through the processes made available to them by the new residency laws and with the help of the Red Cross and their sponsoring families. They were given work permits, established residence and reclaimed their Bosnian identity in exile in 1999.[9] One year after arrival they had all rented houses, found jobs (despite an 11 percent unemployment rate at the time), bought cars, sent their children to local schools where they learned to speak and study in Catalan while their mothers learned Castilian Spanish. Three of their husbands were found and joined them. The men's adaptation has been fraught with gender issues, among which depending on their wives for financial, social and linguistic support are salient. Only one family has returned to Bosnia and that was through the husband being able to translate for Spanish UN peace-keeping forces with Serbian military personnel. The others feel settled and are making viable lives again.

The treatment provided for the Bosnians I described here was, I believe, unique. The provision of all their essential needs: housing, employment, food subsidies, doctors, dentists, schooling etc. allowed them to settle in without the many problems and set-backs so many other refugees to Mallorca encounter. Most said language was the greatest barrier. However, being involved with their 'foster' families and immediate employment submerged them into Castilian Spanish at all levels. The children learned both Catalan and Castilian and helped their mother, often translating for her when she was unable to make herself understood. One woman explained how at first she thought she recognised words but often mixed up those that sounded similar. For example, soon after their arrival whenever she went out with her young daughter people would greet her with *Hola* (a usual Castilian greeting) and she would reply 'no Olla' (her daughter's name). Another time, she was told that representatives of the shoe factories in Inca (the centre of the island) would be bringing *zapatos* (shoes) for them, so when a man came to the house the next day and asked if she wanted *patatas* (potatoes) she eagerly replied, 'si, si'. When he returned carrying a 20 lb. sack of potatoes over his shoulder, she was quite embarrassed.

They are reminded of 'home' through regular telephone contact, when they visit or send money to family in Bosnia, or when grandparents come to visit, but they do not want to return. The myth of returning is produced by the host society and seldom shared by the refugee if economic security and resettlement have been possible. New opportunites have been found and reveal how identity is formed and reformed in different circumstances and locations, how symbolic and spatial boundaries take on new meanings as a result of war and migration, and how socio-cultural, ethnic, regional and national identities merge against a backdrop of national and European economic and political conditions.[10] The categorical exclusion imposed by terms like refugee, immigrant, ethnicity, culture etc. can be devastating or drawn upon in the struggle to resettle. What this means in everyday life and for the future is not clear. There are still limited social exchanges amongst themselves or with the host society, work opportunities are mainly in the service sector and recognition of previous training or professions is full of bureaucratic pitfalls with delays of five years before professional papers (many of which they cannot get from Bosnia) can be processed.[11]

Clearly local activity on Mallorca is almost 100 percent dependent on global politics and processes and the lives of the Bosnians and other immigrants discussed here reflect this. War in Bosnia-Herzegovina displaced thousands of people and, in 1992, Mallorca, a thriving tourist/service-oriented economy was able to offer hospitality to the Bosnian refugees and work opportunities for immigrants from many other countries no longer able to provide for their livelihoods 'at home'. The prosperity of the Balearic Islands is a 'light at the end of the tunnel' for many. Emigration from 1920 to the 1960s to more developed countries of western Europe improved living standards and demand for goods and services. The shift over the last thirty years from an agricultural to an industrial, service economy and the increasing influence of other lifestyles have all contributed to a the Balearics' heightened per-capita income (among the highest in Spain).

The Balearic society has experienced a sensation of 'de-structuring' of their society since tourism and its accompanying developments began in the 1950s. Mainland Spanish, foreign residents, immigrants and refugees add up to a multicultural, -racial, and -ethnic society unlike the vision natives have of themselves as 'Mallorquins', an identity which has many definitions depending on the circumstances and who is speaking (Waldren 1996). Cosmopolitan after years of being a haven for tourists, expatriates, artists, writers etc. from around the world, Mallorcans are trying desperately to maintain, recapture and re-invent their history and culture while participating fully in the global social, material and economic advances at their disposal. They need a migrant work-force to meet the demands of an ageing society and one of the lowest birth-rates in Europe and that means absorbing thousands of immigrants who come needing aid, work and hope for their futures.

These are issues that now dominate the European continent. We have seen how global economic and social trends are borne out in local encounters and, most of all, how gender differences in the experiences of migration and the specificities that women bring to the migration process need to be built into policy and practice.

## Notes

1. Over half a million Bosnians were displaced to countries in the European Union. Almost 60 percent were located in Germany and a further 30 percent in Austria, The Netherlands and Sweden; seven thousand went to Britain (Al-Ali 2002).
2. The terms 'refugees', 'foreigners' and 'immigrants' are used broadly based on the comments made by those we have interviewed. One might be a refugee when arriving under the auspices of an agency, governmental or NGO. However, immigrants, those who come into the country as tourists and then get 'lost', also refer to themselves as refugees seeking home, hearth, income and futures they could not find in their countries of origin whether for political, ethnic, religious or economic reasons.
3. Similarly, the majority of Bosnians who went to Germany, Britain and The Netherlands chose to remain in these countries and become citizens or permanent residents (Ali-Ali 2002).
4. Eastmond notes: 'Social class and local identities (region, town or village) were often more relevant in most spheres of daily action (*among Bosnians in Sweden*) than ethnicity.' (Eastmond 1998: 75)
5. Ribas-Mateos (2000) found a 'more acute reduction in status' was experienced by women migrants than by men in her study of migration to Spain. I think this refers to the Moroccan women she studied, although she did not make that distinction.
6. Pre-war Bosnia was a regional identity, not politically relevant or ideologically backed as a territorially based 'nation': rather it straddled, but did not subsume, its component national or ethnic religious communities (Muslims 44 percent, Serbs 31 percent, Croats 17.5 percent). After the war, 'Bosnian' carried anew and politicised connotations. Today, 'Bosnian' refers to an ideological multi-ethnic position (Bringa 1995: 166).
7. The term 'refugee' is often rejected by migrants. The Palestinians in Lebanon referred to themselves as 'returners' but later embraced the term refugee as a strategic necessity for bargaining with international agencies and governments for recognition of their rights.
8. Residence permits were not available for most of 2002 due to a huge backlog and applications were not accepted for one year.
9. This is an identity based on culture, background and history rather than territorial boundaries.
10. As James Fernandez noted, the interpretive space for categorical shifting and interpretation of self and otherness indicates the ambivalence of the categories in their use (Fernandez 1997: 728).

11. A recent improvement on this front is the Red Cross Aula Planeta, which is a location where computers donated by the hotel chain Sol Melia are made available for immigrants' use free of charge. They can access the Internet, send e-mail, read their homeland newspapers and search for various documentation they need to complete their paperwork for work permits, residency, titles etc. The only set-back is that it is only open on Saturdays from 10 a.m. to 12 noon, a rather limited time-span for thousands of refugees.

## REFERENCES

Afsar, H. ed. 1991. *Women, Development and Survival in the Third World.* London, Longman.

Al-Ali, N. 2002. 'Loss of status or new opportunities? Gender relations and transnational ties among Bosnian refugees'. In *The Transnational Family: New European Frontiers and Global Networks*, eds D. Bryceson and U. Vuorela. Oxford, Berg.

Amit, V. 2000. 'Introduction: Constructing the field'. In *Constructing the Field: Ethnographic Fieldwork in the Contemporary World*, ed. V. Amit. London, Routledge.

Anthias, F. and G. Lazaridis. 2000. *Gender and Migration in Southern Europe: Women on the Move.* Oxford, Berg.

Aziz, M.A. 2000. *Diario de Mallorca.*

Buechler, H. 1987. 'Spanish Galician migration to Switzerland'. In *Migrants in Europe*, eds H.C. Buechler and J.M. Buechler. New York, Greenwood Press.

Buijs, G. ed. 1993. *Migrant Women: Crossing Boundaries and Changing Identities.* Oxford, Berg.

Callaway, H. 1987. 'Women refugees: Specific requirements and untapped resources'. In *Third World Affairs*, ed. G. Altaf. London, Third World Foundation for Social and Economic Studies.

Delamont, S. 1995. *Appetites and Identities: An Introduction to the Social Anthropology of Europe.* London, Routledge.

Gregory, D. and J. Cazorola Perez. 1985. 'Intra-European migration and regional development'. In *Guests Come to Stay*, ed. R. Rogers. Boulder, CO, Westview.

Eastmond, M. 1998. 'Bosnian Muslims in Sweden'. *Journal of Refugee Studies* 11, no. 2: 161–81.

Fernandez, J. 1997. 'The North-South axis in European popular cosmologies and the dynamic of the categorical'. *American Anthropologist* 99, no. 4: 725–28.

Indra, D. 1989. 'Ethnic human rights and feminist theory: Gender implications for refugee studies and practice'. *Journal of Refugees Studies* 2, no. 2: 1–22.

Pandzo, A. 1993. 'War Time'. *Mediterraneans* 7: 199–201.

Suárez-Navaz, L. 2004. *Rebordering the Mediterranean: Boundaries and Citizenship in Southern Europe.* Oxford, Berghahn.

Waldren, J. 1996. *Insiders and Outsiders: Paradise and Reality in Mallorca.* Oxford, Berghahn.

# Part III:
# Localising Europe

# Chapter 9
# Claiming the Local in the Irish/British Borderlands: Locality, Nation-State and the Disruption of Boundaries

William F. Kelleher, Jr.

### Introduction

The Belfast Agreement signed on Good Friday 1998 and often referred to as 'the Good Friday Agreement' created new political institutions in Northern Ireland. Designed to foster peace and reconciliation among the majority Protestant unionist, pro-British population, their Catholic, Irish nationalist fellow citizens, and the British state, these innovations have met with challenge, resistance and accommodation from all three sides. Northern Ireland's Irish nationalists have embraced the initiatives the most wholeheartedly because they perceive the agreement and the institutions it fosters as their best hope for equality, a status they believe the State has denied them previously, and for the eventual unity of the island of Ireland's two States.[1]

Like those who planned the institutions of the European Union to prevent war and engender peaceful cooperation, the architects of Northern Ireland's new order hoped to foster reconciliation at regional and local levels. The new institutions were designed to transform the relations among Northern Ireland's complex histories of colonial and anti-colonial violence, the memory of those histories, and the ethno-national boundaries that demarcate regions and neighbourhoods and hinder communication between the largely Protestant, British unionist population and the largely Catholic, Irish nationalist one (see Mitchell 1999). Like the European institutions that have, in part, inspired them, these innovative British/Irish organisations have produced paradoxical effects. New categorical divisions have introduced novel ambiguities into everyday social life. Reconfigured institutional arrangements have both reduced and exacerbated tensions while they have produced spaces that foster the reorientation of political, cultural and class identities.

This chapter shows such everyday struggles over boundaries and identity categories. It depicts social spaces opened up by the Northern Ireland peace process and demonstrates the ambiguities and uncertainties that arise in them. The chapter does not hold that the processes described have come to any particular conclusion: people continuously re-work them. To demonstrate this, it focuses upon the efforts of one Irish nationalist woman, whom I shall call Mary McKeown, to find the truth about the killing of her brother, Liam McKeown, by British security forces in 1988.[2] Liam was shot in the heart as he walked to play a Gaelic football game on a field situated at the border between the British State, the United Kingdom of Great Britain and Northern Ireland, and the Irish State, the Republic of Ireland. The death of Liam Mckeown occurred at the edge of his town's (Tullyman's), Gaelic sports field, on a major cross-border road that was, until recently, heavily militarised.

Since the killing, Mary has worked tirelessly to discover the truth behind Liam's death. In doing so, she has engendered a series of new associational ties that have disrupted several pairs of received oppositional categories that characterise social scientific studies not only of Ireland but of Europe more generally: tradition and modernity, local and national, male and female, Protestant and Catholic. This chapter presents a partial enumeration of the events that constitute this story not only by trying to account for the reverberations of Liam's death at the local and national levels but also by developing analytical tools that enable their understanding (see Kelleher 2000).

## Ireland in Europe and the World

Although fully ensconced in the European Union, Ireland and Northern Ireland fit awkwardly into the categories that anthropologists of Europe have deployed. The two Irelands hold this status because they are social and political formations with complex colonial histories, European spaces that have endured both pre-modern and modern colonialisms. As such, they bear some of the qualities of both sides of the pair, 'the west and the rest,' and the transformations in the two Irelands today are marked by this complicated history.[3] This colonial history – materialised in segregated institutions of social reproduction in Northern Ireland, such as schools and residential neighbourhoods, and realised in such social facts as the relatively high rates of unemployment among Catholics, the descendants of 'the natives' – suggests that different categories of analysis need to be applied or, better, that the prevailing categories for the anthropological study of Europe demand questioning in order to understand the multiple dimensions of social, cultural and political change in this anomalous territory.

This chapter tries to capture this historical legacy and the transformational work of Northern Ireland's constitutional rearrangements at the levels of the person and the locality. It tries to understand Northern Ireland's fractious movement from a place of long-term conflict to one of peace through analytical categories, primarily concepts of transformation and social worth, being developed by scholars of central and eastern Europe who are struggling to understand changes in those anomalous, socialist/capitalist social spaces. In this work, conceptualisations have moved from the notions of transition in modernisation theory where a society undergoing the change from 'tradition to modernity' is imagined as a progressive movement from one order in stable equilibrium to another with a liminal state in between, to concepts of transformation that understand the emergence of new elements as the adaptations, rearrangements, permutations and reconfigurations of existing social and cultural forms.[4] In this recent usage, actors are thought to survive rapidly changing environments by redefining and recombining resources that include organisational forms, habituated social and cultural practices, and both official and informal social ties.

Studying transformation, then, requires a focus on the problems, relationships, and interweavings of multiple orders rather than the movement of one order to another that the notions of the transition from tradition to modernity or from war to peace imply. For ethnographers interested in everyday life, working on transformation requires understanding how actors in particular locales and settings succeed or fail in rebuilding a new order with the instruments of the old as they reconfigure those tools. Tradition and the social and cultural instruments of war do not disappear but get rearranged and studying them necessitates an assessment of how people evaluate these instruments and use them to reconfigure social worlds. In these conditions, ethnographers must account for the changing senses of social worth that develop as people rank persons, places and the technologies of social practice differently during moments of re formation. Again, familiar instruments of judging value and calculating it do not disappear. People re-cognise and re evaluate them as they use them to confront and address novel situations.

In order to illustrate these adapting evaluative practices at the levels of both the person and the social world, I borrow a concept of social order developed by economic sociologist David Stark that attempts to foreground the instruments people use to evaluate their situations as well as the sociality that marks them (Stark 1994).[5] Social order, from this position, is understood as the intersection of social ties, networks and accounts – the narratives, instruments of economic calculation, and legalistic/judicial accountings among others –

that mobilise each other. Social ties mobilise accounts by transporting them across settings through networks of affiliation, while accounts mobilise ties by linking social persons in rank orderings with measuring instruments that inscribe value and justify the principles of association that underlie the social relationships and networks that people form.[6]

In modern societies, there is always more than one such order and in Northern Ireland there exist at least three major orders: the Irish nationalist order that has questioned the legitimacy of the State and has valued protesting against State wrongdoing if not rebelling militarily against it; the unionist, British nationalist social order that accounted for itself by foregrounding its historical loyalism and support for the state while protesting state acts that its members believed did not reciprocate that loyalty to the extent required; and the social order of the British State that accounted for itself as a universal agent that represented society as a whole and intervened for the sake of all citizens in the nationalist and unionist orders.

## Remaking the Social Order(s) in Transforming Northern Ireland

These different orders are the product of a colonial past that lives in the present. As numerous ethnographers have found, both the urban and rural landscapes of Northern Ireland are saturated with memories of the distant past.[7] Both Protestants and Catholics remember past atrocities through stories marking geographical spaces and are acutely aware of difference through practices like 'telling', which is the reading of bodies in everyday social encounters in order to decipher whether the stranger encountered belongs to one's 'side of the house' or not, whether those persons are Protestant or Catholic.[8] For Irish nationalists, these practices mark them as lesser and index the inferior social position they have held in the history of both the colonial State and the devolved State of Northern Ireland. They often refer to this history when attempting to understand the nearly thirty years of political violence they and their Protestant fellow citizens suffered as the twentieth century drew to a close in Northern Ireland.[9]

Catholics read these practices of telling as indices of their otherness in the eyes of their Protestant/British fellow citizens. Irish nationalists knew they held the rights of citizenship but did not trust the State's or their neighbours' commitments to upholding them. They identified with the State, as historian Marianne Elliott writes, through a sense of 'resentful belonging' (Elliott 2001: 431–82). Many Catholics questioned the State's legitimacy and found it difficult to vehemently condemn acts of violence against it even though they thoroughly objected to violence as a political instrument.

In Tullyman, the border town that is home to the McKeown family, this anger and doubt about belonging and the ambivalence about violence that often accompanied it characterised Catholic structures of feeling and was emphasised in Protestant readings of their fellow townspeople. Citizens in the town recall the past through a variety of technologies of remembering that range from story-telling to frequent summer-time commemorative marches to music sessions in pubs, but Catholics, primarily, recuperate the history of their inferior position in the region through stories and cultural practices that represent the national border. For them, the Irish border signifies their otherness in the State in which they live. Created in 1920 by the Government of Ireland Act but materialised along with the state of Northern Ireland in 1921, the border separated Northern Ireland's 430,000 Catholics, most of whom were Irish nationalists, from their fellow nationalists in the twenty-six counties that eventually became the Republic of Ireland, and instead joined them with the 820,000 Protestants, most of whom were British nationalists, who lived in the six of the nine counties of Ulster that became Northern Ireland (Elliott 2001: 373). In the memories of Tullyman's Catholics, the inclusion of their town in the new Northern Ireland State constituted a particular affront because in the 1920 local elections they had voted for a majority Catholic council that had, in turn, pledged its allegiance to the republican Government in Dublin. In fact, most of the border regions had voted for Irish nationalist councils loyal to the Dublin Government. The counties of Fermanagh and Tyrone, the southern regions of Counties Down and Armagh, and Derry City or Londonderry as Protestants call it, returned Catholic majority councils that pledged loyalty to the new Irish political entity based in Dublin.[10]

The traditional province of Ulster consisted of nine counties. Six of those counties, the largest geographical area that would preserve a Protestant majority for the foreseeable future, were carved from Ulster to create the Northern Ireland State. Two of those counties and significant regions of three others had voted for representatives whose allegiance was to a different State. To Northern Ireland's Catholics, then, the boundaries of the new State were not based on democratic principles but on demographic ones: the boundary commission decided to give Protestants the largest territory possible where they could maintain a majority for the foreseeable future. Many of the Tullyman region's Catholics perceived this history and the eighty-two years since as the continuation of life with a colonial identity, an identity imposed upon them not one based on either democratic choice or self-determination. Catholics in Tullyman, especially those who were republicans and believed that violence was justified to overcome this historical legacy, narrated these formative events and their anti-democratic nature to demonstrate the illegitimacy of the State in which they lived and to account for the violence of the IRA that they believed defensible.[11]

In the 1990s many Catholics in Tullyman, especially republicans, remembered this history and made sense of their experiences during the last third of the twentieth century through its narration. The recent past, in their view, only reinforced their notion that the Northern Ireland State positioned them as lesser and, in their representations, the border added personal insult to political injury during the violent years from 1969 to 1998. During the conflict between the IRA, local Protestants and the British State, Tullyman became a flashpoint between 1972 and 1994. IRA guerilla fighters organised armed attacks on the British Army and the Royal Ulster Constabulary (RUC), the Northern Ireland police force, from Republic of Ireland areas at the edge of Tullyman. The IRA attacked army and police installations and assassinated members of the security forces in their border-area homes, particularly vulnerable Protestant citizens who were either members of the RUC or the Ulster Defence Regiment (UDR), the locally recruited, part-time unit of the British army.

This strategy led to a British army counter-strategy of closing off border roads, making them impassable by blowing them up to create craters that could not be driven around or through. The military nature of this strategy was not the aspect remembered as most significant by area Catholics, however. Most border Catholics I interviewed emphasised the moral wrongs engendered by these practices: the holes in the road unduly blocked the interrelationships of families because most Catholic townspeople's kinship networks extended across the Irish border. Surveillance systems put family get-togethers under suspicion and farmers no longer had direct access to pasture lands they used on the two sides of the border. Daily economic practices became suspect, and, since Catholics accounted for the State in terms of its undemocratic, immoral foundation, they evaluated these State practices, like the obviously military acts of road blocking, through a similar moral-political discourse. Catholics saw this surveillance as an ethical affront that put innocent, everyday practices under suspicion. Protestants perceived these State practices as reasonable means to insure their safety. The gap between Catholics and their Protestant fellow citizens in the region increased as Catholic moral accountings such as the border-roads stories, narratives tinged by Irish republican ideology, circulated and developed a moral critique of the militarised State with which local Protestants identified.[12] Protestants in the Tullyman area interpreted these moral critiques of the State and the use of them to justify the IRA's killing of their police and security force community members as immoral. They perceived local members of the security forces as friends, kin and neighbours, not as abstract agents of the State.

These conflicting accounts articulated (in the double sense of giving voice and linking different phenomena) relations of family and kinship to border security and national/international politics. Tullyman's citizens, people who value family relations, subsequently produced discourses questioning the morality of murder on a regular basis. After the army made the roads impassable, travellers had to cross the border by a single road that had a high-security, heavily militarised checkpoint on the border's northern side. Passers-by and motorists had to go through this inspection site to get to the Republic of Ireland and these sojourns had a disciplinary effect on Tullyman's Irish nationalists.

Area Catholics who worked south of the border learned to accept routine questions and occasional insults as they went through the checkpoint. They did not want soldiers to detain them and make them late for work, family appointments or the various and sundry activities that people performed in the Republic. Those who resisted the queries of the soldiers, deflected them or responded ironically as they answered the same questions daily, or even several times a day, suffered consequences. Most Catholics quickly learned to keep their heads down, answer the questions, however intrusive, and drive off. Catholics noticed that once members of the changing regiments knew the Protestants of the area, those soldiers waved those citizens through the checkpoint without interrogation. Catholics who talked back to the soldiers or refused to answer questions beyond the legally based ones, 'Who are you? Where are you going? Where are you coming from?' were mocked, put under bodily inspection along with their vehicles and often threatened. Liam McKeown was one of these people, and local Catholics have used the story of his death as a metonym for the predicament of Catholics in the town and the surrounding border areas. His death, a single event, stood for the whole and took on, through the agency of his sister, important historical significance.

## The Death of Liam Mckeown

Liam McKeown was shot and killed in 1988, on the edge of his hometown, Tullyman. It was, as the weekly newspaper in the Republic's County Monaghan stated in its front-page headline, 'a controversial shooting'. Liam was twenty-three, a young man the paper described as 'universally popular, particularly with the members of the staff of Monaghan Poultry Products, Ltd. where he worked and was Union Shop Steward.' He was shot dead by a single bullet minutes after walking through the British Army checkpoint on his way to play in a Gaelic football game on Tullyman's home field, a pitch situated in the short space between the checkpoint lookout and the then 69-year-old border.

The shooting was 'controversial' not only because the bullet came from this army fortification, but also because the official version of what happened changed in less than twenty-four hours. Right after the shooting, the British Government's official spokesperson had called Liam's death an accident. Two soldiers changing posts had exchanged a machine gun at the checkpoint and the weapon had accidentally gone off during the transaction. By Monday night that story was re-articulated. Now British officials said that an eighteen-year-old British soldier from England had cleaned his machine gun and was returning it to the centre of a checkpoint window when 'his finger slipped onto the trigger and three shots were fired' (*Dungannon Observer*, 26 February 1988). According to this story, one of these bullets ricocheted off the road and struck Liam in the chest, the heart specifically, killing him instantly.

This border region's Roman Catholics did not believe either Government version. People living in the predominantly Catholic housing estate next to the checkpoint said they heard three machine-gun shots fired on Monday, the day after Liam's death, shortly after soldiers stopped traffic coming and going across the border. This, they believed, was to create three bullet marks in the road to conform to the Government's second story. The State, in this narrative, constructed facts to confirm its agents' previous utterances. Many Catholics believed the State's representatives did not construct the story from the facts, and all factions in the Northern Ireland Catholic community voiced disbelief in the Government account. The spokespeople of no Catholic group granted that story legitimacy. The *New York Times* did (23 February 1988): Francis X. Clines wrapped Liam McKeown's death into a front-page story that focused on the growing rift between the Governments of the Republic of Ireland and the United Kingdom of Great Britain and Northern Ireland. Clines attributed the inter-Governmental tension to 'the Stalker Affair', a name which in Britain and Ireland refers to a series of events: police shootings of unarmed civilians in Northern Ireland, the attempted cover-up of these by high-ranking police officials, the investigations of Manchester Deputy Chief Constable John Stalker into these shootings, the official obstruction of justice that followed, and Stalker's dismissal by the Thatcher Government on the pretence of unfounded corruption charges as he sought to obtain a damaging piece of evidence against the police and army.[13]

Clines, of the *New York Times* did not detail these events, but he did mention that tensions between the two Governments were exacerbated when the British Attorney General announced, the week before Liam McKeown was shot, that the security force killers investigated in the Stalker Affair would not be prosecuted for 'national security reasons and the public interest.' Clines did not specify what happened to Liam McKeown either, concluding his story with the rift between London and Dublin, a relationship he described as 'ever-fragile' and fraught with 'centuries old enmity'.[14] Clines wrote:

> Tensions were only worsened over the weekend when an unarmed nationalist was shot and killed as he walked past a British Army checkpoint in Northern Ireland. The army apologised and said it was a firearms accident, but the incident would be used to foster the contention of the outlawed Irish Republican Army that the British–Irish agreement was proving worthless in its goal of better protecting the rights of Northern Ireland's Roman Catholic minority.

Clines represented British Government concerns as social facts. Worried about American opinion, the British Government directed much attention to the U.S. Press on such matters. There was a trans-cultural element in the statements and re-statements by the non-British Press on such events as reporters accepted the translation of events offered by British Government information officers.[15] Clines duly represented the dominant narrative of the State, and he inserted a national and trans-local element into representations of this event.

As he did in covering the Stalker Affair, Clines reported no information about the McKeown shooting. His writing articulated well with the British Attorney General's discourse. That man would not hear the cases marshalled against the security forces by Stalker for reasons of national security and 'the public interest.' When Clines did not bother to gather the stories surrounding Liam McKeown's death he served these same interests. Unwritten but implied in his speculations about the uses to which the IRA would put this shooting was the idea that the 'British–Irish Agreement' of 1985 did in fact protect the rights of the minority who identified themselves as Irish not British. In no place did Clines mention data, then available, that raised serious questions about the merits of the agreement, a pact that recognised the Irish border as legitimate and as an expression of the will of 'the majority', a group created when the six north-eastern counties of the island of Ireland, 16 percent of the island's territory, were marked off and instituted as a State in 1921.

## The Border, Violence and Accounting for It

From the perspective of Tullyman area Catholics, many of whom, but not the majority, are, as local people call them, 'republican minded', the Irish border and Clines's story are acts of violence and describing them ethnographically requires writing not only the representation of violence and its politics, but also the violence of representation and its politics (Armstrong and Tennenhouse 1989: 1–26). The border and Clines's representation of both it and Liam's death constitute violent representations in the sense that they work to maintain a pattern of dominance.

Liam McKeown, born and raised in Tullyman, resided in the type of borderland Gloria Anzaldua calls 'a vague and undetermined place', a social space that Homi Bhaba, remembering Fanon, names 'alienation within identity'; a space marked by 'a Manichean delirium'. Liam was one of 'the prohibited and forbidden' in this space (see Anzaldua 1987: 3 and Bhaba 1989: 131–48). Neighbourhoods, housing estates, individual fields, village roads and hinterland ones were marked as 'no-go areas' by both Aughnacloy's self-defined British (Protestant) and other-defined British (Catholic) subjects. Trust did not extend across great distances; borders proliferated; and, in the 1980s, dividing practices pervaded everyday life.

It was not only social space where boundaries proliferated. Time and bodies were split as well. Such splits – Fanon's 'Manichean delirium' – of colonial spaces were often the themes of the many after-'Sunday lunch' walks I took with male members of Liam McKeown's extended family in 1985 and 1986. We never crossed certain streets, went to the end of specific roads or entered particular fields. These men marked those Protestant-owned spaces as other along with the places where the army and police stopped people. Time, too, entered these walks. My fellow travellers marked the places present before the sixteenth-century colonial conquest as decidedly different from those habitations that came after the colonial State settled the area.

We avoided the security force's presence, but I can remember no walk in which they were absent. Always at some point on our journey, usually in the borderland areas, someone would say something like 'There's some Brit lookin' at us through the scope of a gun now, sure!' But it was not only the security forces that rendered social space ambiguous. History and memory, the past in the present, did so as well. On the first tour I had of the area, I was shown an old cemetery out on Tullyman's margins, in an almost entirely Protestant residential area. Liam's brother-in-law, like him a trade union shop steward, toured me through and talked about the grown-over area in the first person. I remember several of his statements:

'We buried our people here and built this church.'
'They took the chapel away from us.'
'They cut off the Celtic crosses from the tops of the gravestones and they fly the British flag here to annoy us.'

This site was the first I was shown in Tullyman; 'I'll show ye what our "wee town" is about,' I was told, and, as these remembered quotations show, Tullyman was about conquest, appropriation and forced identification from this particular nationalist's perspective. What he and his 'side of the house' called 'our wee town' could not have comprised more than 30 percent of its territory, and the boundaries surrounding that Catholic locality were seldom, if ever, transgressed. Catholics did not readily move across the boundaries within Tullyman. One reason they did not was because these borders were inscribed on bodies in Tullyman. The history of violence that accompanied both the seventeenth-century settler colony of the Ulster Plantation and the State of Northern Ireland was embodied in how people walked, pursed their lips and talked, in body postures, clothes and hairstyles. People read bodies in Tullyman. Those read as 'other' were, for the most part, not spoken to, not recognised. Telling made borderland crossings a dangerous activity within and around the town. People said they could tell who people were just by looking, and if people were recognised as out of place they could be in danger. Liam McKeown's life and death exemplified this.

Liam had the reputation for being quite often, if not permanently, out of place. This identity did not come from any trait in his character but from the fact of his performances in everyday life. Not able to find work north of the border, Liam worked in the Irish Republic. He had to cross the border twice every day to get back and forth to work. British soldiers routinely interrogated him and he often incurred their wrath. He never answered any of their questions except those he was legally obliged to, and he seldom, if ever, gave much more than one-word answers. Stories about him seem to have passed from regiment to regiment. Over the period I saw Liam often, from 1984 to 1987, his relations with those soldiers deteriorated dramatically. He received many threats and started to keep a record of hostile encounters that he wanted to file with a lawyer. Here are some excerpts from one:

> On Saturday, the 28th of September, 1985, I was crossing the border to go home to Tullyman, my sister was driving her car, a Volkswagen Passat. She is a learner driver so I sat in the front of the car with her, I being a qualified driver. My other sister, Nora, and my girlfriend, Brigid O'Neill, were in the back of the car. We approached the Tullyman checkpoint at approximately 8:30 P.M. My sister stopped at the traffic lights and then when the light turned green approached the middle hut, she was asked for her driver's license, which she showed to the soldier. She was then told to pull the car into the shed. The soldier then came over to the shed and asked Mary to get out of the car and open the boot. He then walked away, approximately ten minutes later he returned with another soldier and told Brigid and Nora to get out of the back of the car. Mary got out and opened the door for them as the car is fitted with child-proof locks. The soldier asked them both their names and addresses, and they were told they could leave. After they left the soldier made us stand outside the car for approximately fifteen minutes. There was a policeman at the middle hut and I asked the soldier to get him, but he refused. Approximately five minutes after this a police car came and took the policeman from the checkpoint. We were then told by the soldier to get into the car as we were being taken into the search centre. Two land rovers then arrived. Two soldiers got out of one of them and came over to the car, one of them carrying a large baton. He told me to get out of the car and into the land rover. I told him that I couldn't as my sister was a learner driver, and I had to sit with her while she was driving. At this the other soldier said 'smash a fucking window if you have to, but get that bastard into the jeep'. The soldier carrying the baton tried to get past my sister to get at me, he was waving the baton, he then shouted at me 'get into the jeep mate now'. I refused to move. My sister who at this time was still requesting that I be allowed to stay with her as her qualified driver moved forward to prevent the soldier from reaching me. He then moved back from the car saying 'let them go in the fucking car'. Two soldiers then got back into the jeep while another two got into the car, and with one jeep in front of us and one behind we were escorted to the Tullyman army search centre. There we were questioned and searched and also the car searched for approximately two hours. We were then released.

Border incidents like this characterized Liam's everyday life. He made complaints to the police, but they did not investigate. The British–Irish Agreement of 1985 was supposed to ameliorate army abuses by ensuring that a policeman be present to mediate encounters such as these, and the Government south of the border was supposed to represent the rights of the nationalist people of Northern Ireland should such infringements continue. Liam's case showed lapses in these matters.

The day before he died, an event took place that continued this pattern of surveillance. His mother described this day and the events that occurred when Liam drove her 'home' to the north from her brother-in-law's wake in her 'homeplace', her birthplace and her extended family's primary residence south of the Irish border:

> On Saturday morning we were left there standing beside the car at half eight and then two land rovers came and took us down the search centre. And there was a soldier got into the back of the car and had a rifle pointed at us, and I asked him if he'd mind not doing that and the soldiers took us over to the search centre and searched Liam and searched the car. They took us until five past nine in the cold after sittin' up all night at the wake.

The next day, just after Liam brought his mother home from the funeral, a soldier shot him dead. The Irish Government, amid the tension between themselves and Britain that Clines wrote about and hearing the stories from the borderlands, requested permission to examine Liam's body. Liam had already been buried several days by the time they made this request. The family's desire to know the truth overruled their pain, and the body was exhumed.

The Irish coroner found several discrepancies between the body and the Northern Ireland coroner's published report. Most significantly he found that Liam's body had not been returned whole. Part of the ribcage, Liam's heart and his breastplate were not returned to the family. Judging the exact nature of the shooting that killed Liam was difficult, if not impossible, due to the lack of evidence. Nevertheless, on appeal, the Irish Republic's coroner was allowed to examine these wrenched out body parts in Belfast, Northern Ireland. He did not make the results of his examination known to the family.

Although his fate has remained unknown, people in and around Tullyman remember Liam. They recall a young man positioned by the border and the discourses around it and recognise that his performances on that boundary made, for the security forces, his identity. His resistance in that location made him 'other' – nationalist, Roman Catholic, republican, pro-IRA – words which used in the Irish borderlands meant different things to different people. To the British soldiers who patrolled this border and the British citizens who lived around it, they meant identity in alienation. His identity as 'other' was inscribed upon Liam in everyday life. His daily border crossings made him readable in resistance while, simultaneously, those who inspected him understood his performance as non-sense.[16] His actions did not make sense to them because they took up colonial discourses and understood him not as a person shaped by the long record of colonial and anti-colonial violence that had marked the area's history, but as an irrational subject.

Two days before the soldier killed Liam, a bomb was found in a culvert outside Tullyman. The soldiers dismantled it, but local people said that stories circulated that the security forces believed Liam brought it across the border. It is unclear whether they believed it after Liam's death. In the very first news report after his murder, a Government spokesperson implied that Liam was a member of the IRA. The State never repeated that report. No-one has uttered it in the media since. The IRA, generally regarded to acknowledge all their members on death, never claimed him as theirs. Liam, who was positioned, positioned himself, was inscribed upon, and read à la Fanon's 'Manichean delirium' in life cannot be read in death. Silence ruled, and the violence of representation and its politics continues.

## Remembering and Engendering

Liam McKeown's murder functioned as a metonym for the border experiences of Catholics living in Tullyman and its environs in the 1970s, 1980s and early 1990s because the stories around it associated the most potent signifiers of both their twentieth century history and their practices of everyday life. The border, secret State actions, the lack of State accountability, the power to make truths, the insertion of the State into everyday taken-for-granted acts, the restrictions of bodily movement and the lack of freedom that followed, the difficulty of creating a home when identity was alien, and the difficulties of producing locality in a conflicted terrain were figured into local narratives of this event. Paradoxically, now, some Tullyman area citizens have begun to use this critical event and accounts of it to start remaking their troubled social world. Mary McKeown, Liam's sister, and other women in the area have forged this new beginning. Their actions, particularly Mary's, have initiated a tenuous beginning toward a civil society that these women so desperately desire in the Northern Ireland of the continuing but faltering peace process.

For these female Tullyman area citizens, this longed-for reconfiguration focused on making a home and constructing locality. They have worked hard to make 'home,' understood not as the establishment of a stable, still and safe physical centre whose space must be controlled, but as the institution of a set of practices, routines and everyday reactions that enables self-recognition, makes boundaries and signifies identity to others both within and outside its limits (Rapport and Dawson 1998). Catholic/nationalist women believed the State and loyalist/unionist social orders worked against the establishment of such home-making practices by Catholics in their town. Tullyman's Irish nationalist women explained that they were marginalised by the home-making practices of their Protestant neighbours who formed over two-thirds of their border town's population and suspected any incursions by Catholic strangers into their physical neighbourhoods, including the town's central public spaces. They pointed to the fact that a number of Irish nationalist, Catholic, young people from the town had settled across the border in the Republic of Ireland in recent years as one piece of evidence, among a variety of others, that everyday discrimination had material effects and that home-making, for them, was limited.[17]

In the 1980s, Mary, along with many Irish nationalists in her border area, said that the solution to this problem was the dissolution of the Irish border. Many of these women, not all, supported Sinn Féin, the political party affiliated with the IRA because it most directly campaigned for the dismantling of the border that was constantly patrolled by the British army and was regarded as a geographical moral stain on the Irish landscape. During the 1980s and 1990s most nationalist women in this area were entrenched in their particular social order, their intersection of social networks and the accounts that mobilised their diminishing social ties. As the political violence wore on from the 1970s to the 1980s and into the early 1990s, they did not often move beyond their physical neighbourhoods, and the people in the housing estate next to the checkpoint felt the most bunkered in of all. With high unemployment rates, not many people had the means to travel away from their increasingly enclaved existence. Women from this place, and the number of single mothers grew in this particular housing estate as the conflict continued, were increasingly subject to the State through their need for welfare benefits at the same time as the State corralled them. These social facts prevented mobility in its double sense of moving up the class ladder and travelling across social space.

Tullyman's Catholics, both men and women, accounted for their identity in alienation and for the British nationalisation of their neighbourhood spaces through stories about the border and the soldiers who maintained it. The soldiers and police patrolling the area regulated social space and Irish nationalists seldom congregated in Tullyman's public settings except in the Roman Catholic Church and the town's Catholic pubs during the 1980s and 1990s. Most Catholics understood the public spaces in the town's central area as British and unionist. Catholic Irish nationalists did not consider it wise to put their collective cultural practices to work in those places. They did not feel that they could mark them with the practices that form what Arjun Appadurai calls 'the production of locality', the phenomenological property of social life that works to socialise space and time and to produce not only local subjects but also 'the very neighbourhoods that contextualise those subjectivities' (Appadurai 1996: 180).

## Producing Locality in Tullyman

The production of locality, as Appadurai emphasises, does not come naturally. It is a social and cultural process and requires the application of technologies to transform either physical or virtual spaces into places that foster meaningful and enduring social lives and make communities. These communities of action and interaction, in turn, make up a neighbourhood, a spatial or virtual entity where certain, specific kinds of subjectivity, agency, sociality and reproducibility are organised and instituted (Appadurai 1996: 178–9). 'Locality, as a dimension or value, is variably realised' in neighbourhoods, and it gives them a teleology or general purpose (Appadurai 1996: 179). The technologies and social practices of locality, then, constitute and reproduce meanings, and, therefore, it is important to depict and understand their contextualisation (Appadurai 1996: 182–8).

All practices directed to the production of locality, as historically grounded acts, produce contexts: they extend social and cultural work across space and create not only places but also the structure of feeling that people live by. Ethnographic accounts of small-scale societies, Appadurai indicates, usually describe such practices in the form of ground-breaking rituals for houses, gardens, villages and the pathways that connect neighbouring residential sites. Such studies take up the social fact that local subjects construct neighbourhoods in opposition to another ecological or social domain and impose a phenomenological aspect onto their environment through the assertion of 'socially (often ritually) organised power' (Appadurai 1996: 184).

The Tullyman Catholics' techniques of locality described above show the significance of such practices in Northern Ireland and their connection to power, but, as Appadurai notes, the context of locality differs significantly in modern nation-states. In small-scale societies, the practices of locality generate contexts. As people extend their localising practices to new ecological or social spaces, they make them amenable to their previously established techniques, but those techniques themselves are dialectically transformed in the new environment. Modern nation-states rearrange this pattern of context production. Dialectical relations remain between a neighbourhood's techniques of locality and State technologies of control, but the relative power of the nation-state often drives the contexts of less powerful locations, places like Tullyman, as the nation-state works to create not only homogenous space and time but also cultural homogeneity (Anderson 1991). Local subjects, then, although they remain context producers, become context driven: they remain subjects of local history but the nation-state makes them objects of its context-producing activities.

Catholics experienced this push during the 1980s in Tullyman where time and space were not homogeneous. Catholics did not cross a variety of local and national boundaries freely and they divided time into what came before the British State and what followed. They challenged the contexts produced by the State. The State had not succeeded in organising homogeneous spaces. There were, and still are, heterogeneous spaces in Tullyman, and both Protestant townspeople and agents of the British State, police and soldiers, interpreted these spaces of difference and the people who lived in them not only as other but also as dangerous. As a result the Catholic housing estate and the row of Catholic houses at the north end of the town were marked. In this situation, Catholic neighbourhoods took on the identity of institutions such as prisons, army barracks or airports – organisations that create spaces of distinction against what Appadurai calls 'the homogeneous space of nationness' – but, whereas barracks and airports become sites of State celebration and distinction, prisons and enclaved neighbourhoods, like Tullyman's Catholic places, became sites of degradation (Appadurai 1996: 189). All such sites, of course, work to make the nation-state meaningful. Nation-states produce meaning by integrating some sites while marginalising and opposing others.

When citizens from recalcitrant Tullyman localities, people like Liam McKeown, insisted on their communities' context-producing practices to engage agents of the State in their everyday border-crossings, they met a power-laden counter-production. If they did not accept or become subservient to State forces, they suffered the consequences as Liam did for a long time before that unnamed soldier killed him. These everyday practices that drove the context of nationalist neighbourhoods degraded his family and community.

## Women's Knowledge and the Transformation of Context

The relatively unrelieved condition of being context-driven rather than context-producing engendered a sense of social worthlessness in the Tullyman Catholic community during the 1970s, 1980s and early 1990s. People seldom ventured into local public spaces and young people chose to emigrate across the border or to the United States when they could. This, of course, did not apply to every Tullyman Catholic citizen and Mary McKeown was chief among these. In the mid-1980s when I met her, she worked in the Sinn Féin Advice Centre in a town nearby in order to help people with welfare benefit claims and a variety of other complaints against the State. She was asked to run as a candidate for that party in 1985, but she left the party soon after because it did not address local social issues to her satisfaction, especially those surrounding the situations of women.

After the British soldier killed her brother Liam, she campaigned tirelessly to find out the truth. Both the British and Irish States' official inquiries proved unsatisfactory so she went to the media – television, radio and newspapers – at every opportunity. Her stories about Liam's death and the likely military wrongdoing that led to it provided the drama that television producers desired. Her narrative about everyday police and army violence and the difficulties of getting beyond the State's official accounting of events, of getting 'the truth', began to gain legitimacy among nationalists and provided journalists with 'a good story'. In 1991, she along with other Catholics who had family members killed by the State, began organising a victims' group that sought the truth and contested the State's accounting of their loved ones' deaths.

This group's efforts put the stories of Catholic victims of State violence into the public arena. The media had highlighted security-force victims of Irish republican violence more thoroughly than they did the victims of the security forces, but debate did take place when Mary and others in her group appeared. Hegemonic, mainstream media functioned as context-producing for Tullyman's Catholics once Mary appeared on television and radio with some regularity. Neighbourhoods constitute contexts for people, but they require contexts beyond those they produce to establish locality: they require development of a relational consciousness of other neighbourhoods. Dialectically related, the locality-producing activities of neighbourhoods or of a supraneighbourhood like a State result in an entanglement of context-driven and context-generative practices.

The media events in which Mary McKeown participated demonstrated this. She spoke at one, for example, that considered the experiences of victims from all three sides – the British Protestants, Irish nationalist and the State. In this 1998 televised forum, Mary shared an awareness of the other sides' sorrows. She spoke of the need for all victims to know the truth. Her critical accounts focused on the security forces' treatment of her brother, the failure to investigate loyalist criminal behaviour against Catholics and the necessity that the IRA reveal its logic for specific political killings of Protestants in her region. This made a difference.

Mary had appeared on several television programmes over the years, but this 1998 forum was particularly significant because the British Prime Minister, Tony Blair, participated in order to represent the spirit of the peace agreement that had been signed that year. On the programme, Mary and other relatives of people killed in the Troubles engaged Blair on issues of healing social wounds and the responsibility for them. She addressed the importance of recognition and remembrance of the injuries of all sides in any successful peace process. Only she, however, questioned the Prime Minister about the State's accountability for the conflict. She expressed the view that it was not only paramilitary organisations that had to recognise the hurt they caused and tell the truth in the interest of healing, but also the State had to tell the truth about the illegal murders they carried out. Blair demurred. He seemed flustered and did not answer her queries and demands well. Tullyman Catholics believed she got the better of Blair and showed up the State. Her statements were understood by local and regional nationalists not only to have revealed the State's need to account for its actions but also to have shown its reluctance to apply the rules of law to itself in the way it directed them to its citizens. Catholics around Tullyman felt she showed the British Prime Minister up by using local techniques of representation, Tullyman context-producing practices, and this delighted them. Tony Blair, in their view, did not provide an answer to her queries about this contradiction between State and people.

When she returned home from this event, Mary's answerphone was full of messages from local Catholics praising her for her performance and for making the need for 'the truth' public. This local value opened boundaries. Two Protestant women whom Mary did not know approached her to compliment her performance and to share their stories of family tragedy. One, Ronda, contacted Mary at her workplace. She followed Mary into the room where she worked, closed the door behind her, and told Mary this story, which Mary told me:

> And she says, you know, 'I want to talk to you!' She says, you know, she says: 'My brother was shot by the SAS too.' She says that they were waiting, the undercover unit, for the IRA to come along, and her brother and this other person went duck hunting. And they were going across the bogs and the SAS popped up and shot her brother dead. She said: 'His body lay in the bogs for a day before they would allow any of them, even the priest, to go in,' ach not the priest, 'the minister, to go in near his body.' And she started to challenge what was happening and everything, and they nearly drove her mad. They nearly drove her insane. They actually tried to get her locked up as a mental case ...

A second Protestant woman approached Mary about the Blair programme. Mary recounted her dialogue with this woman, Ruth:

> And the next thing she goes, 'you know, every word, every word you said was true,' and I goes 'oh, aye, I know,' and ye know the way and you're there and you're kind'a standing around, and she says: 'Maybe me and you will get a wee coffee some morning,' and I says 'aye, no problem,' you know, and she says 'you know I'm not a Catholic.' And she says 'my brother,' and the tears were in her eyes, she said her brother was killed, and she says: 'To this day we blame the police.' And she says: 'We haven't been able to find the truth.' And the tears were just sitting there you could see this pain. And she says: 'I'm so proud of what you said.'

This Protestant unionist woman took up some of the discourses that Mary used to criticize the State, and she was proud that a woman from her local area was brave enough to confront the British Prime Minister. Neither of these women felt free to meet Mary in public or organise with her although they identified with her on the basis of having brothers killed by the State-organised 'shoot to kill policy' of the 1980s (see Asmal 1985). Ronda and Ruth seemed to be secret supporters of Mary's group, and, perhaps, the intricacies of their hidden solidarity can be illuminated by recalling the contextual relations surrounding the production of locality and the conditions of subalternity that affected women in this border area.

These two women did not know Mary but knew of her. Mary said she had seen them before but did not know them and never spoke to them. These two women came from neighbourhoods that were antagonistic to Mary. Yet, these women took up her stories about Liam and the State border performances that provided a context for his death. This sharing of discourse and the desire it produced in these women to let Mary know that they supported her, indeed identified with her, related to the process of contextualisation. As outlined earlier, practices and techniques of locality produce the contexts through which a neighbourhood constructs its own *telos* and extends contexts for action by both its members and those of opposed neighbourhoods.

In this dialectical dynamic, subjects from one neighbourhood must be aware of the localisation practices of those neighbourhoods for which they generate contexts and those that generate contexts for them. So, Ruth and Ronda possessed some knowledge of the practices of locality in Mary's segregated Tullyman neighbourhood and Mary knew theirs because their neighbrhood's practices of locality and the powerful State they identified with drove her neighbourhood's sense of place and the activities that constituted it. A trans-cultural process occurred in this polarised situation as it did in the *New York Times* story cited earlier. Clines accounted for the death of Liam McKeown in the terms of the British State's storyline. This accounting permeated Tullyman's Catholic community via the local Media, and Catholics constructed their accounts in dialectical relationship to it. Mary, in turn, believed that Protestants in Tullyman reproduced such State ideologies without question, but she learned from her participation in Media events and through encounters like those with Ronda and Ruth that Protestants were not as homogeneous as she expected.

Mary learned that the British State order was dominant but contested in the Protestant neighbourhoods that abutted her area of Tullyman and its region. She realised that there were Protestant women, too, whose knowledge about the interrelations of people and State could not be articulated publicly or were voiced in secret. The problem for these women, and Mary's efforts to get the Media and the State to recognise her knowledge of State/people relations index this, was not so much the problem of speaking but the problem of having their subaltern, local knowledge occluded. The problem for these women was that the point of intersection of the knowledge they all possessed was not made public and did not become context-producing for either their communities or the State. Their combined knowledge circulated under cover and, as women's knowledge, was interpreted as local and outside the realm of truths that demanded the attention of political struggle. Nonetheless, these women struggled on and, however slightly, they reconfigured their neighbourhoods, their contexts and the nation-state they inhabited.

## Conclusion

The women, Protestant and Catholic, described in this chapter have addressed the binarily opposed social orders in which they live by addressing the State that often drives the political and cultural conflict between them. In Northern Ireland, this contestation of hegemonic power, although minimal, offers a glimpse into the processes of reconciliation that may be required to establish not only peace but also a functioning civil society where all citizens can engage each other on vital issues. To do this will require a dramatic transformation of Irish nationalist senses of belonging and British unionist senses of inclusion and exclusion. The British State in Northern Ireland, its colonial past and ambiguous post-colonial present, has contributed powerfully to Northern Ireland's conflict as the stories here show. Criticising the State and its powers of determination along with the other groups that have committed violence offers a starting point toward a reconfiguration of the opposed social orders that have generated Northern Ireland's conflict.

The three women whose stories end this chapter have started such a critique. Through narrative forms that have endured in Ireland, they have demanded the truth and have supported a 'truth commission', an institution that the State, the unionists and the Irish nationalist republicans do not desire. By doing so, then, these women are challenging the three powerful social orders that make the promises of the Belfast Agreement, the Good Friday peace agreement, difficult to keep. At the time of writing, early 2003, the new institutions that the agreement stipulates are suspended yet again. The movement of civil society has not been strong enough to sustain them. Protestant and Catholic social orders cannot seem to sustain an intersection of social ties and accounts that enables full democracy. Local institutions have come under the direct rule of Westminster and this rule, with its foundation in the colonial State, makes it difficult for citizens to enact full citizenship rights. The emerging practices of the Tullyman women described here challenge this formation. They have used older cultural forms, narratives of family responsibility, to identify with one another and make demands of the State. Their political work needs to be reproduced in a wide variety of Northern Ireland neighbourhoods to have an effect. Work like theirs, not necessarily the work of the State, is likely to bring a reconfiguration of social orders and a lasting peace in Northern Ireland.

## Notes

1. Ed Moloney (2002) describes the divisions between Sinn Féin and the Irish Republican Army (IRA) in the negotiation of the peace process and the formation of the strategy for equality.
2. All names of people and places in this chapter are fictional. Although a peace of sorts has been established, persons in Northern Ireland are still vulnerable to violence.
3. For discussion of what he names 'anomalous states', see Lloyd (1993: 1–9).
4. David Stark presents these concepts in Stark (1994).
5. I understand sociality in this chapter as the predisposition to learn and accept the categories and concerns that give group identity to a person.
6. The meaning of 'accounts' in this chapter differs somewhat from the usage of John Borneman (1997). His work deals with issues of violence and justice as does this chapter, but the emphasis here is more on the use of accounts in forming networks and rearranging social ties and beliefs, and not on accountability. Of course, the issue of accountability is not tangential to the story presented here and could be the organising concept for this series of events.
7. Allen Feldman (1991, 1997) and Begoña Aretxaga (1997) describe the articulation of the past and the present and the instruments of everyday life that people use to remember colonial history in urban areas. Dominic Bryan (2000) describes ritual performances that bring the values of British colonisation to life. Kelleher (2003) describes the production of colonial memories in rural Northern Ireland.
8. Frank Burton (1978, 1979) describes these practices of telling. Aretxaga (1997), Feldman (1991) and Kelleher (2003) detail them and connect them to the processes of colonisation and memory.
9. Marianne Elliott (2001: 429–82) discusses the history and subjectivity of inferiority.
10. Oliver MacDonagh (1977) describes the legacy of the Act of Union, passed in 1800: this history enables understanding of these local historical beliefs. He elaborates on the production of these narratives and values in relation to Irish constructions of time in MacDonagh (1983).
11. In local parlance, 'republican' refers to people who support Sinn Féin and the IRA. The word describes people who support violence against the State. It is seldom used to describe a republican in the sense of desiring a republican form of government.
12. It needs to be emphasised that, except for a very few Catholic residents of the town of Tullyman, members of this group did not freely reveal their accountings of the political events surrounding them. A few Irish republicans, local members of Sinn Féin, made theirs public, but few others did. I was able to collect stories in the privacy of people's homes, but most people did not allow me to audiotape them.
13. See John Stalker (1988) for the fullest account of this series of events.
14. On the positioning of ethnographic subjects out of time, see Fabian (1983).
15. For descriptions of the relations between the U.S. Press and British information officers, see Thomas (1988, 1991).
16. On non-sense and colonial representation see Bhabha (1990: 203–18).
17. On women making home in the Tullyman area, see Kelleher (2000)

## References

Anderson, B. 1991. *Imagined Communities: Reflections on the Origin and Spread of Nationalism.* London, Verso.

Anzaldua, G. 1987. *Borderlands/La Frontera: The New Mestiza.* San Francisco, Aunt Lute Books.

Appadurai, A. 1996. *Modernity at Large: Cultural Dimensions of Globalization*. Minneapolis, University of Minnesota Press.
Aretxaga, B. 1997. *Shattering Silences: Women, Nationalism and Political Subjectivity in Northern Ireland*. Princeton, Princeton University Press,
Armstrong, N. and L. Tennenhouse. 1989. 'Representing violence, or "how the west was won"'. In *The Violence of Representation: Literature and the History of Violence*, eds N. Armstrong and L. Tennenhouse. New York, Routledge.
Asmal, K. ed. 1985. *Shoot to Kill?: International Lawyer's Inquiry into the Lethal Use of Firearms by the Security Forces in Northern Ireland*. Dublin, Mercier.
Bhaba, H. 1989. 'Remembering Fanon: Self, psyche and the colonial condition'. In *Remaking History*, eds B. Kruger and P. Mariani. Seattle, Bay View Press.
Bhaba, H. 1990. 'Articulating the archaic: Notes on colonial nonsense'. In *Literary Theory Today*, eds P. Collier and H.G. Ryan. Ithaca, Cornell University Press.
Borneman, J. 1997. *Settling Accounts: Violence, Justice and Accountability in Postsocialist Europe*. Princeton, Princeton University Press.
Bryan, D. 2000. *Orange Parades: The Politics of Ritual, Tradition and Control*. London, Pluto Press.
Burton, F. 1978. *The Politics of Legitimacy: Struggles in a Belfast Community*. London, Routledge & Kegan Paul.
Burton, F. 1979. 'Ideological social relations in Northern Ireland'. *British Journal of Sociology* 30, no 1: 61–80.
Elliott, M. 2001. *The Catholics of Ulster: A History*. New York, Basic Books.
Fabian, J. 1983. *Time and the Other: How Anthropology Makes Its Object*. New York, Columbia University Press.
Feldman, A. 1991. *Formations of Violence: The Narrative of the Body and Political Terror in Northern Ireland*. Chicago, University of Chicago Press.
Feldman, A. 1997. 'Violence and vision: The prosthetics and aesthetics of terror'. *Public Culture* 10, no. 1: 24–60.
Kelleher, W. 1994. 'Ambivalence, modernity and the state of terror in Northern Ireland'. *Political and Legal Anthropology Review* 17, no. 1: 31–40.
Kelleher, W. 2000. 'Making home in the Irish/British borderlands: The global and the local in a conflicted social space'. *Identities* 7, no. 2: 139–72.
Kelleher, W. 2003. *The Troubles in Ballybogoin: Memory and Identity in Northern Ireland*. Ann Arbor, University of Michigan Press.
Lloyd, D. 1993. *Anomalous States: Irish Writing and the Post-Colonial Moment*. Durham, NC, Duke University Press.
MacDonagh, O. 1977. *Ireland: The Union and Its Aftermath*. London, Allen & Unwin.
MacDonagh, O. 1983. *States of Mind: A Study of Anglo-Irish Conflict 1780–1980*. London, Allen & Unwin.
Mitchell, G. 1999. *Making Peace*. London, William Heineman.
Moloney, E. 2002. *A Secret History of the IRA*. New York, W.W. Norton.
Probyn, E. 1990. 'Travels in the postmodern: making sense of the local'. In *Feminism/Postmodernism*, ed. L. Nicholson. New York: Routledge.
Rapport, N. and A. Dawson eds. 1998. *Migrants of Identity: Perceptions of Home in a World of Movement*. Oxford, Berg.
Stalker, J. 1988. *The Stalker Affair*. London, Harrap.

Stark, D. 1994. *Recombinant Property in East European Capitalism*. Ithaca, Cornell Working Papers on Transitions from State Socialism (No. 94–5).
Thomas, J. 1988. 'Bloody Ireland'. *Columbia Journalism Review*. May/June, 31–7.
Thomas, J. 1991. 'Toeing the line: Why the American Press fails'. In *The Media and Northern Ireland*, ed. B. Rolston. London, MacMillan.

# Chapter 10
# Boundary Formation and Identity Expression in Everyday Interactions: Muslim Minorities in Greece

Venetia Evergeti

### Introduction

The problem of researching and defining ethnic identities and the geographical and symbolic boundaries that define them is one of the central themes in sociological and anthropological literature. Lately, the study of national and ethnic identities becomes even more important with the rapid developments towards the European integration. One of the main issues that academics, politicians and lay members are facing relates to the formation of a 'European identity' and its relation to the already existing national identities (Macdonald 1993). Within this context, issues related to ethnic identities of minority groups within European States become very sensitive. In other words, if we are talking about a 'unified European identity', where, then, do minorities within respective countries stand? What kind of European manifestations will they develop and how?

Given this background, in this chapter I wish to address the notion of 'boundaries' in relation to the social processes of identity formation within specific minority groups, namely the Muslim minorities in western Thrace, Greece. Using empirical data from my ethnographic study in the area, I will examine the way people understood, defined, maintained and negotiated their ethnic boundaries in the local context of their village. My data presents a situation where a small Muslim minority, close to the current geographical borders of Europe, consists of three different ethnic groupings. They all share the same religion and the status of a minority, but they also have distinct and very subtle cultural differences. Furthermore, the formation and maintenance of a unified minority identity in contrast to the Greek (Orthodox) national identity is not without tensions and conflicts. On many occasions it requires the competent crossing of categorical symbolic and geographical boundaries and the negotiation of various identity elements. When seen from a 'European' perspective, the issue of their identity becomes even more topical and problematic as some of the Muslim minorities in the area have a Turkish origin. In this respect, the group represents both 'European' and 'non-European' political and cultural elements.

Important questions are raised from such a situation: first, in what ways do people understand and express such cultural differences and how do they represent them in geographical boundaries? How do they cross 'categorical boundaries' – especially in the cases where they live in small rural establishments so close to the current European borders? When are such boundaries maintained and when are they modified? And finally, and most importantly, what does this process of negotiation tell us about the everyday reality of European integration? In what follows, I intend to address these questions by presenting two examples from my case study. Focusing on such a complex microcosm on the borderlines of Europe can, I believe, offer us a significant insight into the social processes involved in the formation of diverse elements of European identifications.

## Theoretical Framework

The search for 'objective traits' that characterise and differentiate one social group from another has been the empirical basis of many approaches. Often, statistical information is provided in order to show how the concentration of some cultural characteristics relates to a specific group. Such approaches, however, fail to provide an understanding of complex situations of ethnic diversity and the process through which contrasting identity elements are acquired. Rather, they produce what Graham Watson (1981) calls 'reifications of ethnicity'. That is to say, ethnicity and identity are not fixed properties to be quantified with statistics.

In this chapter, I take as my starting point a notion of ethnicity as an emergent feature of ongoing social interaction. As Graham Watson (1981) has suggested:

> Ethnicity, like age and gender, is an emergent property of an ongoing interpersonal bargaining process. Claims, implicit or explicit, verbal or non-verbal, are made, made by somebody, and assessed, accepted, rejected or shelved by somebody else. (1981: 453)

In exploring social affiliations and the choice of identities they necessitate I adopt what Schwartz and Jacobs (1979) have termed 'the sociology of the "inside"'. More specifically, I employ the interactionist perspective,[1] and in particular the notion of a negotiated interactional production of identity. The concepts of identity and ethnicity that I employ are the ones referred to and described by the members of the group under study. Furthermore, the themes related to identity are generated from the lived experiences and activities of the participants. In this respect, the theoretical framework within which this work is organised is an ethnographic naturalistic analysis informed by a descriptive and inductive study of the experiences of those under study.

The purpose of this approach is to reveal the interactional dynamics of group identity and boundary formations within a particular socio-cultural setting and explore its various manifestations (ethnic, gender etc.) in social contacts. At an empirical level, this work is informed by my ethnographic study of the Muslim minorities of Thrace, in Northern Greece. In particular, I attempt to describe and analyse the process of ethnic identification within minority groups and the way people used local knowledge in producing, maintaining, negotiating and even transforming their status. The analytical emphasis is on what Ryle (1990) has called 'knowledge how' as opposed to 'knowledge that'. In other words, I am interested not only in 'what' the features of the 'master statuses' or identities under study were, but more importantly in 'how' these were communicated through everyday interactions. Hence, my focus is not only on elements of the ethnic identity of my ethnographic group, but also on the communicative resources and reasoning procedures used by members in their 'presentation of self' in given situations (Goffman 1990b).

According to Barth (1970), cultural differences between ethnic groups do not necessarily mark the boundaries formed between them. In a similar way the reduction of such differences does not correspond to a breakdown in boundary-maintaining processes. If this is the case, the question is: What is the relationship between ethnic/cultural differences and ethnic boundary maintenance? I argue here that there is an interrelationship between boundary maintenance and identity formation and expression. Their connection is not linear but a complex one that is manifested through everyday interactions. Furthermore, I aim to show that ethnic boundaries are not always stable and continuing as Barth argued. On the contrary, in their social encounters, people are able to manipulate and effectively cross social and ethnic boundaries.

## Socio-Historical Establishment of the Minority

My case refers to an area in Northern Greece (known as Western Thrace) where a small Muslim minority is located. In what will follow I will provide a selective account of some important socio-historical elements concerning the establishment and recognition as a minority of the Muslim people in the Greek part of Thrace. This information is rather important in understanding the issues related to the historical formation not only of the categorical boundaries of the minority communities but also of the current European border.

## The Balkan Predicament

The history of the Thracian minority is influenced by three different but interrelated historical heritages. It is highly connected not only with aspects of Greek history but also with the overall history of the Balkans, as well as some aspects of Ottoman/Turkish history. This is a very important detail to keep in mind, as in what will follow I will be referring to conflicting nationalisms in the area. Not only does the particular minority (as with every other social group) carry its own specificity but it is also 'burdened' with the so-called multi-ethnic mosaic of the Balkan peninsula. Also referred to as the 'melting pot', this is the centuries-long inter-mixing of many different ethnic groups in the area. Dimitris Kostopoulos states that borders and ethnic group relations in the Balkans have been the object of a long standing argument between history and geography, in which history seems to be the winner at geography's expense (1993: 11). Whether or not this is true is the topic of another debate; however, the fact remains that the area is rich in turbulent historical developments which have affected the States involved and even more so the many minorities within them (Poulton 1994).

The patchwork of minorities that one will find all over the Balkans has created a traditional feeling of insecurity among those minorities. At times such insecurity tends to drive minorities to seek affiliation with or help from their 'purified' motherland. However, the countries of the peninsula of Aimos have historically been anything but pure. The various ethnicities have always, in one or another way, inter-mixed with each other. After all, the four-hundred years of coexistence under Ottoman rule left their mark resulting in continuous ethnic mixing that any 'nationalist exorcism' cannot break (Kostopoulos 1993: 11). The struggle for 'purification' in the Balkans is thus older and deeper than any other struggle for independence of small ethnic groups in the area. Unfortunately Greece and particularly the northern parts of the country suffer from the same 'spell'.

The Muslim communities in the area, once part of the Ottoman Empire, were given the status of a minority within the different countries that accommodate them through conventions and treaties between the newly established countries. Today, some of these groups are identifying themselves with Turkey as far as it is seen as the remainder of the old Ottoman Empire, or at least the closest country to their own Islamic traditions. Such is the situation with the Muslim minorities in Bulgaria and parts of the Muslim minorities in Greece.

## Establishment of the Minority and the Treaty of Lausanne, 1923

The Muslim minority in Thrace was established through the Treaty of Lausanne, signed in 1923. A separate convention provided that there should be 'a compulsory exchange of Turkish nationals of the Greek Orthodox religion, established in Turkish territory, and of Greek nationals of the Muslim religion established in the Greek territory'. The only exceptions to the exchange were the members of the Greek population of Istanbul and the Muslim population of western Thrace, who could prove that they were established in the respective areas prior to October 1918. The convention imposed upon Turkey a number of minority obligations that Greece, too, had to respect vis-à-vis the Muslim minorities found in its territories.[2]

Since then the issue of the minority in western Thrace has played a significant role in the developments of the Greek–Turkish relations.[3] Also, the area of western Thrace has a strategic military position and Greece has often expressed her fears that having a Muslim minority living so close to the borders of Turkey, with a Turkish ethnic consciousness, could result in a situation similar to that in Cyprus.[4] Therefore, the Greek authorities adopted an assimilation policy towards this heterogenic population that lives across the Greek frontier, because it was (and still is) considered as a constant threat in the area. However, this view is also connected to the important role the traditional Greek Orthodoxy has played in the construction of the modern Greek national identity.[5]

Although the Treaty of Lausanne recognised the minority as a religious one and safeguarded its rights accordingly, the members of the minority in Thrace have formed, through different historical developments, not only a different religious but also a different ethnic identity from that of the 'dominant group'.

Taking this into account, there exists a peculiar 'antithesis' between the Greek national identity and the minority's ethnic one: the Muslim and especially Turkish ethnic identification of some members of the minority communities represents for the Greek majority the 'non-European' 'other' against which their 'Europeanised' national identity has been *officially* defined. In other words, some elements of the Greek Orthodox identity[6] have been portrayed in contrast to the Muslim Ottoman element that occupied the country for four hundred years.

## Negotiating Identities and Crossing Boundaries

The Muslim minority in western Thrace is estimated today to be about 120 thousand people living in the three provinces of Evros, Rodope and Xanthi. Nevertheless, there is disagreement as to the exact number, as Greece does not include questions regarding ethnicity and religion in the national census.

Furthermore, the Greek State refuses to recognise them as an ethnic, specifically Turkish minority, a fact that has also attracted the interest of public opinion and organisations of minority rights.[7]

However, both the Greek State and the different minority rights groups have underestimated the complexity of the issue of the ethnic origin and identity of the people of the Muslim communities in western Thrace. For many years, following the Treaty of Lausanne, they have been characterised as a 'religious minority' and at the same time they are considered as homogeneous in terms of language and origin, a fact that is seen as specifying the cultural unit. Nevertheless, the minority consists of three different ethnic or cultural groupings. These are the self-defined Turks, Pomaks and Gypsies (Roma). As it became apparent from the organisation of the village where I was staying during my fieldwork, these ethnic differences were negotiated and displayed by my informants in their everyday experiences (as will be illustrated shortly).

The Pomaks live mainly in the highlands of Rodope in the diocese of Xanthi. Although it is very difficult to define their origin, as Kanakidou (1994) suggests, they were one of the first populations in the Balkans and most specifically in the area of Rodope. They speak their own Slavic-Bulgarian dialect, and it has been said that in their customs one can recognise elements of Christian culture.[8] They are considered the most religious of the three groups with a very traditional lifestyle.

Their origin is obscure and at times has been interpreted differently by Bulgarian, Greek and Turkish historians. Each of these countries, depending on its own historical research and national interests, appears to claim for itself the origin of a part or the whole of this ethnic group.[9] According to the Greek point of view, the Pomaks were nomads of Thracian tribes, that were 'Hellenised', 'Slavicised', 'Christianised' and were finally converted to Islam after the fall of Konstantinopole. Some Greek historians refer to them as Ahrianes, a term that referred to the best fighters in the army of Alexander the Great (Papathanasi-Mousiopoulou 1992–1994). Some others even attempted, with the help of blood group testing among Pomaks, to prove that Pomaks were by no means related to Turks and were therefore Europeans.[10] On the other hand, Bulgarian historians refer mainly to the Pomak language, which constitutes a predominantly Bulgarian dialect. However, this dialect also contains many words from Turkish and Greek, as well as linguistic patterns of its own. Officially, in northern Thrace (in Bulgaria), they are called Bulgarian Muslims. Finally, the Turkish historians do not pay attention to such linguistic and cultural aspects but emphasise the common factor of religion, Islam. There is also the view that Pomaks and Turks are not only related by religion, but Pomaks are the first and oldest Turkish population in Europe. 'To put it mildly', as Seyppel (1989: 44) suggests, 'each of the national historical schools involved, presents 'history' as serving its own national fiction'.

If asked about their origin, the Pomaks will refer to all the different speculations we just saw above, but will mostly connect themselves with the history of the Ottoman Empire. Nevertheless, the Pomaks represent a separate cultural-linguistic group within the minority. The Treaty of Lausanne dealt with a Muslim minority, and indeed there existed a *religiously* homogeneous minority group. However, this group was not *linguistically* or *culturally* homogeneous as well.

On the other hand, there is little 'national' interest in the case of the Muslim 'gypsies' or Roma (as I will be referring to them here because of the negative connotations the word 'gypsy' has). They are a nomad group who most of the time move from town to town, rather than staying in one place. This has been referred to as the main reason for the non-existence of precise figures for them in the population census of Greece. They speak the Greek and Turkish languages, but have also their own dialect, which is a mixture of Romany and Turkish. Within the people of the minority they are considered as the least faithful Muslims because of their changeable lifestyle. When I was in my field site I met a Greek researcher in the area who has written extensively about the Pomaks and their distinct language (Liapis 1995). At the time, he was involved in a research project on the Roma of the area. He explained to me, that there is racial prejudice against the 'gypsies' (coming both from the minority as well as the wider Greek society), who do not even have an official recognition of their distinct culture, which is mostly connected with the art of *kalathoplectiki* (making baskets from cane). Actually, there exists a very peculiar system of racial prejudice within the minority. The Roma are considered as the most 'inferior' by both the other groups (the most usual stereotype is that they are dirty and lazy – even though they are working in the fields of the others). The Pomaks are considered as 'inferior' and 'backward' from the Turkish population, because they are very religious and have large families. Most of the Imams and the Hotzas in the Muslim villages are Pomaks, and this sometimes results in antagonism between the two groups. For example, when I asked people in the village if they agreed with what the Hotza was preaching in the mosque, some would reply: 'Are we going to listen to a Pomak now?... He is only a Pomak, they are very religious anyway.' However, the way in which these differences are realised and defined by the members of the minority is very important in understanding the processes involved in their identity formation and presentation.

The third group, the Turks, is perhaps the one that is seen as the most problematic, since their ethnicity is not officially recognised. My ethnographic material is based mainly on this group as the village I was staying in was predominantly Turkish.

## Politicising Identities

It would be true to say that with few exceptions the literature I found on the issue of the minority in Thrace falls under one of two main categories, both insisting on the 'unbiased and objective' truth of their views. In this respect, we have on one side the 'official Greek point of view'[11] which is very nicely and somehow ironically summed up by Dimitras.[12] On the other hand, there is the Turkish 'assessment' of the situation which supports the view that the minority is homogeneous and that its 'separation' into three different ethnic groupings is a construct of Greek propaganda aiming at the rejection of the 'Turkishness' of the minority. Both of the sides exclude the minority members in a selective way, meaning that they only refer to the people's views on an issue when it is 'relevant' to their own political interests.

Seen within such a framework, the members of my case study would be either of Greek national consciousness and therefore loyal to Greece or of Turkish origin and national consciousness and therefore loyal to Turkey; to be loyal to Turkey would mean to be an enemy of Greece. In this respect, we would come to the conclusion that a member of the minority can be either one or the other, but never both. However, taking an interactionist approach and, furthermore, emphasising the importance of the flexible, negotiated order of identity formation, we see that one can be both. Identities are not fixed: rather, they are open to interpretation and change depending on the social context. Through a process of interpretation or definition, members of the minority communities would show competence in moving across categorical boundaries and articulating the ethnic identities within them.

I am not trying here to de-politicise the situation. On the contrary, even if one wanted to take the political element away, this would not be possible, as it is not only part of the historical developments in the area but also an important component of the everyday life of the people. My aim, then, is to understand the significance of these political or other properties for the formation of these people's identity. In this respect, one might wonder which of all the above elements is prevailing and is stronger in the ethnic formulation of identity of the members of the minority in general, and more specifically those of the village where I conducted my fieldwork. It is my contention that the understanding of identity formation in general, but also in the case of the Muslim minorities in western Thrace, lies in the recognition of the 'negotiated order' (Strauss 1963) through which members define themselves, depending on their understanding of the situation.

The question then arises: How do the people from the minorities in western Thrace achieve their ethnic identity within such a politically charged environment? As I soon realised, the issue of their ethnic identity was a consciously problematic one; they had to present it and maintain it in their everyday reality. Nevertheless, they competently managed their presentation of self, depending on the social situation. 'Greece is my country, Islam is my religion, Turkish my origin' or 'I am a Greek citizen of Turkish descent' were frequent answers to my questions about identity. My informants were not either only Greeks or only Turkish. They were both and even more, depending on the situation and the social circumstances. Their identity negotiations were neither simple nor without tensions. They were, however, flexible in a way that theoretical frameworks, which emphasise dichotomies and bi-polarities, would not have been able to address.

## A Methodological Note

My ethnographic fieldwork lasted approximately six months and involved participant observation, informal interviews, and discussions with the inhabitants of one of the Muslim villages of the area. During the months of my stay in the area I lived with one of the families of the village, which provided me with information about the everyday life of the group that I would have not been able to gather otherwise.

For most of my informants, particularly in the beginning of my stay, my questions were treated with suspicion – this was connected with their orientations towards my 'Greek identity'. Most people thought that I was 'checking up on them' to see whether they were loyal or not to their country, Greece, and that I had probably been sent by the police or the state to see if there was any threat to regional stability and security. Their suspicion, though, revealed another important facet of the way they were defining their ethnic status. To refer to themselves as the 'Turkish minority' was not accepted by the Greek authorities. Thus, a very significant element of their identity was not legitimately and publicly recognised. Nevertheless, such ethnic characterisations were in use in a daily basis. Thus, because some aspects of self-identification were not openly acknowledged by the dominant majority, I had to look for the spheres and forms of social interaction within which the minority communicated and maintained their identity. These spheres could be separated in the closed sphere of interaction of the village and the public sphere of the wider area of Thrace and its towns.

During my fieldwork I witnessed numerous occasions where contrasting elements of polarised entities (for example Greek/Turkish, modern/traditional, European/non-European etc.) were reproduced when crossing social boundaries and formulating distinctive identities. Examples were instances of intermarriage and celebrations of both Greek and Turkish national and religious festivals (where Turkish or Pomak students would be taking part in the school marching, holding the Greek flag). However, for the purposes of this discussion I will concentrate on two different ethnographic examples that are particularly illustrative of the way ethnic identities and geographical boundaries were negotiated in everyday life. First I will describe the ethnic organisation of the village and then I will illustrate how the presentation of self changed depending on the member's definition of the social boundary as modern/cosmopolitan or traditional/rural.

## The Village Map and Interethnic Relations

As most of the other villages in the area, Mikrohori was divided into a number of quarters called *mahalle*. These were like different neighbourhoods, but had no clear boundaries. For example, people tended to define the borders of a specific neighbourhood in different ways depending on which side of the village their house was situated in. In general, the way people talked about their *mahalle* displayed a degree of loyalty, especially in the cases where close relatives lived near each other and therefore had some kinship unity as well. However, the only *mahalle* that seemed to have more commonly defined borders was the end of the village, which was occupied by some Roma families. That part of the village was described to me as somewhere between the final borders of the village. There were two reasons for that. Firstly, it was a mark of the distinct ethnic identity between the so-called 'gypsies' and the rest of the village. Secondly, the particular neighbourhood was next to the cemetery, which was perceived by the people of Mikrohori as situated outside of the village. Furthermore, some of the Roma families were not living permanently in Mikrohori and it was often suggested that because of their nomadic life, they did not consist an integral part of the village.

These separations are more evident in the village map (Figure 10.1). The couple I was staying with drew the map, in order for me to use it in my study. The school, the mosque and the cemetery are distinctively designated on the map, while the circles with numbers in the middle indicate the houses of the village. Every evening for about a week we all sat down, Aleck and Annie drawing the map, and me keeping notes on the information they were giving me for each house they were numbering. Amazingly, they knew every family in their village and could give me detailed information on almost every family's history. However, when it came to the Roma neighbourhood the circles were left empty, and no information was given (see Figure 10.1 around house 87). More specifically, wherever there was a house of a 'gypsy' family it was labelled as such, i.e. γυφτοι or γυφτικο ('gypsies' or 'gypsy family'). The circles designating their houses were left empty and a general label (γυφτοι) was given at the top, followed by ditto marks underneath for the rest of the houses in that street (see Figure 10.1). In this way, the neighbourhood of the 'gypsies' was defined in the abstract, implying a degree of anonymity.[13] Whereas the rest of the houses had an identity, so to speak, specified by their numbering, the Roma houses did not. Moreover, the

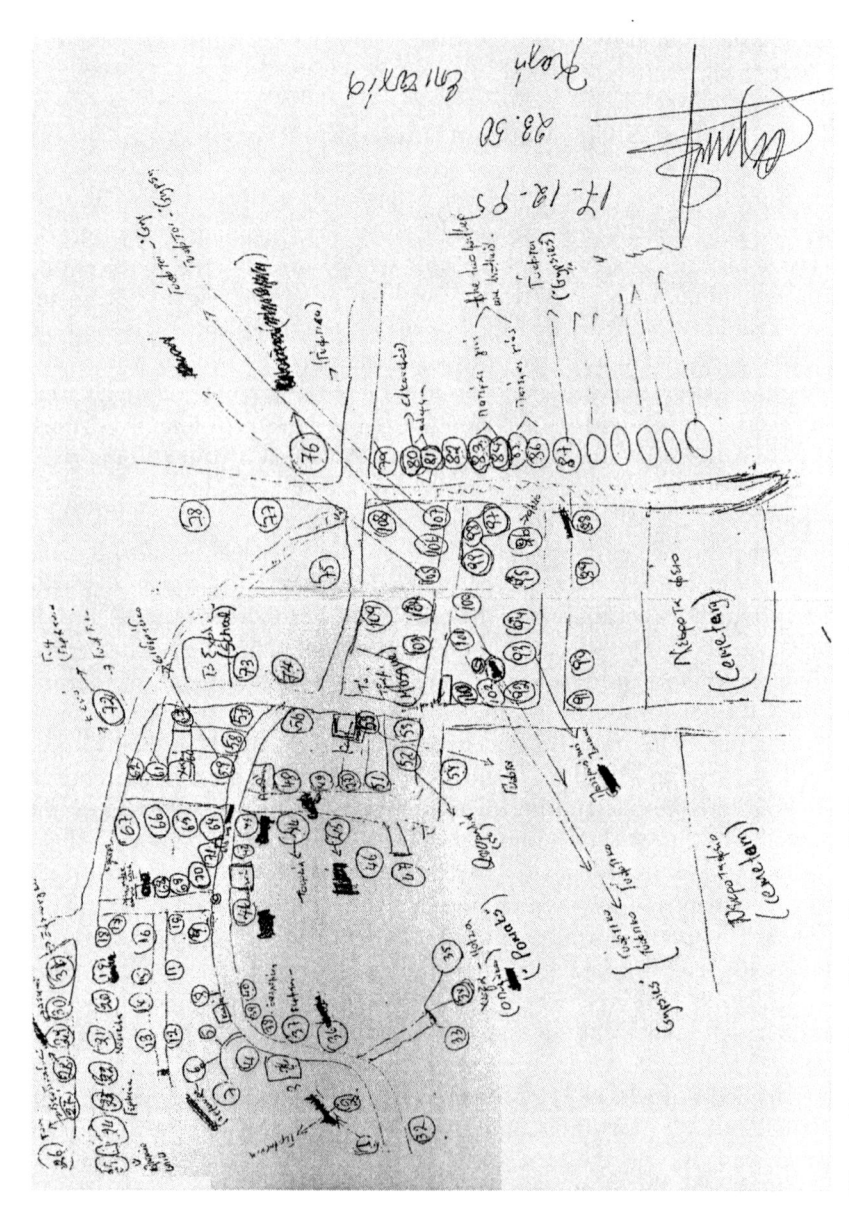

Figure 10.1  Map of the village of Mikrohori drawn by its inhabitants.

information that was given to me for the Roma families in the village (especially for those living next to the cemetery) was limited, because it was perceived as being unimportant. As my hosts put it, 'There are only gypsies living there. You don't really need information about them do you? Most of them come and go, depending on the work in the fields.'

In general, the Roma were employed by the rest of the villagers as seasonal-wage workers in their fields. As it was explained to me: 'Most of them are hard and reliable workers. They move all the time, though. At the end of the season they move to the towns, where they do other things, mostly work in street markets.' However, that was the case only for those Roma living next to the cemetery. The few families that were scattered around the village (again labelled as *γυφτοι* on the map) were permanent inhabitants of the village.

In a similar way, the houses of the Pomak families were also pointed out to me, but were not so clearly designated on the map itself (apart from a small neighbourhood where the Hotza lived – houses 33, 34 and 35 on the map).

The Pomaks and the Gypsies were described as a minority within the village, not only because of their limited number (in comparison to the Turkish majority), but also because of the existence of an inner hierarchy. Those who claimed to have a Turkish origin considered themselves as being at the top of the ranking, with the Pomaks coming second – who were sometimes admired for their religious commitment, but other times described as being 'backward' (see the quotation below). In any case, Pomaks were seen as not 'pure Turks'. Third in line came the Roma, who were treated differently and in some instances socially excluded from the other two groups.

As mentioned above, the Pomaks and the Roma were normally fluent in Greek and Turkish, as well as their own ethnic languages. This was not always welcomed by the Turkish people in the village, mainly for two reasons. First, it seemed to me that there were signs of envy, because the Turkish people did not always speak fluent Greek but this was only my assumption. Secondly, as mentioned earlier, the ethnic Turks wanted to be recognised as an ethnic Turkish minority, and therefore did not like the distinction between the three groupings within the minority. They often saw this separation as a 'tactic' of the State in order to characterise the minority in religious terms.[14] In this respect, there were many people that refused to recognise the Pomaks as a separate ethnic group (this, however, was not the case with the Roma, who were recognised and referred to as a separate group). Consider, for example, the following statement:

> The division of the minority into three different Muslim groups in Thrace is a strategy followed by the Government, in an attempt to show that the Turkish population is not so large. There is not really such an ethnic separation among us. The Pomaks are also Turks. They educate them [meaning the Pomaks] in the special Muslim academy, in order to differentiate them from the Turks. They do it on purpose, to change their ethnic consciousness.

The above was the viewpoint of the *Mufti* (the religious administrator of the minority for the prefecture of Rodope) when I asked him about the Pomaks. However, the above view was not shared by the Pomaks in the village. When I visited one of the Pomak families in Mikrohori and asked what the identification 'Pomak' meant, one of the older sons of the family, who was at the time studying to become an Imam (religious leader), replied:

> Pomaks are the people of the mountains of Rodope. There are Pomaks in Bulgaria and Turkey as well, so I don't know why the Turks don't want to accept us. Our people dress differently and use their own language. The others [meaning the Turks] don't like it because they can't understand it. There are many theories about our race, some say we are the descendants of Alexander the Great [he laughs] … I like this interpretation. Oh I don't really know, we are what we are, we are what you see [pointing to himself and his family].

The way these definitions were achieved was through their everyday contacts inside the village. In many respects, because of the small size of the village, everyone knew to what ethnic category everyone else belonged, but the way these categories were recognised and communicated publicly depended on the conditions of the situation. As Eidheim has suggested,

> What perpetuates the axiom of an identity cleavage, is the fact that people are able to identify each other as belonging to separate categories on the basis of their performance of any role in the public sphere. This reinforces the syndrome of signs attached to ethnic categories, as well as the notion that separate identities are mirrored in the social landscape. (Eidheim 1970: 48)

Furthermore, the boundaries between the three ethnic groups were not fixed, but were negotiated according to people's interpretations of various social encounters. For example, sometimes the Pomaks were defined to me (by Pomaks and Turks alike) as being closer to the Turks (rather than the Roma), in terms of their religion and their culture. At other times, the Turks would suggest that the Pomaks were very traditional, and therefore did not integrate with the group as much as the Roma did. In any case, both the religiosity as well as the fluency of the Greek language was often mentioned as a quality of the Pomaks, one that differentiated them from the Turks.

However, the use of the Pomak or Roma language in public was not welcomed by the Turkish-speaking population. Interestingly enough, by not recognising the distinct identity of the Pomaks, the Turks were performing what they had described to me regarding their own relations with the Greeks as a discriminatory act. Nevertheless, when it came to their relations with the Pomaks, the situation was defined differently, depending on their understanding of the inter-ethnic relations. Perhaps the sphere where these ethnic boundaries were more evident was in the marriage patterns within the minority. In general, intermarriages between the three racial groups were avoided. They were, however, more common than marriages between people from the minority and Christian Greeks.

On a final note regarding interethnic relations, it would have been interesting to also get a representation of the village in a map made by the Pomak and Roma families. This could have provided an understanding of whether (and if so how) the village *mahalle* would have been portrayed differently but also whether Pomaks and Roma would have constructed the map with their houses more centrally depicted.

## 'Now You See It, Now You Don't'

No matter how obvious or subtle the ethnic differences and borders were, it was not until a later stage in my fieldwork that I was able to observe everyday events and through my own socialisation into the community I became more sensitised to the reality of ethnic identifications. After the initial 'testing period' of my fieldwork, people started trusting me and being more open about their dilemmas of identity.[15] A dilemma that was frequently referred to was the modern/traditional dichotomy and the analogous presentation of self in the public spheres of the towns as opposed to the closed spheres of the villages. This was best illustrated in the way the veil was or was not worn by women on different social occasions.

For example, when going out in the nearby cities or in a bigger village where there would also be Greeks, many women (especially the younger ones) would be dressed in modern clothes and only cover their head with a scarf (instead of the full traditional black coat and veil), which in some cases would also be removed once out of the village. The first time I saw this was when I went with Annie and Aleck (the couple I was staying with) to the celebration of the establishment of the Turkish Republic. Annie was very well dressed, because, as she had explained to me, there would be a lot of important people and diplomats from the Turkish Consulate of Komotini at the party. Just before we went out, Annie put on a scarf and ran to the car while looking around to see if there was anyone in the small street. Once we were in the main avenue, away from the village, she removed the scarf and started fixing her hair and make-up in a small mirror. As Aleck explained:

> All the women will be open and well dressed where we are going. Only the very backward ones would be wearing a veil in such an occasion … [while laughing and joking with his wife] You see, it goes like that: modern woman, modern husband.

In other words, when one's wife was more open and modern, it signified that her husband was also modern by allowing her to go out without the veil.

Indeed, there were very few women on that occasion that were covered and all of them were wearing what was considered to be a modern scarf. Aleck and Annie pointed them out as an example of being inappropriately dressed for the occasion. This is a remarkable example of the way people would take into account different (sometimes conflicting) expectations arising from changes in their social surroundings, and formulate their appearances accordingly in order to fit in. Thus, by being careful that no-one would see her in the village, Annie was acknowledging the responses that her 'modern' appearance could elicit within the close community of the village. On the other hand, by not wearing the veil she was also responding to the social conduct that the celebration demanded. In this respect, she was actively crossing from one social boundary to another and in turn managing and reproducing 'a "fitting" image'.

What Annie did that night was not something unique to that situation. On the contrary, in different degrees, it was illustrative of a general pattern of social action. For example, as I mentioned before, women who wore the full black ferentze inside the village would change to a more relaxed but dressy ordinary long coat and bright scarf when visiting the town. Nevertheless, they were all very careful not to be seen without the veil around the village, even if there were times when they would take it off outside the village. To my questions – Why was it kept so hidden? Why were women so careful not to be seen, since it was such a common act? – the response of Hannah (who had become one of my key and trusted informants in the field) and her husband Mohammed came in the following dialogue:

> *H.* They are afraid that the others will gossip about them. Especially, the older women in the village would talk about it and you don't know what is going to be said about you ... we still live with old traditions.
> *M.* [interrupting] They are all backward, that's what they are. They have nothing else to talk about and they are looking for gossip. In such a small community people are curious to know every one else's business. Many times I said to her [pointing to Hannah] to take it off when we are in the town ... but she's afraid, she doesn't feel comfortable, she says.
> *H.* It's OK for you talking ... well, sometimes I don't know what I am; open, covered, what? When I was living in Komotini [before they got married] I wasn't wearing it. Then when I came in the village all the other women were covered and your parents said I should also wear it. It's difficult to change all the time. I would prefer to either be one or the other at all times.
> *M.* One bird doesn't bring the spring. It needs to come from everyone. It's such a closed society that it will take ages to change.

Thus, putting on and removing the veil, or wearing a more colourful one, involved an active appreciation of whether the social occasion was modern or traditional. As indicated above, the fact that the habit was not publicly acknowledged was part and parcel of that active appreciation of the situation.

It also indicated one's attempts to fit in and therefore not to be singled out as a topic of village gossip. However, the negotiation of those social identities or master statuses does not come without contradictions and dilemmas, or even without tension, as Hannah proposed above. As Shibutani has noted: 'Dilemmas and contradictions of status force one to choose between reference groups. Such conflicts are essentially alternative ways of defining the same situation, alternatives arising from each of two or more perspectives that might be brought to bear upon it' (1962: 140).

Also, it became apparent that in many cases it was the husband who did not want to be seen in the town with his wife covered. If inside the village it was the rule to go out veiled, in the nearby towns the same custom was interpreted in a negative way as being unfashionable or even 'backward'. Mohammed later explained that in the same way that Hannah felt uncomfortable and was afraid of being gossiped about if seen without the veil, he also had similar feelings when they would go out in the town and she was veiled. For example, he expressed 'embarrassment' when Hannah had the veil on and they were passing the central square of Komotini.

> It's a bit embarrassing when we go to the square with all the cafés and restaurants. It's full of young people and university students, sitting outside drinking coffee. Probably they look at us and say 'look at them, the Muslims are old-fashioned'. I would love to go with my wife in places like that. We're still young and we live like old people because of the expectations back in the village.

In this respect, the veil is here transformed into what Goffman has called a 'stigma'. In effect it gives out a readily available social identity, the appreciation of which is based on first appearances. Thus, the symbolic meaning of the veil leads to a rushed characterisation of a 'virtual social identity' ('old-fashioned' and traditional) instead of the 'actual social identity' (young and modern) (Goffman 1990b: 12). Other men also commented negatively on the practice of the veil:

> I would like the women to be open but you can't do it here, you would be an exemption to the rule. You see if all the women got uncovered then it would be easier for your own wife. I believe in God, but I'm not very religious. The *Hotza* overdoes it sometimes with his teachings. He says that uncovering themselves [the women] would be a sin. Well I don't believe that. I think it's more the fear of social outcry.

The above example of the veiling practices does not refer only to the dilemma of choosing between a traditional or a modern outlook. It also points to the dilemma and negotiation of an ethnic and religious identity and the successful inter-crossing of the boundary that entails it. In order for the people of the minority to be able to fully participate in the Greek society, especially for the younger ones, a choice has to be made in terms of their appearance and what this appearance signals. The practice of veiling is a sign of both religious and ethnic difference. In this respect, recognising their own group's publicly acknowledged image and changing between different statuses and boundaries required an active appreciation and management of their identity elements.

## Conclusion

In an era where we are moving rapidly towards European integration, the study of these complex processes proves essential in understanding how people can indeed feel at home in many homes. As discussed above, I carried out fieldwork in the area during 1995 to 1996. Although Greece was at the time and had been since the early 1980s a member of the European Union, the issue of 'Europeanisation' of the area (and even more so European identity) was still considered quite new for the members of the minorities in Thrace. This mainly reflected the problem associated with their own identities, namely the fact that the Greek State would not recognise them as a distinct ethnic entity.

However, even then, there were some political debates as to the 'Europeanisation' of the village and the broader minority. In comparison to Turkey, people from the minority often referred to themselves as more 'European' by the mere fact of being Greek citizens. Nevertheless, on many occasions while complaining about the state of their village in comparison to other Greek villages or other parts of Greece, they would often say that their area must be the less European (meaning modernised) and the most neglected within Europe.

Using specific examples from my ethnographic fieldwork on the Muslim minority in Greece I have tried, in this chapter, to indicate the importance of an appreciation of the flexibility of identity formation and the processes of crossing between social and ethnic boundaries. For the purposes of this discussion, I have been selective in the use of ethnographic material. The actual daily interactions were rich in symbols of identity conflicts. Nevertheless, in order for these symbols to be understood and analysed, they would have had to be seen within the relevance of their local social context. Such fine details call for an ethnographic analysis sensitive to the internal organisation of the milieu. With the examples provided above I have tried to show how ethnic identity is situationally specific. I have illustrated instances where people modified the complex elements of their identities in order not only to cross social boundaries but also to fit into the variety of ethnic settings within which they found themselves. As I maintained earlier, identity and its many manifestations are not firm and static. The varying elements of one's identity are communicated and reaffirmed through an interactional order. In this respect, identity contains both meanings and actions, none of which can be explored through a question/answer technique. Identity is 'an emergent property of an ongoing interpersonal bargaining' (Watson 1981: 453) and as such it requires time and continuous contact with the informants in order to acquire a deeper understanding of its nature.

The material I have presented and analysed here can shed some light on the debated issues surrounding the formation of Europeanised identities. My case study provides a significant insight into the complex processes involved in maintaining different, and sometimes contradictory, ethnic/national elements of social identities. As my ethnographic examples have shown, developing such diverse identity elements requires competently crossing categorical boundaries and occasionally belonging to two (or even more) ethnic groups at the same time. By using local knowledge and orienting themselves towards the cultural expectations of particular groups, social actors can acquire various group memberships while moving beyond geographical and symbolic boundaries. Understanding these complex and sometimes problematic processes is very significant in understanding how people can be at home in many homes and how the notion of European unification can be realised through existing cultural and ethnic diversity.

## NOTES

1. For a comprehensive discussion of the interactionist perspective see Blumer (1969).
2. This meant that there was a condition of mutuality for the protection of minorities in the two countries. Many people, adopting a defensive attitude when asked about the rights of the Muslim minority in Greece, attempt to compare Greece's record with the records of the neighbouring country. The argument they use is that the Greek minority in Turkey is now only 2,500 people compared with the 100,000 following the signing of the Lausanne Treaty.
3. As I explained above, the Treaty of Lausanne established the position of the minority in Thrace as well as the Greek minority in Turkey, which still today Greece and Turkey continue to invoke against each other.
4. The majority of studies on the issue of the Muslim minority in Greece have drawn their conclusions and examples from a comparison between the cases of Thrace and Cyprus. See for example Haralabides (1994: 25–35) on 'learning our lesson' and taking examples from what happened in Cyprus.
5. In many respects the national consciousness was constructed against the Ottoman 'infidels'. Notions of the Μεγαλη Ιδεα (Great Idea) of a unified Greece prevailed during the war of independence and helped in the formation of the nationalist agenda. Greek irredentism aimed at 'nation building' which would include all the lands under Ottoman occupation that were once part of the Hellenic world. Clogg very correctly states that the significance of the fall of 'The City' (Konstantinopole) to the Ottoman Turks was more symbolic than real for the Greek world. For more details see Clogg (1992: 16–42) and Herzfeld (1982: 53–74). Also, see Herzfeld (1995: 218–33) for an acute analysis of the way the Greek modern identity has been constructed on a frame of a 'cultural cleansing' from whatever elements are identified as Oriental, and therefore of Turkish origin.

6. For a discussion on the specificities of Greek national identity and its relation to minorities in Greece see Pollis (1987 and 1992) and Jusdanis (1987).
7. See for example, Helsinki Watch Report, 1990, *Destroying Ethnic Identity: The Turks of Greece*, pp. 31–32; also see pp. 11–29 for Greek violations of the human rights of the minority. See also Minority Rights Group, 1989, *Minorities in the Balkans*, Report no. 82, p.33.
8. According to Hidiroglou (1991), one of these customs is the crossing of the bread before they cut it. Also see Milonas (1990).
9. On the different views on the Pomaks' origin see Seyppel (1989).
10. Magkrioti (1980–1981) tries to prove the 'racial' descent of Pomaks from the Alexander the Great by pointing out that they show the same deep sockets of the eye as in pictures of Alexander and other Macedonians.
11. This is the view supported by Soltaridis (1990) and some other academic scholars in Greece, who choose to promote a certain picture in accordance with the country's nationalist ideals. However, it is quite interesting – and certainly not accidental – that some of the above scholars themselves come from the Greek minority of Istanbul who suffered from Turkish persecution. Nevertheless, there are also academics who follow a more neutral or unbiased line, like Divani (1995) Karakasidou (1993) and others.
12. See Dimitras's comment on Greece's attitude towards her minorities: 'In Greece there is only one minority group, the Muslims. Their standards of living constitute a model for other countries to follow'. This is a synopsis of the official political attitude of the Greek State towards its minorities. Variations of the same view are adopted not only by most of the political parties in the country but also from academics who are supposed to be more sensitive on the issue' (Dimitras 1991). Dimitras argues that although the conditions of the Thracian Muslims in Greece are by far better than those of other minorities in Europe or the Greek minority in Istanbul, still they do not represent the ideal.
13. See Schuetz's (1944) comments on the concept of anonymity in his essay, *The Stranger*.
14. Antonis Liapis (1994) and Polis Milonas (1990) have pointed out in their studies on the Pomaks that many of their informants complained of having been ridiculed by the Turks, for using their language (i.e. Pomak) in public places.
15. I have analysed elsewhere (Evergeti 1999) my changing status during the fieldwork and the way it informed the various stages of the ethnography.

# REFERENCES

Barth, F. ed. 1970. *Ethnic Groups and Boundaries: The Social Organisation of Culture Difference*. London, George Allen and Unwin.
Blumer, H. 1958. 'Race prejudice as a sense of group positioning'. *Pacific Sociological Review* 1, no. 1: 3–7.
Blumer, H. 1969. *Symbolic Interactionism: Perspective and Method*. Berkeley, University of California Press.
Clogg, R. 1992. *A Concise History of Greece*. Cambridge, Cambridge University Press.
Dimitras, P.E. 1991. 'Minorities: An asset or liability in Greece?' *CEA* 4.
Divani, L. 1995. *Ελλαδα και Μειονοτητες* (Greece and Minorities). Athens, Nefeli.
Eidheim, H. 1970. 'When ethnic identity is a social stigma'. In *Ethnic Groups and Boundaries: The Social Organisation of Culture Difference*, ed. F. Barth. London, Allen and Unwin.
Evergeti, V. 1999. Negotiations of Identity: The Case of a Muslim Minority Village in Greece. Unpublished Ph.D. dissertation, University of Manchester.

Goffman, E. 1972. 'The neglected situation'. In *Language and Social Context*, ed. P.P. Giglioli. Harmondsworth, Penguin.
Goffman, E. 1990. *The Presentation of Self in Everyday Life*. Harmondsworth, Penguin.
Goffman, E. 1990. *Stigma*. Harmondsworth, Penguin.
Gold, R. 1997. 'The ethnographic method in sociology'. *Qualitative Inquiry* 3, no. 4: 388–402.
Hall, S. 1991. 'The local and the global: Globalization and ethnicity'. In *Culture, Globalization and the World-System: Contemporary Conditions for the Representation of Identity*, ed. A. King. London, Macmillan.
Haralabidis, M. 1994. *Εθνικα Ζητηματα* (*National Issues*). Athens, Gordios.
Herzfeld, M. 1982. *Ours Once More: Folklore, Ideology, and the Making of Modern Greece*. Austin, University of Texas Press.
Herzfeld, M. 1995. 'Hellenism and Occidentalism: The permutations of performance in Greek bourgeois identity'. In *Occidentalism: Images of the West*, ed. J.G. Carrier. Oxford, Clarendon Press.
Hidiroglou, P. 1991. *The Greek Pomaks and their Relation with Turkey*. Athens, Proskinio.
Jusdanis, G. 1987. 'East is East-West is West: It's a matter of Greek literary history'. *Journal of Modern Greek Studies* 5, no. 1: 1–14.
Kanakidou, E. 1994. *Η Εκπαιδευση στη Γλωσσικη Μειονοτητα της Δυτικης Θρακης* (*Education in the Linguistic Minority of Western Thrace*). Athens, Ellinika Gramata.
Karakasidou, A. 1993. 'Politicizing culture: Negating ethnic identity in Greek Macedonia'. *Journal of Modern Greek Studies* 11, no. 1: 1–28.
Kostopoulos, D. 1993. *Βαλκανια: Η Οικογεωγραφια της Οργης* (*Balkans: the Oiko-Geography of Rage*). Athens, Stohastis.
Liapis, A. 1994. *Η Υποθηκευμενη Γλωσσικη Ιδιαιτεροτητα των Πομακων* (*The Linguistic Specificity of Pomaks*). Komotini, Thrakiki Eteria.
Macdonald, S. ed. 1993. *Inside European Identities*. Oxford, Berg.
Magkrioti, G.D. 1980–1981. '*Πομακοι η Ροδοπιοι*' (Pomaks or Rhodopians?). Thrakika 3: 42–64.
Milonas, P. 1990. *Οι Πομακοι της Θρακης* (*The Pomaks of Thrace*). Athens, Nea Synora.
Papathanasi Mousiopoulou, K. 1992–1994. '*Οι Διαθεσεις των Πομακων της Δυτικης Θρακης*: 1918–1923' (The Orientations of the Pomaks of Western Thrace: 1918–1923). Thrakiki Epetirida 9.
Pollis, A. 1987. 'Notes on nationalism and human rights in Greece'. *Journal of Modern Hellenism* 4: 147–60.
Pollis, A. 1992. 'Greek National identity: Religious minorities, rights, and European norms'. *Journal of Modern Greek Studies* 10: 171–95.
Poulton, H. 1994. *The Balkans: Minorities and States in Conflict*. London, Minority Rights Publication.
Ryle, G. 1990. *The Concept of Mind*. Harmondsworth, Penguin.
Schuetz, A. 1944. 'The stranger: An essay in social phychology'. *American Journal of Sociology* 49, no. 6: 499–507.
Schwartz, H. and J. Jacobs. 1979. *Qualitative sociology: A Method to the Madness*. New York, Free Press.

Seyppel, T. 1989. 'Pomaks in northeastern Greece: An endangered Balkan population'. *Journal Institute of Muslim Minority Affairs* 10, no. 1: 41–9.

Shibutani, T. 1962. 'Reference groups and social control'. In *Human Behavior and Social Processes*, ed. A.M. Rose. London, Routledge and Kegan Paul.

Soltaridis, S. 1990. *Η Δυτικη Θρακη και οι Μουσουλμανοι (Western Thrace and the Muslims)*. Athens, Nea Synora.

Strauss, A.L., L. Schatzman, D. Ehrlich, R. Bucher and M. Sabshin. 1963. 'The hospital and its negotiated order'. In *The Hospital in Modern Society*, ed. A. Friedson. New York, Free Press.

Watson, G. 1981. 'The reification of ethnicity and its political consequences in the North'. *Canadian Review of Sociology and Anthropology* 18, no. 4: 453–69.

# CHAPTER 11
# NEGOTIATING EUROPEAN AND NATIONAL IDENTITY BOUNDARIES IN A VILLAGE IN NORTHERN GREECE

Eleftheria Deltsou

### The Content and Boundaries of Europe

In the social sciences, studies of processes of identity formation have a long record. The study of European societies has followed this interest and raised questions regarding the content of national identities within Europe and of European identities in general (see Macdonald 1993). In this sense, the creation of the EU has raised issues of identity, thereby challenging both the anthropological analytical categories and the subsequent ability to fully grasp, let alone foresee, the political, economic, national, social and cultural developments in the existing European countries (see Goddard *et al.* 1994). In these discussions one primary theoretical and methodological riddle concerns the concept of Europe itself. Issues such as where the boundaries of Europe lie, what Europe stands for, and who decides on the boundaries or about the meanings of Europe have long been in the forefront of discussions in both academic and non-academic contexts. As Goddard *et al.* state (1994: 25), 'answers to the question of "what is Europe" hinge, in many respects, upon the problematic issues of classification and definition; yet these in turn are not only problems of semantics but of ideology and politics. Indeed, the concept of "Europe" has been used and misused, and interpreted or misinterpreted from so many different perspectives that its meanings appear to be both legion and contradictory'. Thus, what is by now taken for granted is that Europe does not constitute a naturally given category but a construct, the content of which is historically determined on the basis of political, economic, social and cultural factors.

Despite all the contradictory conceptualisations of 'Europe' and its constructed nature, the existence of 'Europe' as an hegemonic, dominant rhetoric should not be overlooked. Maps portray 'Europe', politicians, economists, scholars, people in general talk about 'Europe', continuously giving it undeniable substance. Even the actual analysis of 'Europe' as a rhetoric seems not to be able to avoid employing the term one way or another, not just as folk terminology but on some level as a naturally implied and thus given entity. One level of discussion, therefore, concerns the semantics of Europe as a theoretical/analytical category. Without attributing less importance to the ideological, therefore political, implications of academic discourses – to the fact that theories are social acts and that the words of academia are directly or indirectly intertwined with all other discourses, what is currently at the forefront is the analysis of non-academic uses of the concept of 'Europe' and the accompanying binary dichotomies such as East vs West etc., all of them negotiable in terms of their content. As particularly ethnographic explorations of the content of these categories have shown, 'Europe', 'the East', 'the West', 'the Mediterranean' constitute entities, the boundaries of which are formed in relation to conceptions and practices of powerful groups (see Said 1978; Herzfeld 1984 and 1987; Gilmore 1987; Carrier 1992). As systems of signification, these terms constitute shifters, the positive or negative value of which depends on the context. At the same time, as is true for other theoretical dichotomies, they also present and presume the existence of discontinuities between the West and the East, Europe and non-Europe, the Mediterranean versus Europe, etc., hiding, in fact, the existence of relationships of dependence (see Gupta and Ferguson 1992; Deltsou 1995).

## The Construction of Greek Identity as Part of, or in Opposition to a European Identity

One quite well explored example in reference to the significance of Europe and the meaning it carries in relation to the ambiguities of a national identity is that of Greece (see, for example, Danforth 1984). Particularly, the work of Herzfeld (1982, 1987, 1992) has shown how the development of a Greek national identity is a case of 'disemia', as it is caught between a Romeic and a classicist Hellenic identity, between the East and the West, between the Greek perception and/or experience of political marginality as the pariah of the European Union and of historical centrality as Europe's spiritual ancestor (Herzfeld 1997: 18, 92). In this context Greek identity took the form of '*proghonopliksia* (an obsession with the ancestors), ... a symptom,' as Herzfeld asserts, 'of a deeply wounding sense of social, cultural, economic and political dependency' (1997: 105–6) that the Greek State experienced in the past and is still led by either through reality or fear.

The continuing existence of the ambiguities of Greek identity and of the corresponding meanings of Europe are vividly illustrated in the conflict between the Greek Orthodox Church and the Greek Government over the issue of omitting religion from the new State identity cards that broke out in 2000 and still remains unsolved. Leaving aside the reasons for the Archbishop's reaction to the Governmental plans, it is important in itself to notice the kind of rhetoric the Archbishop used in order to mobilise the crowds in his support. One of his arguments was that the EU and globalisation processes in general pose a threat to Greek identity, a threat of cultural – and thus also of or equating to religious – elimination. In the Archbishop's rhetoric, Europe clearly stands in a relation of opposition to Greece. On the other hand, the policies and discourse of the Government appear to support the 'Europeanisation' of Greece. This, of course, implies in the first place that Greece was not yet seen by its own functionaries to be 'European' and that according to their perceptions there are certain characteristics other than geography that make someone 'European'. In the context of the same debate, the Prime Minister himself publicly announced that Greece was European, clarifying that there was no either/or dilemma, being Greek excluding being European and vice versa. In a Greek newspaper a cartoonist commented on the issue by presenting an ID card, where Greek was the first name and European the last name, indicating the Government's view of the segmentary complementarity and not of opposition between the two identities.

The discourses of the State and the Church reveal the ideologies and attitudes of these formal institutions. They do not cover, however, the spectrum of the actual everyday identity experience of social actors. The context in which people realise their identities as Greek and/or European is of course that of multicultural interaction. Particularly in countries like Greece, where the majority of the population has to a large degree successfully developed a Greek national identity, it is interesting to see how the nation-state ideology becomes embodied and practised in conditions of multicultural interaction.

In Greece, immigration provides a multicultural experience. While for most of its history Greece was a provider of economic migrants to other countries, recently it has become a host country to legal as well as illegal economic migrants, the majority of whom come from the former socialist countries. This new experience of multicultural interaction together with the former experience of Greeks vis-à-vis the 'Western Europeans' has put the Greek national identity to the test. As will become obvious, depending on the occasion Greek identity may subsume itself under a European identity or it may exclude or differentiate itself from it.

In the first place, the boundaries of a European, a Western, a Greek identity etc. are not permanent, but negotiable and permeable. This permeability of identity is true as an overall theoretical statement about the construction of identities in general. A social actor as a self actively chooses from a number of identities, all of which are socially constructed and historically determined. These processes of identity formation should not be seen only as constructions of collectivities, but also as parallel perceptions of the 'self' (see Sokefeld 1999). On each occasion that an interaction of identity formation may be taking place, different ethnic groups may try to accentuate their social boundaries by presenting their cultures as deeply incompatible, but they may also establish themselves in conflict because they may have claims to the same identities and the similarities are thus perceived as threatening (Harrison 1999: 239). The aim of this chapter is to show that whatever the context within which identities are being formed and expressed, on different occasions the particular choice of a specific identity may exhibit ambiguity, flexibility or rigidity of boundaries. However, while the option seems to be pretty open, when performances of identity construction take place on occasions in which the superiority of the constructed group is believed to be at stake and the boundaries are drawn to secure distinction, then the boundaries are constructed as rigid and impermeable.

## An Ethnographic Example from Northern Greece

The question of the ambiguity, flexibility or rigidity of identity formation and selection will be explored through an ethnographic example from a northern Greek coastal village, where the national self comes in face-to-face contact with the 'other' and other identities. The contexts for these contacts are provided by tourism and immigration. The identity performances that take place in the village construct different types of national identities: a Greek national identity as a not truly 'European' one and a 'European' identity in juxtaposition to an 'Eastern' identity which, even though it refers to eastern Europe, it is not considered a 'European' one.

In the village the following groups of people can be schematised as agents of interaction. First, people who directly or indirectly have local origin, either through kinship or marriage. Virilocality – the long established, predominant practice of post-marital residence in the village, described in the local discourse as a practice of giving and taking brides – provides the village with new members (mostly but not exclusively women), who are liminally and contextually considered to be members of the community. While marriage does not secure unquestioned membership of the community, origin from the village through kinship does, even in the cases of people who do not reside permanently in the village. Thus people who, for example, live and work in the city of Thessaloniki (about one hundred kilometres away), but may go to their village during the weekend are considered full members of the community and their right to participate in local affairs is not questioned. The second group is the owners of summer houses, either in the old part of the village or in the wider area, a number of whom may go to the village not only during the summer, but almost every weekend throughout the year. Some of these people – and particularly some owners of old houses in the old part of the village – have somehow developed closer relationships with villagers than others, but still none of them is considered a member of the community. Visiting tourists also constitute an obvious group in the summer life of the village, but their transient presence naturally precludes any consideration of community membership. Finally, the migrants, who are long-term if not permanent residents of the village, are also excluded from community membership, even though after a number of years the steady everyday interactions and working relationships that have been developed give them a space of existence within the community, but not membership of the community.

As has become apparent, of all these people only those who relate to the village through a connection of local origin are considered to be real members of the community. In order to discuss how boundaries between the groups are drawn and how the respective identities are constructed, it might be useful to differentiate between practices that aim *primarily* at exclusion and practices that aim principally at the construction of the self. Even though in both cases the outcome is the same, that is, boundaries are drawn and selves are constructed, the agents' emphasis on one of the two leads to a different identity perception by the involved parts. Through a number of practices the community draws clear boundaries around its members, in order to exclude first of all the visiting tourists in absolute terms and second but in less absolute terms the summer-house owners, most of whom in any case live in the village periodically. Those, however, who dramatically experience exclusion from the community are the migrants who are permanent residents of the village. Their exclusion from the community constitutes not only a denial of community identity, but it highlights a different national identity for them. This aspect would not be so important if a significant number of these migrants did not consider themselves and were not officially registered as Greek. As we will see, in the current context of community building the formation of a village identity has incorporated the exclusion of the migrants in it. The ethnic/national[1] identity performances that construct in the village the collective identity of the locals and the sense of community aim at the demarcation of the cultural boundaries that exclude the migrants of the village from membership not only of the community but of the wider national group.

In the village, locals draw boundaries first of all by establishing an exclusive sense of the community. Of course the establishment of a particular community identity is not a practice designed principally toward exclusion of the migrants. Processes of community-building have been present throughout the history of the village and well before the arrival of the immigrants. Locals in the past seemed to strongly demarcate themselves from other neighbouring communities on the basis of assumed collective positive but also negative characteristics. Thus, for example, in the 1970s and the 1980s, locals would emphasise the high number of university students and graduates the village had in comparison to other villages[2] and the fact that most of these 'educated' people used to identify proudly with their village. At the same time villagers used to distinguish themselves (and often still do) from the inhabitants of villages of Asia Minor-refugee origin who exist in the area, on the basis of the 'openness' and 'progress' that Asia Minor refugees have exhibited in their lives. In the process of forming an exclusive village identity the 'development' of the community and the projection of the public image of the village through community performances on a national or even international scale are of major importance. Such an occasion is the the annual swimming competition of the crossing of the Toroneos gulf, which has been organised by the village cultural association and the community for nearly thirty years. The gradual increase in significance of the event over the years is directly associated with the community's public identity, which builds its symbolic manifestation through the presence in the village of the mass Media – and of the village in the mass Media – and of politicians and other public figures, who are invited to participate in the events that accompany the actual competition.

On the other hand, other community projects and developmental plans also aim at the promotion and progress of the village in terms which are not local but national. All the discourse that accompanies the 'village' as a community is directly related to a sense of the national self. This becomes particularly obvious with tourism. Dominant perceptions of development (see Deltsou 2001) target the image that tourists have of the village, revealing that the local/national sense of the self has an imagined outsider, a tourist, as its point of reference. The issue that arises concerns the identity of tourists. In the village the term 'tourist' refers exclusively to non-Greeks. During the first years of tourism, in the mid-1970s and more or less throughout the 1980s, in the village the term 'tourist' was synonymous with that of western European and specifically included Germans and Austrians, fewer Italians, even fewer French and rarely any others from other western European countries. Back then, the term 'western European' or even plain 'European' reflected the political division of Europe between an Eastern and a Western part that was the outcome of the Cold War. In the early 1990s, though, the tourist situation in the village changed, following the political changes in the former socialist countries and so the village started receiving tourists not only from other western European countries but from the former socialist countries, mostly from the former USSR. Since then the use of the term 'tourist' in the village requires further clarification, which is accomplished by distinguishing between *Evropeous* and *Anatolikous* (Europeans and Easterners).

Obviously in this case as well, 'Europe' does not contain in its boundaries any central or eastern European countries, all of which are seen by locals as uniform in one sense: that they experienced a different political and economic regime from that of the 'West',[3] that is, of 'Europe'. This is not, however, just a matter of conceptualisation. Even though systems of ideas are practices in themselves, particular ideas about 'Europe' and 'Easterners' materialise in other practices as well. In the village the attitudes of most businessmen involved with tourism differ significantly toward 'Easterner' tourists from those toward the 'Europeans'. Despite the fact that, as local professionals admitted, 'Eastern Europe' constitutes the new promising market, still they do not want 'Eastern' tourists in the same way they want the 'Europeans'.

The explanation for this preference of the 'Europeans' over the 'Easterners' also clarifies the content of 'Europe', which is set on the basis of the political and economic principles their past and present represent. The current conditions of economic devastation and political and economic corruption in the former socialist countries are attributed to having missed, during all these years, the 'train of capitalism'. As an outcome of different historical experiences, the behaviour of 'Eastern tourists' is juxtaposed with that of 'Europeans'. The 'proper' tourist behaviour of 'Europeans' is seen as outcome of an embodied practical consciousness that derives from the political and economic system in which they have been raised, namely capitalism and Western democracy. 'Easterners', on the other hand, are seen to have a certain 'impertinence' as, according to some businessmen, they demand luxuries and services that their tourist packages do not pay for. This impertinence is also respectively explained as the embodied practical consciousness that was the outcome of communism both as a political and an economic system.

This, however, is just one side of the story. The other side concerns 'European' tourism, before which locals feel 'wanting'. In comparison to them locals experience the ambiguity of the Greek national self: they are rightful members of Europe, while at the same they are not. Europe – the place where Greeks belong to because they are its spiritual ancestors – is perceived as civilised, a place of high culture (Herzfeld 1997). Greece, on the other hand, exhibits signs of lack of 'civilisation', which make Greece into Europe's 'Other'. Interestingly enough, as Greeks accept the standards of 'civilisation' that are represented by 'Europe', they also accept the hegemonic part of the relationship and they thus 'otherise' themselves. As becomes obvious, even though the 'other' is usually defined by the dominant 'Western' self, here the group 'Otherises' itself, as it uses the points of view and criteria of the 'Western' self in order to measure its own spatial, temporal and therefore social distance from it.

Regardless of how strongly 'European tourism' is desired, Greece is perceived to be somehow ill-suited for the 'Europeans'. A local businessman said, 'Europeans cannot stand the garbage, the dirt, the bad services at the customs offices, the delays'. In agreement with what Herzfeld (1997: 103) asserts that 'Greeks... look to more powerful countries for approbation and this is the source of their deep preoccupation with issues of cultural intimacy' – the businessman's statement reveals the dirty laundry that Greece should try either to hide or to change. This perspective 'otherises' the national self, the national identity, by applying a rhetoric similar in its principles to that applied to 'otherised' outsiders. This 'otherisation' of the national 'us' is an expression of cultural intimacy, a national identity that constitutes a source of external embarrassment, while it simultaneously turns these people into a nation (Herzfeld 1997). All, however, that constitutes the Greek cultural intimacy and that needs to be changed or hidden does not target the Greeks themselves, but the 'Europeans' who will come and see. This concern with the public image of the Greek culture seems related to what has been testified about family life by the first anthropologists who worked on Greece: that family members fought hard to control the image of the family to outsiders (see Friedl 1962; Skouteri-Didaskalou 1984). After all, it is a well known Greek threat that one might reveal someone else's dirty laundry ('vgálane ta aplita sti fóra').

Towards immigrants, however, the expressed Greek national identity in the village not only does not present, but does not seem to have any dirty laundry. In the village, locals use two categories to distinguish between immigrants: Albanians[4] and Russian-Pontics.[5] Of the two groups, Russian-Pontics provide the best example to illustrate how locals become 'Europeans' when before them. The particular process of identity difference and thence identity formation is all the more important, because the people who are supposed to be truly Russian-Pontics are of Greek origin. Back in the late 1980s and in the 1990s, when the former Soviet Union was dissolving into its constituent parts with all the difficulties and dangers this process entailed for its residents, this ethnic/national identity gave the Greek-Pontic populations the right to come 'back' to the 'mother country'. One of the major issues, however, which has caused not only a theoretical problem as to whether this constitutes a repatriating group, a group of refugees or one of economic immigrants (see Voutira 1991), but also problems of perception and acceptance by the local populations, derives exactly from the fact that the people who came to be called Russian-Pontics had never set foot on mainland Greece before.

Despite the originally intended meaning of the term Russian-Pontic as a Pontic who came from the former Soviet Union, in practice the term has acquired in the village a generic meaning, covering all immigrants, except for Albanians.[6] Even though the term presumably alludes to the ethnic/national origin of the people, in fact it is a socio-economic term that describes their status as economic migrants from any eastern European country, practically irrespective of the specific ethnicity/nationality that they have. Thus in discussions amongst locals about chores that need to be done the expression 'Get a Russian-Pontic to do it for you!' clarifies the socio-economic group one should employ, while the need for a decision as to whom in specific to hire often brings in the discussion the particular ethnic/national or regional origin of the individuals.

The main characteristic of the Russian-Pontic Eastern identity, which is defined in opposition to a European identity, is defined in the context of work. Locals consider Russian-Pontics to be 'lazy'. As a local man said, 'Unless someone tells them specifically what to do, they sit there all day long, doing nothing.' The explanation for this attitude relied on the basis of the existence of an-other source of dirty laundry: that of the political and economic system Russian-Pontics lived in. 'In the socialist system where Easterners lived, people needed supervision in order to do their work,' the local man said.

> When you live and work in a country of the Eastern bloc, whether you do your work or not, you'll have to eat, you'll have your place to go. And in order to do what you have to do, you'll have a supervisor over your head. And if you get to slip away, it will be your accomplishment. Because in either case, you'll eat the same; no matter whether you work or not. Here it's different.

The excuse is clearly the rationale of a true capitalist: the economic system where Russian-Pontics lived in failed, because it was not free and competitive enough to encourage personal involvement and initiative. Thus in the face of a presumed practical consciousness that locals assume derives from a failed economic system, they become not just the conveyors but the representatives of the capitalist economics that are associated with 'Europe' and the West.

The term Russian-Pontics, on the other hand, particularly for the ones who are truly ethnic Greeks, initially meant nothing. The term was coined for them when they came to Greece, drawing for most Greeks a dividing line between 'true Greeks' and those others who present themselves as 'somehow Greeks'. In a number of cases some locals denied Russian Pontics the Greekness of their origin, saying: 'If they are Greeks, then what are we?' Such statements are emblematic of the nationalist ideology in Greece that in the first place does not see any difference between the national and the ethnic and second assumes the existence of cultural homogeneity.[7] Despite the fact that the homogenisation of Greek culture by the State was neither uniform nor fully effective (Leontis 1995, Tziovas 1994) because the strive toward cultural homogeneity was deemed necessary in order to prove Greece's right to nation-state sovereignty, the dominant rhetoric emphasised and taught the existence of cultural homogeneity.

On the basis of the above ideology, the contemporary experience of multicultural interactions has set locals' belief in cultural homogeneity to the test. To them, people who behave in ways that are foreign to them cannot be Greeks. In these instances one of the idioms that locals used to separate Russian-Pontics from the larger national group was that of anti-Turkishness. Some locals by associating the unknown (to them) cultural practices of the Russian-Pontics with the most dominant idiom of exclusion, that of Islam and Turkey, characterised them as 'Turks' and prohibited them from any attempt toward incorporation.[8]

The anti-Turkish idiom partly originates from the fact that for locals, certain practices of the Russian-Pontics are not recognisably Christian in comparison to their own practices. Much like state-nationalists and certain social theorists who see distinct language and cultural practices as markers of distinct ethnic groups, locals identify cultural differences with ethnic, hence, national differences and boundaries. They thus figure those unrecognisable practices to be Muslim and contemplate that Russian-Pontics must be 'Turks'. The identification, however, is achieved by reversing an already existing symbolic identification, namely that of Turkishness with Islam. Cowan (1997: 157) mentions that in the pre-national period in Sohos, the term 'Tourki' (Turks) had a 'religious rather than a national connotation'. The villagers, by simply turning Islam from a signified of Turkishness into a signifier of Turkishness, associated on a discursive level the unrecognisable practices of Russian-Pontics with Islam. The fact, therefore, that the perceived difference between the mainland Greeks and the ethnically Greek Russian-Pontics is seen to be ethnic/national in nature, actually shows that the villagers in this occasion have been good students of the teachings of a Greek nationalism of homogeneity: since Russian-Pontics exhibit cultural differences, then they are not Greeks.

## Conclusion

Russian-Pontics do not let local views about their presumed ethnic/national characteristics and the also presumed superiority of the mainland Greeks go unchallenged. They question the superiority of the locals on the basis of their ideas and behaviour, which for the Russian-Pontics signify uneducated, ignorant individuals. The fact that Russian-Pontics came from a social system that valued mass education highly and provided several of them with the opportunity to get university degrees gives them a sense of superiority over locals, whom they consider if not literally then practically uneducated. Together with this goes their belief that they actually have better manners than locals, something that they do not explain as an issue of belonging to different cultures, but as an issue of being 'cultivated'. The most important element, however, that actually proves to them the uneducated state of the locals is their confused views about the Russian-Pontic identity. A Russian-Pontic said: 'Being a Russian-Pontic is not an ethnicity/nationality. We're Greeks by ethnicity/nationality. Everybody there knew it.' All these elements set for Russian-Pontics new terms in which they attempt to validate their identity and claims to incorporation. As much as they may challenge, however, and reinterpret their position in this village in specific and in Greece in general, in terms of power Russian-Pontics definitely constitute the weak part of the relationship.

What this chapter has tried to show is that the Russian-Pontic identity that is attributed to the economic immigrants is a follow-up to the formation of a Greek identity. The everyday local construction of a Russian-Pontic identity reshapes not just the former geographical/political categories of the West vs the East, but especially the ambiguous position of Greece in this dichotomy. Until recently, Greece was politically, culturally and economically at the margins of Europe, being classified as Mediterranean, southern European or Balkan. Under the new circumstances, Greeks have suddenly found themselves on the other side of the boundary, representing the West, democracy and capitalism vis-à-vis the economic refugees, rigidly excluding all 'Easterners' from incorporation.

When it comes, however, to the ambiguities of Greek identity as not truly 'European', since the content of the Greek dirty laundry is believed to exclude Greece from being 'European', local people perceive the boundaries as permeable and have the option open for the future. A local said 'We're ten, twenty, thirty years behind in comparison to Europe. And, even though we're ahead in comparison to Africa, we still occupy an in-between place.' Some, however, see this period of marginality also as a period of transition toward Europeanisation, which is not just negotiated, but currently – particularly in terms of formal politics – under construction. For them this is reflected in the efforts of the Greek Governments of the last twenty-five years to make Greece 'rightfully' a full member of the EU.

As has become clear, while locals negotiate their ambiguous position and identity with regards to 'Europe', at the same time they construct their European and Greek identity in relation to 'Easterners' and Russian-Pontics as rigid and non-permeable. The whole issue, of course, starts from and relies on the premise of the power of 'Europe'. That's why in the analysis of identity issues that concern 'Europe' one should not forget the question Herzfeld (1997: 105) has asked: 'why – by whose fiat – certain cultural traits must be seen as negative. Whose narrative of progress is called into being by the very mention of Europe?' In this analysis I have tried to show how 'Europe' is the implied centre around which selves, others and 'others' are constructed. I fear, however, that even efforts aiming at the deconstruction of 'Europe' may not manage to undermine its essentialised power.

## Notes

A different version of this chapter appeared in Deltsou (2000).
1. As explained in Deltsou (2000) and will become obvious in this chapter as well, in non-academic Greek the terms 'ethnic' and 'national' are both expressed by the term *ethnikos*, a fact that adds to the complexities in the processes of identity formation. In order to depict the convergence of the two terms in everyday Greek I will systematically put them together as ethnic/national.
2. Villagers compare their accomplishments not to all other villages in the region, but mainly to those of *dopji* (locals). The term *dopji* that in other parts of Greece is used to signify Slavic speaking communities, here refers to (and distinguishes from) the Greek-speaking populations that resided in the region before the arrival of the Asia Minor refugees in 1922.
3. On the construction of the 'West' as a category see Carrier (1992).
4. In the village, the category of 'Albanians' includes Albanians by ethnicity or citizenship. The differentiation refers to the people who are Greek-speakers and reside in the southern part of Albania or, as Greeks call it, the northern part of Ipiros. This is why in Greece they are called *Vorio-Ipirotes*. Even though people tend to be more sympathetic towards them, some view them with suspicion, as after so many years their identity as Greeks has incorporated an Albanian part into it. It is often argued also that assuming the identity of a *Vorio-Ipirotis* constitutes an effective strategy for ethnic Albanians to migrate to Greece.
5. The term 'Russian-Pontic' is a direct translation of the Greek term *Rosopontii*. The use of the term in the text repeats the local usage without any intentions to justify the use of the term.
6. As already mentioned, Albanians constitute a separate category of immigrants in themselves. This separate categorisation is not irrespective of the fact that during its communist era Albania was considered to be politically sui generis.
7. On the issue of the Greek nation as an homogeneous body see Danforth (1995), Karakasidou (1993), Liakos (1997), Tsoukalas (1995).
8. For a more detailed analysis of the process of distantiation and the 'anti-Turkishness' idiom see Deltsou (2000).

## References

Carrier, J. 1992. 'Occidentalism'. *American Ethnologist* 19, no. 2: 195–212.
Cowan, J. 1997. 'Idioms of belonging: Polyglot articulations of local identity in a Greek Macedonian town'. In *Ourselves and Others: The Development of a Greek Macedonian Cultural Identity Since 1912*, eds P. Mackridge and E. Yannakakis. Oxford, Berg.
Danforth, L. 1984. 'The Ideological context of the search for continuities in Greek culture'. *Journal of Modern Greek Studies* 2, no. 1: 53–87.
Danforth, L. 1995. *The Macedonian Conflict*. Princeton, Princeton University Press.
Deltsou, E. 1995. Praxes of Tradition and Modernity in a Village in Northern Greece. Unpublished Ph.D. dissertation, Indiana University.
Deltsou, E. 2000. '"Tourists," "Russian-Pontics", and "Native Greeks": Identity politics in a village in Northern Greece'. *Anthropological Journal on European Cultures* 9, no. 2: 31–52.

Deltsou, E. 2001. 'The rhetoric of "development" as a discourse for the construction of place and politics'. In *Semiotics and Culture, vol. II: Ideology, Science, Art, Architecture*, ed. G. Paschalidis and Å. Hontolidou. Thessaloniki, Paratiritis.

Friedl, E. 1962. *Vasilika: A Village in Modern Greece*. New York, Holt, Rinehart and Winston.

Gilmore, D. 1987. *Honor and Shame and the Unity of the Mediterranean*. Washington DC, American Anthropological Association (special publication) no. 22.

Goddard, V., J. Llobera and C. Shore eds. 1994. *The Anthropology of Europe: Identity and Boundaries in Conflict*. Oxford, Berg.

Gupta, A. and J. Ferguson. 1992. 'Beyond "culture": Space, identity, and the politics of difference'. *Cultural Anthropology* 7, no. 1: 6–23.

Harrison, S. 1999. 'Identity as a scarce resource'. *Social Anthropology* 7, no. 3: 239–51.

Herzfeld, M. 1982. *Ours Once More: Folklore, Ideology, and the Making of Modern Greece*. Austin, University of Texas Press.

Herzfeld, M. 1984. 'The horns of the Mediterraneanist dilemma'. *American Ethnologist* 11, no. 3: 439–54.

Herzfeld, M. 1987. *Anthropology Through the Looking-Glass: Critical Ethnography in the Margins of Europe*. Cambridge, Cambridge University Press.

Herzfeld, M. 1992. *The Social Production of Indifference: Exploring the Symbolic Roots of Western Bureaucracy*. Chicago, University of Chicago Press.

Herzfeld, M. 1997. *Cultural Intimacy: Social Poetics in the Nation-State*. New York, Routledge.

Karakasidou, A. 1993. 'Politicising culture: Negating ethnic identity in Greek Macedonia'. *Journal of Modern Greek Studies* 11, no. 1: 1–28.

Leontis, A. 1995. *Topographies of Hellenism: Mapping the Homeland*. Ithaca, Cornell University Press.

Liakos, A. 1997. *Η προσκόλληση στο Μεγαλέξανδρο* (The Fixation with Alexander the Great). Βήμα, Newspaper (23 January 1997).

Macdonald, S. ed. 1993. *Inside European Identities: Ethnography in Western Europe*. Oxford, Berg.

Said, E. 1978. *Orientalism*. Harmondsworth, Penguin.

Sokefeld, M. 1999. 'Debating self, identity, and culture in anthropology'. *Current Anthropology* 40, no. 4: 417–47.

Skouteri-Didaskalou, N. 1984. 'Τα εν οίκω μη εν δήμω και αντιστρόφως' (Home affairs should not become public and vice versa). In *Ανθρωπολογικά για το Γυναικείο Ζήτημα* (*Anthropological Approaches to Women's Question*), Athens, O Politis.

Tsoukalas, K. 1995. 'Ιστορία, Μύθοι και Χρησμοί: Η Αφήγηση της Ελληνικής Συνέχειας' (History, myths and oracles: The narration of Greek continuity). In *Εθνος Κράτος Εθνικισμός* (*Nation-State-Nationalism*), Athens, ΕΣΝΠΠ.

Tziovas, D. 1994. 'Heteroglossia and the defeat of regionalism in Greece'. *Cambridge Papers in Modern Greek* 2.

Voutira, E. 1991. 'Pontic Greeks today: Migrants or refugees?'. *Journal of Refugee Studies* 4, no. 4: 400–20.

# Chapter 12
# Claiming a 'European Ethos' at the Margins of the Italian Nation-State

Jaro Stacul

### Introduction

This chapter seeks to analyse the meanings attached to the current concept of 'Europe' in northern Italy, as well as put forward some hypotheses about the role of human agency in the interpretation of Europe itself. Ideas of European identity, modernity and culture have become an object of debate as a consequence of the emergence of a new communitarian ideology and of the EU's attempt to create a 'people's Europe'. In his recent book on the construction of Europe, Shore (2000: 26) examines the nature of this 'people's Europe'. He observes that if this, too, is a cultural construct, then the issues surrounding it include how it is being imagined and whose images prevail. Among the multiple images that the current notion of 'Europe' is meant to conjure up in popular imagination, that of the removal of barriers, leading to freedom of movement, is one of the most powerful. Removing boundaries and enabling people to move across Europe is one of the conditions for the construction of a supra-national European identity and 'culture', and a European model of society (Bellier and Wilson 2000: 3).

In countries that have just joined the EU or are candidates for EU membership, European identity and 'culture' are also believed to be tantamount to a common, European ethos associated with modernity and bureaucratic efficiency (Mitchell 2002: 155). Apart from modernity, it has been observed that the content of the idea of European identity remains largely vague and, as a political programme, it is contested and rife with contradictions (Shore 2000; Stråth 2000: 13–14). The same holds true for the notion of a 'European culture': the idea of a common European cultural heritage, besides being associated with unity and cohesion, may promote new forms of cultural chauvinism (see Holmes 2000). Likewise the promotion of a 'European culture' through the creation of exclusive European Schools has the effect of strengthening class boundaries (Shore and Baratieri, this volume).

Europe as a set of institutional discourses manifests itself in different ways. Perhaps the most intriguing aspect underlying the definition of the new Europe is that while ideas of modernity, efficiency and rational management inform a social democratic discourse in the area of economic and social policy, they are also present in a neo-liberal agenda (Delanty 2000: 224). The dichotomy between these different discourses raises various issues. More importantly, it opens up the question of the meanings that this notion of Europe conjures up to the people who are now part of a Europe without barriers, and points to the role of social actors as interpretants: Cohen (1996: 805) made a similar point in relation to Scottish nationalism, and noted that individuals are not passive recipients of political messages, but they appropriate them for their own requirements. The same applies to the new Europe: Europe may have clear meanings within the institutional boundaries of the EU, but for those who do not participate actively in political life or seldom travel, Europe may instead be conceptualised (and appropriated) by means of their cultural categories or through the lens of the 'local'. Despite the considerable amount of literature on constructions of Europe by the elites, politicians, party spokesmen etc., very little anthropological thought has been devoted to an analysis of Europe as it is conceptualised and understood by social actors, and a consideration of the role of human agency is largely missing.

The other related issue raised by the current concept of Europe is the contradictory nature of the idea of European identity it conveys. Claiming a European, supra-national identity entails crossing a boundary (in the metaphorical sense) and acknowledging the existence of a collective identity. Yet the new politics of Europeanisation is also exhibited in neo-liberal technocratic ideologies (Delanty 1995: 8): at a time of removal of boundaries people are caught between a vision of Europe that conjures up ideas of cohesion and solidarity, and the neo-liberal ideas of modernity, efficiency and competition around which the notion of Europe, as a technocratic regulatory State, revolves. But the current issue that European identity raises is that solidarity has become the victim of neo-liberal theory and practice (Bauman 1999: 30). How can these two coexist, in the minds of the people, at a time when the idea of collective identity is being deconstructed? How do social actors come to terms (and cope) with the tension between the ideas on which the new Europe is built? To this issue I turn first.

## Coping with Europe

Among the countries that have been affected by the advancement of Europe as a regulatory State, Italy represents an interesting case. Until the early 1990s the Italian State used to play an important part in imposing an organising principle on society and the economy. In the early 1990s, by contrast, the economic crisis, the corruption scandals that led to the demise of the governing Christian Democratic Party (DC), the division of the Italian Communist Party into two parties and the subsequent transformation of the Italian party system, resulted in a new political landscape. These transformations, along with the competitive pressures the EU (most notably the Maastricht Treaty of 1992) and globalisation placed upon the Italian economy, had the effect of questioning the legitimacy of state centralism (Diamanti 1999): they were accompanied by several privatisation initiatives taking place all over the country and brought to the fore the dichotomy between the rich north and the poor south.

It is against this background that Italy saw the growth of new political parties that quickly adjusted to the demands of a society disillusioned with politics. Among these parties the *Lega Nord* (Northern League) was the most successful. When it came to the fore, in the early 1990s, it contested the idea of national identity and the legitimacy of a nation-state seen as corrupt (see e.g. Diamanti 1996; Giordano 2000) and even succeeded in capturing the vote of many former supporters of left-wing parties (Cento Bull 2000: 18). It had on its agenda the transformation of Italy into a federal State and, for some time, even the territorial division of the north from the south of the country. Its leader, Umberto Bossi, championed the idea of northern Italy as partaking of a 'European culture' because of northerners' supposed efficiency and attitude to hard work, as opposed to a 'Mediterranean' one of a putative slack and state-subsidised south (Cento Bull 1996: 177; Giordano 2000: 458–64), which was earmarked as the main cause of Italy's economic crisis. This 'European culture' was expressed by a work ethic consisting of entrepreneurship, a spirit of sacrifice and a high propensity to saving (Cento Bull 1996: 177) and was imbued with Thatcherism.[1] In scapegoating the south, the Northern League attempted to convey the conviction that Italy's place in Europe was undermined by corrupt politicians, resulting in the country's possible exclusion from European markets (Allum and Diamanti 1996: 153).[2] The definition of northern Italian identity in opposition to the south seems to echo the construction of national identities in the context of nineteenth century nationalisms, because with the definition of national (and regional) units came the definition of what the nation (or region) is not (McDonald 1993: 226).

The advent of the Northern League gave to northern Italian identity a political dimension by essentialising the idea of northern Italy participating in a 'European culture'. The idea of Europe advocated by the Northern League was not that of a geographical entity made up of nations, but of a cultural one divided into regions. According to the Northern League's spokespersons, 'northern Italian culture' was not only threatened by the presence and influx of southerners in the north, but also by the waves of immigration from non-European countries, and so its preservation was deemed necessary. Despite its racist overtones, this emphasis also reflected one of the contradictions in the construction of Europe: free movement within the EU was counterbalanced by the idea of concentrating checks at the Community's external borders, thereby evoking the image of a 'fortress Europe' (Shore 2000: 80). Italy is not the only European country that experienced the advent of parties with such agendas, for others with very similar political programmes were coming to the fore elsewhere in Europe. What unites most of them is a political discourse revolving around the notion of culture (see e.g. Stolcke 1995: 4), that is to say one expressed by a rhetoric predicated on cultural diversity and incommensurability, which reifies differences of cultural heritage. This discourse does not express fidelity to the idea of the nation but draws authority from a wide range of collective practices (Holmes 2000: 13). It expresses a 'redefinition of the notion of culture as a political process of contestation on the power to define key concepts' (Wright 1998: 14) and has been deployed and mobilised to stress (and create) difference. Yet in Italy being European did not only entail stressing distinctiveness between West and East, Christianity and Islam, but also involved contesting the inner 'cultural' boundaries of Europe by casting southerners as the 'other'. But did this notion of 'European culture' have the same meaning for those who chose to identify with these autonomist parties? What is this notion built on outside the centres of EU decision-making and the headquarters of political parties?

## Getting Closer to Europe

In an attempt to illuminate the questions asked at the outset, I will analyse the impact of the current notion of 'Europe' not as an abstract concept, but rather as an idea that can be appropriated and accommodated to local-level discourses. The context in which I have conducted research is the Trentino region in northern Italy, in which autonomist parties achieved considerable appeal in the 1990s. Trentino represents a special case in that it is one of the most affluent regions in Italy thanks to the special autonomous status that it enjoys and to the subsidies it receives from the Italian State. Italian and Italian dialects are the main languages spoken there, but because it was part of the Austro-Hungarian Empire until 1918, Trentino also shares a common history with the neighbouring German-speaking regions.

The rise of regionalist movements in the area cannot be understood unless it is borne in mind that, given the significant degree of autonomy of the province, in most of Trentino the State does not have the same significance that it has in other Italian ordinary regions. In this respect, the limited presence of the State apparatus at the local level has influenced the people's 'sense of place' to a significant extent, as it is the municipality (*comune*) and the province (*provincia*) which loom largest in the lives of most of Trentine people.[3] The overwhelming majority of the public offices are owned by the *provincia* itself, whose logo (an eagle) can be noticed in almost every corner of the provincial territory. Both the economic and political crisis of the 1990s and the advent of autonomist parties had considerable impact in Trentino. They furthered the belief that the economic system Trentino inherited from the Italian State, along with the subsidies granted from the Italian State itself, hindered the economic potential of the province instead of giving it a boost (Turato 1998: 105). This idea, affected by the propaganda of the Northern League, engendered the conviction that Trentino could be better off economically by relying on its own means, and by establishing economic relationships with the regions north of the national border (i.e. with central Europe) instead of with the rest of Italy.

The Trentine-Tyrolean Autonomist Party (PATT) benefited from this situation:[4] it championed the creation of an Autonomous European Region of Tyrol encompassing Trentino itself, South Tyrol and the Austrian region of Tyrol (Alcock 1996: 83; Luverà 1996) and appealed to the idea of 'Europe' to legitimate self-determination. This project necessitated the definition of a regional, local history and 'culture'. One possible horizon on which a regional history could be constructed was that of pre-1918 Trentino, when the province was part of a larger region of Tyrol under the Austro-Hungarian empire (Alcock 1996: 83). In the PATT's rhetoric the political and cultural distinctiveness of Trentino was not predicated upon the existence of a putative authentic Trentine culture, but on common culture and unbroken history with the neighbouring German-speaking regions, even though German is not spoken in Trentino. Thus, central to the rhetoric of the PATT (and of the Northern League too) was the prominence given to regions as constituent parts of the new 'Europe' in which national boundaries have less significance: claiming Trentino's place in Europe involved looking beyond national frontiers just as it meant hardening the boundary with the Italian provinces to the south.

The Vanoi valley, an Alpine community at the eastern edge of Trentino, is a context in which the meanings of 'Europe' became an object of debate because of the transformations just discussed. The valley, like most of Trentino, used to be a stronghold of the Christian Democratic Party (DC), the party that could exercise its power through its networks and the capillary infrastructure of the Catholic Church. The Italian Communist Party (PCI) was the DC's major antagonist, but apart from a couple of occasions in the 1970s it never posed a serious threat to its supremacy in the valley. The inhab-

Figure 12.1   Tyrol: Pathway to Europe. (Photo: Jaro Stacul).

itants of the area may be described as post-peasants, as until the 1960s they lived by a combination of agriculture, forestry and animal husbandry. They negotiated the intrigues of industrial wage work, peasant farming, the bureaucratic apparatus of the Italian State, as well as the material (and symbolic) allures of consumerism and globalisation. Most of them engaged in migration across central and northern Europe in search of employment and eventually came back to the valley. They are full participants in the Italian body politic: they vote in national elections, they read the national and regional press, they watch television and, in 2001, various people in the valley had access to the Internet at home. Despite their long-standing commitment to wage-earning outside agro-pastoral activities, they never developed a working-class consciousness and they still call themselves 'peasants' (*contadini*). With the demise of agro-pastoral economy in the 1960s, the population of the valley dwindled. The falling price of timber in the 1990s placed a heavy strain on the local economy, and now only the subsidies of the regional government keep people on the land. The present-day population (scarcely 1,700 inhabitants) includes for the most part retired agriculturalists (mainly women) and lumberjacks (men) who earn a pension from the State, and people who work in various kinds of manual trades. They have direct control over land, even though a substantial part of it has been alienated to the city dwellers who come to the valley to spend summer vacation.

In the 1990s the valley experienced a severe economic crisis. The main activity, forestry, was declining, and the provincial government presented a proposal to shut down the local sawmill on the grounds that it was unprofitable.[5] Because of the very few job opportunities in the valley, most of the able-bodied who resided there sought paid work elsewhere and so spent the working week outside the area. Moreover, the ageing population was growing steadily and after the 1960s the number of births was not enough to replace those who died. The other problem was control over land, for a substantial amount of landed property was being sold to people who were neither ordinarily resident nor related to locals. Although the transfer of landed property to outsiders (largely of the nearby Veneto region) was not a novel phenomenon, it was in the 1990s that it took on unprecedented dimensions. In this respect, the presence of outsiders owning land in the area was viewed as a breach of a symbolic boundary of the community, as it challenged the idea that the village belongs only to those who have kinship ties in the valley. More importantly, it questioned the widely shared view that a landholding should be owned by the same family group and handed down from one generation to the next (Stacul 2003).[6]

When I went to the valley in 1995, the Northern League and the PATT were achieving considerable appeal. That period found the people of the valley caught between disillusionment with national politics and the bureaucratic system of the Italian State, and the conviction that becoming part of Europe could bring about the order and efficiency that were seen as lacking at a time of economic and political crisis. Locals were increasingly distrustful of the intentions of the politicians in Rome, were looking to 'Europe' as a sort of ideal model of 'modernity' to be emulated, and welcomed the possibility that the north of the country could have greater autonomy from Rome itself in order to be closer to 'Europe'. The longing for European efficiency was expressed by a desire to get rid of inefficient politicians and by the conviction that what Italy and Trentino needed to be an integral part of Europe was not politicians, but experienced entrepreneurs.

Several people shared the conviction that the subsidies of the Italian State created obstacles to the economic development of the valley. According to some, subsidies engendered an economic behaviour and a 'mentality' (*mentalità*) that were far from entrepreneurial. This conviction represents a cultural explanation of the economic crisis that was very popular in the valley and throughout Italy and is reminiscent of a situation recorded in some eastern European countries after the demise of Socialism (see Heintz 2002: 8–9). The director of the local rural credit institution made this point very clearly when he said that while in the past Trentino did not have an entrepreneurial mentality, 'now that we are in Europe we can no longer rely upon subsidies.' This longing for entrepreneurship did not only apply to the political arena, but also to the practical organisation of life. One woman of the village of Caoria, for instance, complained about the absence of an entrepreneurial ethos in the valley when she noted that the choice of products in the local store was somewhat limited. 'We are in Europe now' she remarked, 'and he (i.e. the shopkeeper) must become competitive.'

The rise of regionalist parties and their stress upon efficiency and entrepreneurship engendered a discussion about the nature of regional and local identity: if Trentino was part of 'Europe' and of a would-be European region, then the idea of an 'Italian culture', on which Trentine identity used to be built, could no longer be taken for granted. This idea made many people believe that, since Trentino was under Austrian sovereignty until 1918, locals used to have the efficiency and work ethic ascribed to the Germanic world, and that these were lost after Trentino's annexation to Italy. This idea was epitomised by the conviction that before the First World War 'things used to work'. Thus, order and efficiency had to be recovered. Many villagers, for example, expressed their yearning for a lost order by describing themselves as belonging to an 'Austrian breed', and postcards portraying the Austro-Hungarian emperor, Franz Josef, or stickers carrying the emblem of the Dual Monarchy could be noticed in various places in the valley. It must, however, be noted that categories such as 'Italian' and 'Austrian' do not necessarily convey ideas of ethno-linguistic identity, at least at the local level (Stacul 2003: 109–16). The idea of an 'Austrian breed' did not involve a commitment to language learning, given that German has never been spoken in the area: rather, it was associated with a biological model of kinship and with a notion of ancestry. The fact that various people proudly showed me photographs of their ancestors wearing the uniform during military service in the Austro-Hungarian army further suggests that the idea of Austrian identity is also embedded in an idiom of kinship. One man of Caoria, now in his seventies, expressed this view when he proudly told me that his father had attended the state schools of the Austro-Hungarian empire: unlike the Italians living across the national (now regional) border, he could read and write. Education was very important, he said, because 'the more you know, the less likely you are to be given orders by someone else'. Thus, evoking the Austro-Hungarian past did not represent mere nostalgia, but conjured up ideas of modernity, efficiency and autonomy.[7]

## A 'European Ethos'?

As has been noted, the context in which autonomist parties found fertile ground was a community that was undergoing profound changes. However, the impact of the Northern League's construction of northern Italy's 'European culture' and of the PATT's construction of a Trentine identity cannot be accounted for unless we allow for their interpretations at the local level. 'European culture' represented one of the main tenets of the propaganda of these parties, yet in the valley this emphasis had the effect of generating a debate on the nature of local identity, on the 'local character', rather than on the north/south dichotomy. Thus, the question of what distinguished the people of one village from those of another suddenly became one of the favourite topics of debate. Interestingly, in the course of most conversations it emerged that the nature of the 'local character' and 'culture' was not predicated on differences in language or dialect, but on attitudes towards work. In all likelihood this emphasis stems from the fact that in the area studied the capacity to sustain hard work is impressive and highly praised. Even now it is rare to see people sitting on a bench and doing nothing, and in Caoria working hard is a constitutive part of local identity. As a man of Caoria said, '[We] Caorians are uncouth people, but also hard workers.' In the villages of Caoria and Ronco, for example, the idea that locals have always worked hard and have never asked for other people's help to solve a problem looms large in local discourse: it mirrors both a spirit of self-sacrifice and a conceptualisation of work as the means of increasing the stock of one's property under the control of oneself which has been recorded elsewhere in the Alps (Heady 1999: 117). The dichotomy between hard and slack workers also asserts the moral integrity of the community of the past and suggests that not working hard is construed as a source of loss of personal dignity: as a woman of Caoria said, 'If they [the young people] had to work as hard as we did, they would probably die.'

Most of the discussions to which I listened or in which I participated provided opportunities for the people of these villages to contrast their self-reliant character with the putative inability of those of the neighbouring communities (notably the municipal seat of Canal San Bovo) to work hard and solve their problems. As a man of Caoria said, 'You see, they sit on a bench in a square, watching who is coming and who is going, and doing nothing.' Underlying this denigration is also the view that because many of these people work in offices (and do not pursue any manual trades), they should not be considered workers at all. In local discourse clerical workers typify those who are employed by the State (referred to as *statali*): they are usually described as people who 'do not do anything at all' because they rely on a wage earned from the public administration and not on their own means and on hard (i.e. manual) work. Although the denigration of clerical workers has a long history in the valley, it was in that period that it took on a political dimension, for clerical workers were associated with the contested bureaucratic system of the Italian State.

In denigrating State management and bureaucracy, the people of the valley contested the idea of public welfare as a form of collective insurance extended over individual members of the Italian state, hard and slack workers alike. In a sense, the denigration of the Italian State mirrors a conceptualisation of work typical of late modernity, which casts the welfare state as a politically motivated conspiracy against a hard-work ethic (Bauman 1998: 46). Such ideas also echo a model of society based on individualistic ambition and a determination to succeed through hard work (Pahl 1995: 12).

The discredit projected on the Italian State and its agencies and the renewed interest in regional and local 'culture' and identity also fuelled a renewed discussion of local history, especially of widely shared ideas about the area's agro-pastoral past. One of the most frequently debated themes was the hardship that locals had to endure in the past as a result of their living in a mountainous area, and how communities succeeded in making a living in the face of such hardship. As a woman said, 'We used to work as much as we could. [We were] always busy, always, always.' However, I found that a discussion of local history did not simply represent an act of remembering, but meant rereading the past in light of present concerns. In the accounts I solicited of their local past various men and women did not present the image of a united and harmonious community, in which people help each other, that often emerges in anthropological studies of rural villages: what was emphasised was instead a vision of a community inhabited by self-reliant people. When talking about the damage that a flood brought about in 1966, for instance, a woman of Caoria said 'They (her fellow villagers) did not wait for other people's help, they did everything themselves.' This idea of self-reliance is epitomised by the dictum *Aiutati che Dio t'aiuta* ('Rely on your own means, and God will help you'), which would be reminiscent of a 'Protestant' ethic if it were not for the fact that the area is Catholic, at least nominally.[8] Other accounts I heard in Caoria also abound with comparisons between Caoria itself and the municipal seat of Canal San Bovo and centre on Caorians supposed self-reliance as opposed to the putative inability of the people of the other village to rely on their own means and solve their problems.

The construction of a local, Trentine 'European' identity and culture also implied the construction of the 'other', that is to say those who are not 'European' and do not have the same 'culture'. On the one hand the 'other' is typified by the corrupt politician; on the other, it is someone who does not belong to a territorial community, that is to say an outsider. But what is the relationship between the two? Perhaps an analysis of the meanings that the phrase 'eating' conveys can provide a partial answer. There is an interesting parallel, in local discourse, between attitudes towards these various meanings, which revolve to a significant degree around the notion of 'eating'. In the valley, as in most of Italy, this notion is associated with exploitation of resources or illicit appropriation of money. That politicians (notably those formerly affiliated to the DC) are believed to 'eat', stems from the fact that they can avail themselves of substantial amounts of public money which they have the power to use to pursue private goals. They are not looked upon as 'workers', but they are believed to be 'fed' by taxpayers. It is not pure coincidence that in the Vanoi valley the municipal administration is jokingly called the *laip*, a dialectal term referring to a trough which in the past served to feed pigs. In making this association, social actors project onto the local government (the municipality) the characteristics that are deemed typical of the public (i.e. State) administration, those of a domain controlled by people who 'eat' common resources.[9]

To a certain extent, the association of the *laip* with the public administration is reminiscent of the stigma attached to those who do not belong to the 'community'. In settling in a place that is not theirs, outsiders are believed to exploit the host country (or community), which in turn has to 'feed' people who wait for subsidies and neither work nor pay taxes. The same applies, to a certain extent, to those who have bought a house in the valley, on the grounds that they bring everything from their place of origin, they are entitled to receive timber and subsidies from the municipality, but they never go to the local supermarket to purchase foodstuffs. Paradoxically, both politicians and outsiders belong in the same category, for they are believed to 'eat' the resources that do not belong to them. Underlying this view is the idea of autonomous work carried out outside the public administration, which is aimed at satisfying one's own needs and not at 'feeding' others. While this conceptualisation of work represents a stigmatisation of those who 'eat' without working, it also draws a boundary between a 'community' of workers and outsiders along ethnic and cultural lines: it also defines a territorial community sharing some values of neo-liberalism that marginalise those who are not competitive in the labour market.

Given the valley's proximity to the Veneto region, the differences in cultural heritage between Trentino and the nearby region became another topic of discussion, yet they revolved around very similar ideas. Although similar dialects are spoken in both regions, villagers stated that people across the regional border were different, because they had a different 'culture'. The origin of this difference, as one informant claimed, was the different landholding systems: Trentine people have had control over landed property since time immemorial, whereas in the neighbouring region farmers used to work in landholdings owned by someone else. In stating this, locals were giving historical foundation to this sense of autonomy: since they were under Austrian sovereignty they have always had direct control over property, and they have not had to work for absentee landlords. Although this view is largely idealised, it points to the association social actors establish between property and work: it suggests that autonomous work and property convey the same meanings, for they serve to invoke the self-reliant character of locals.

Self-reliance became an object of discussion when the PATT proposed the creation of a European region. Closer contacts with northern regions, in particular, were believed to bring benefits to the local economy: as I noted, one of the problems with which the valley was faced was the fragmentation of landed property and its alienation to outsiders; by contrast, in the neighbouring German-speaking South Tyrol this was not a problem, since an economy based on tourism and agriculture, that is to say a 'local' economy, continued to thrive in spite of the economic crisis (Turato 1998: 88–9). This was due to the existence, in the past, of a system of impartible inheritance that enhanced the development of agriculture as a viable economic activity. The economic gap between Trentino and South Tyrol that the economic crisis brought about had the effect of furthering the conviction that Trentino had to follow the example of South Tyrol and develop a 'local' economy: the introduction of a system of impartible inheritance would have enabled farmers to remain on the land and prevent the alienation and fragmentation of property. In stating this, locals implied that the local economy could be given a boost if landowners were to get rid of the system of inheritance, imposed by the Italian State, which prescribes the division of landholdings into equal parts among heirs. In other words, preventing the fragmentation and alienation of landholdings meant an entrepreneurial ethos, individualism and greater autonomy from the State. Eventually the inheritance system did not change, but the social actors' views about it further suggest that both self-reliance and landed property centre on the same ideas, and define the changing nature of local 'culture' in late modernity: a set of shared ideas revolving around the notions of autonomous work and private property.

Although control over landed property is unlikely to convey ideas of autonomy given the small size of landholdings in the valley (see Zaninelli 1978), it nevertheless enables social actors to cast work as something that cannot be alienated. This conceptualisation of work is epitomised by the often-heard statement 'We are always working, but we do it for ourselves, not for the others'. Work is conceived as autonomous work, a set of activities carried out to achieve and preserve autonomy on the one hand, and to protect one's private domain on the other. At a time when the putative inefficiency of the State's bureaucratic machinery and its employees was pointed to as one of the main causes of the national (and regional) economic crisis, appealing to a hard-work ethic also served to reconcile the past and the present, that is to say the hard work performed in the past in the pursuit of manual trades and the capacity (and willingness) to sustain hard work as a requirement for success in late modernity. On the one hand this attitude reflects a conceptualisation of work in terms of family production and moral community; on the other hand, this ideal does not clash with a conception associated with the wage economy, but is a reconciliation of the two. To put it in Marxist terms, 'real' work is conceived as work alienated from production for large landowners or factory managers, and is associated with the private domain. Clearly, the Northern League's stress upon individualism and the capacity to sustain hard work as distinguishing the north from the south of Italy (and Europe from the Mediterranean) was not altogether new: rather, it replicated a feature of separatist claims. Yet the idea was not superimposed, but was accommodated to local-level discourses, and mobilised themes already existent in 'local culture'.

In the late 1990s the project of the establishment of a European Region, undertaken in 1993, was dropped. The popularity of the Northern League and of the PATT gradually declined, and both their unsuccessful management of the regional government and the advancement, at the national and local level, of Berlusconi's *Forza Italia* dealt them a severe blow. When I went to the valley in 2000, the term *Lega Nord* had virtually disappeared from the political vocabulary. Yet although 'Europe' was no longer deployed as a tool to stress distinctiveness, people's concerns remained the same. The economic situation of the valley was worsening, young people had to look for jobs elsewhere and more and more houses were sold to strangers. Locals still expressed disillusionment at the agendas of politicians and were growing suspicious of the Centre-Left coalition governing the country, which was imposing new taxes.

The eve of the national elections held in May 2001 found the people of the area caught between a longing for 'order', which only autonomist and regionalist parties were believed to provide, and the awareness that their choice was in fact limited to either the Centre-Left or the Centre-Right coalition led respectively by the former mayor of Rome Francesco Rutelli, and by the Milanese media tycoon Silvio Berlusconi. A few days before the elections I heard various discussions about whether it was sensible to vote for Berlusconi, given his failure to separate clearly business and political interests. There was a widely shared feeling that this was not a real issue: if anything, it was believed that Italy needed an entrepreneur to solve its economic problems, particularly someone who is not a politician. The Roman candidate of the Centre-Left coalition, by contrast, was not considered a suitable candidate: as one man said, 'Rutelli? He has never worked in his life.' Moreover, it was assumed that a candidate from Rome (as opposed to a Milanese) could not be interested in what happened in the north of the country. Eventually Berlusconi's control of the media, his self-ascribed reputation as a 'worker' and his promise to reduce taxes and raise the minimum State pension proved decisive, and even in the valley his party won the majority of votes.

Thus, the north/south dichotomy and emphasis upon work figured prominently in local discourses despite the declining popularity of autonomist parties. Voting for one candidate or another did not mean involvement in politics and public life, but rather involved a withdrawal from these. Supporting a candidate pointed to as a worker (as was the case of Berlusconi) conveyed neither ideas of solidarity nor of class struggle but, on the contrary, entailed support for a coalition that promised an Italian version of Thatcherism, and that achieved its appeal by heralding the idea of autonomous work as a frame of identification that supplants class.[10] What prevailed was also a conceptualisation of work as something owned by the worker, from which a politics that is party driven should be excluded (for a French comparison, see Ulin 2002: 704–6). On the one hand this reflects a definition of work as a value created in the act of possession, enhanced by withholding it from the market and other impersonal forces (Lampland 1995: 102); on the other hand (and somewhat paradoxically) this conceptualisation is functional to the technocratic ideology of neo-liberalism.

## Conclusion: European Modernity at Issue

Although the Trentine case study does not do justice to all the meanings attached to the current notion of 'Europe', nonetheless it provides some answers to the questions asked at the outset. It has suggested that if we shift our focus from 'Europe' as an official discourse to the meanings that the concept conveys to those who are not political activists, we will find that social actors draw selectively on such a concept: they interpret and understand it through the lens of the 'local' and in light of present concerns. Claiming a 'European ethos' did not entail movement, but involved instead establishing an association with Europe and casting the encompassing Italian State as the 'other'.

If we were to confine our analysis to the ways Europe is imagined in the centres of EU decision-making or in the headquarters of political parties we would commit ourselves to an interpretive framework which overlooks human agency: we would be led to believe that the 'European ethos' to which social actors appeal merely replicates the neo-liberal discourse of the single market. That neo-liberalism has affected local-level views about Europe is a truism, for the 'Europe' social actors talk about largely represents a set of ideas revolving around the concepts of autonomy, efficiency and modernity. However, the Europe they appeal to is not the EU either, but is instead a powerful symbol to be appropriated and manipulated to invert one's subordinate status. In this sense, support for the Northern League and emphasis upon efficiency and the capacity to sustain hard work does not mean subscribing to all the values of neo-liberalism.

Such values, as we have seen, may serve to invert the valley's subordinate status to a position of distinction in the face of economic and political changes. Appealing to them did not imply accepting an Italian version of Thatcherism, nor did it entail evoking the image of a 'fortress Europe' inaccessible to non-Europeans. Rather, it involved redrawing the inner 'cultural boundaries' of Europe, especially the local ones. Giving 'local culture' a 'European flavour' mainly meant pushing the Italian State out of locality. Likewise, appealing to a 'European culture' enables social actors to reconcile past and present: it gives legitimacy to the widely shared belief that partaking of a European ethos requires a recovery of the values of the past that fell into oblivion after Trentino's annexation to Italy. It enables social actors to look for the roots of their 'European culture' in their rural past, to hold on to the belief that independence from outsiders has long been an integral part of local (and regional) identity and 'culture', and to distance themselves from the image of the 'deferential worker' (Newby 1977) ascribed to those who have to alienate their work. Paradoxically, it was in a post-peasant society that the neo-liberal ideology of work became appealing, because it is congruent with many of the values and beliefs that already pervade local discourses: the values of late capitalism legitimated the boundary between those who 'work' and those who 'eat' by reifying a different cultural heritage. Thus, at local-level Europe, hard work, autonomy, efficiency and modernity form part of the same set of ideas.

The ethnographic information discussed so far suggests that we cannot assume that the category of Europe, like those of nation, region or political party, is over and above social relations: it seems clear that it represents a legitimising discourse, yet we have to acknowledge the fact that it is discourses and practices that are part of everyday life that help social actors make sense of Europe itself. An understanding of the meanings attached to the current concept of Europe has to allow for human agency. Europe represents an 'invention' at an institutional level (see e.g. Delanty 1995; Shore 2000: 40–64), but it is not an 'invention' of the pure kind when social actors make sense of it by drawing (selectively) upon their own interpretive categories, and if it embodies widely shared values.

This brings us back to the other question asked at the outset: how far the idea of a supra-national, collective European identity can coexist, in the minds of the people, with the ethic of individualism of late modernity. It seems arguable that the individualistic values that the Northern League, the PATT and even *Forza Italia* champion can coexist with an idea of European identity and culture because at the local level they evoke the image of a 'community of autonomous workers', or that of a mosaic of privately owned lots to which strangers should not have access. It represents a territorial community, but it can hardly be understood by reference to the concepts of solidarity and class: rather, it is a community from which a party-driven politics associated with the working class should be excluded.

In appealing to such values, a boundary with a putative 'modern' Europe is crossed and another one with the Italian State is created. Taking a hint from

Herzfeld (1992: 12), we can suggest that while (European) modernity is largely defined by a commitment to rational management and efficiency, the rhetoric of modernity is redolent with powerful symbols and metaphors that can be appropriated by social actors, and that can serve the values that Europe, as a 'modern construct', purports to deny. Seen 'from below', the notion of Europe may represent a translation of the culture of property, which implies and shapes a dissociative relation: it represents a dissociative relation because property comes into being with the effective exclusion of others (Abramson 2000: 13). Europe made sense because it was embedded in a set of values that already informed local discourses, albeit in a different form: it combined past and present, tradition and modernity. What holds together different images of 'Europe' is a renewed commitment to a distinctive 'culture of property'. This 'culture' emerges as a result of the decline of the State as a frame of identification and of political ideologies. Thus, a 'European ethos', far from embodying the values of unity and solidarity, may instead be appropriated and manipulated for different ends and expresses the complexities of a new entangled politics of which the idea of modernity is just one aspect.

## Notes

This work is based on fieldwork conducted in Trentino in several spells between 1995 and 2001. I would like to thank the British Academy, the European Commission, the Accademia Nazionale dei Lincei, and the University of Trieste for supporting my research. I am particularly grateful to Susan Drucker-Brown, Helen Kopnina and Christina Moutsou for their constructive criticism with respect to the argument developed in this article.

1. Interestingly, the promise to introduce an Italian version of Thatcherism was central to the propaganda of *Forza Italia* (Let's Go Italy), the Centre-Right party created by the Media magnate Silvio Berlusconi, which protects the interests of entrepreneurs. In its propaganda the party asserted the primacy of the family as the centre of solidarity and entrepreneurship, and promised greater choices for citizens, competition and efficiency in public life and a residual welfare state (Ginsborg 2001: 291).
2. It is not purely coincidence that the Northern League's slogan was 'Away from Rome, closer to Europe'.
3. Local particularism in the field of law has also played an important part in affecting this feeling, given that the province, together with the nearby German-speaking South Tyrol, has retained some laws that date from Austro-Hungarian times, especially with regard to the use of land and natural resources.
4. It heralded a Trentine identity at a time when the political and economic crisis in Italy entailed the risk, for Trentino, of losing the status of special autonomous province.
5. The sawmill was shut down in late 2002.
6. The gradual erosion of village autonomy had repercussions in the local political sphere too: at a time of local elections, for example, the preservation of local identity and the necessity of preventing the land from being alienated to non-residents became high on the agenda of those

running for election to the municipal council. Some candidates promised that, if elected, they would strive to prevent the land from being sold to outsiders, and to call back to the valley the natives who live and work elsewhere. In making such promises they also championed a political programme focussed on the protection of locality. They heralded the community of the 'old days', a mosaic of private properties ideally inaccessible and controlled by people who were born and bred in the community itself.

7. Heady (1999: 210) recorded the same situation in the Carnic Alps.
8. Catholicism has played a significant role in instilling this hard-work ethic, but it would be misleading to infer that this ethic is a product of Catholicism, given that those who describe themselves as hard workers have very little or no interest in religion (for a comparison see Abrahams 1991: 18).
9. Ironically, despite the villagers' emphasis upon self-reliance and their denigration of slack workers, in the nearby communities the Vanoi valley is talked about as a municipality 'eating' regional subsidies, on the grounds that despite being heavily subsidised by the public administration it does not produce wealth.
10. This situation contrasts somewhat with the rural areas of southern France where, in the face of the changes that have altered societies and cultures in late capitalism, 'class' remains both a subjective and an analytical category (Lem 2002).

## References

Abrahams, R. 1991. *A Place of their Own: Family Farming in Eastern Finland*. Cambridge, Cambridge University Press.

Abramson, A. 2000. 'Mythical land, legal boundaries: Wondering about landscape and other tracts'. In *Land, Law and Environment. Mythical Land, Legal Boundaries*, eds A. Abramson and D. Theodossopoulos. London, Pluto Press.

Alcock, A. 1996. 'Trentino and South Tyrol: From Austrian crownland to European region'. In *Europe and ethnicity: The First World War and Contemporary Ethnic Conflict*, eds S. Dunn and T. Fraser. London, Routledge.

Allum, P. and I. Diamanti. 1996. 'The autonomous leagues in the Veneto'. In *Italian Regionalism: History, Identity and Politics*, ed. C. Levy. Oxford, Berg.

Bauman, Z. 1998. *Work, Consumerism and the New Poor*. Buckingham, Open University Press.

Bauman, Z. 1999. *In Search of Politics*. Cambridge, Polity.

Bellier, I. and T. Wilson. 2000. 'Building, imagining and experiencing Europe: Institutions and identities in the European Union'. In *An Anthropology of the European Union*, eds I. Bellier and T. Wilson. Oxford, Berg.

Cento Bull, A. 1996. 'Ethnicity, racism and the Northern League'. In *Italian Regionalism: History, Identity and Politics*, ed. C. Levy. Oxford, Berg.

Cento Bull, A. 2000. *Social Identities and Political Cultures in Italy: Catholic, Communist and 'Leghist' Communities between Civicness and Localism*. Oxford, Berghahn.

Cohen, A.P. 1996. 'Personal nationalism: A Scottish view of some rites, rights, and wrongs'. *American Ethnologist* 23, no. 4: 802–15.

Delanty, G. 1995. *Inventing Europe: Idea, Identity, Reality*. London, Macmillan.

Delanty, G. 2000. 'Social integration and Europeanization: The myth of cultural cohesion'. *Yearbook of European Studies* 14: 221–38.
Diamanti, I. 1996. *Il Male del Nord. Lega, Localismo, Secessione*. Rome, Donzelli.
Diamanti, I. 1999. 'Ha ancora senso discutere di nazione?' *Rassegna Italiana di Sociologia* 40, no. 2: 293–321.
Ginsborg, P. 2001. *Italy and its Discontents: Family, Civil Society, State 1980–2001*. London, Allen Lane, The Penguin Press.
Giordano, B. 2000. 'Italian regionalism or "Padanian" nationalism – the political project of the Lega Nord in Italian politics'. *Political Geography* 19, no. 4: 445–71.
Heady, P. 1999. *The Hard People: Rivalry, Sympathy and Social Structure in an Alpine Valley*. Amsterdam, Harwood Academic Publishers.
Heintz, M. 2002. Changes in Work Ethic in Post-Socialist Romania. Unpublished Ph.D. dissertation, University of Cambridge.
Herzfeld, M. 1992. *The Social Production of Indifference: Exploring the Symbolic Roots of Western Bureaucracy*. Chicago, University of Chicago Press.
Holmes, D.R. 2000. *Integral Europe: Fast-Capitalism, Multiculturalism, Neo-Fascism*. Princeton, Princeton University Press.
Lampland, M. 1995. *The Object of Labor: Commodification in Socialist Hungary*. Chicago, University of Chicago Press.
Lem, W. 2002. 'Articulating class in post-Fordist France'. *American Ethnologist* 29, no. 2: 287–306.
Luverà, B. 1996. *Oltre il Confine: Euregio e Conflitto Etnico: tra Regionalismo Europeo e Nuovi Nazionalismi in Trentino-Alto Adige*. Bologna, Il Mulino.
McDonald, M. 1993. 'The construction of difference: An anthropological approach to stereotypes'. In *Inside European Identities*, ed. S. Macdonald. Oxford, Berg.
Mitchell, J.P. 2002. *Ambivalent Europeans: Ritual, Memory and the Public Sphere in Malta*. London, Routledge.
Newby, H. 1977. *The Deferential Worker: A Study of Farm Workers in East Anglia*. Harmondsworth, Penguin.
Pahl, R. 1995. *After Success: Fin-de-Siècle Anxiety and Identity*. Cambridge, Polity.
Shore, C. 2000. *Building Europe: The Cultural Politics of European Integration*. London, Routledge.
Stacul, J. 2003. *The Bounded Field: Localism and Local Identity in an Italian Alpine Valley*. Oxford, Berghahn.
Stolcke, V. 1995. 'Talking culture: New boundaries, new rhetorics of exclusion in Europe'. *Current Anthropology* 36, no. 1: 1–13.
Stråth, B. 2000. 'Introduction: Europe as a discourse'. In *Europe and the Other and Europe as the Other*, ed. B. Stråth. Brussels, PIE-Peter Lang.
Turato, F. 1998. 'Il Trentino Alto Adige'. In *Idee del Nordest: Mappe, Rappresentazioni, Progetti*, ed. I. Diamanti. Turin, Edizioni Fondazione Giovanni Agnelli.
Ulin, R.C. 2002. 'Work as cultural production: Labour and self-identity among southwest French wine-growers'. *Journal of the Royal Anthropological Institute* 8, no. 4: 691–712.
Wright, S. 1998. 'The politicization of "culture"'. *Anthropology Today* 14, no. 1: 7–15.
Zaninelli, S. 1978. *Un'Agricoltura di Montagna nell'Ottocento: Il Trentino*. Trent, Società di Studi Trentini di Scienze Storiche.

# Notes on Contributors

**Daniela Baratieri** is a Researcher at the European University Institute (Florence) and is completing a Ph.D., under the guidance of Prof. Luisa Passerini, exploring memories and oblivion concerning 'Italian colonialism' in Italian culture from the 1930s to the 1960s. Her most recent publications are concerned with Italian popular visual representations of Africa in the years of de-colonisation: with G. Finaldi and N. Labanca, 'L'immagine fotografica dell'Africa: rassegna dei periodici illustrati 1955–1965' In *AFT Archivio Fotografico Toscano* (xvi, June–December, 31/32, 2002); and 'La re-edizione di Bengasi e L'assedio dell'Alcazar negli anni 50', in S. Bernardi (ed.) *La storia del cinema italiano vol. IX* (Venice: Marsilio, forthcoming).

**Eleftheria Deltsou** is a Lecturer in Social Anthropology at the University of Thessaly, Greece. Her work has focused on the use of the tradition/modernity and urban/rural dichotomies in the contexts of nationalism, tourism, consumption and upward social mobility. Her analyses show how these dichotomies constitute 'politics of culture' that establish social inequalities. Her more recent work focuses on cultural politics, eco-tourism, agro-tourism and development in the context of the European Union.

**Venetia Evergeti** received a Ph.D. in Sociology from the University of Manchester. Currently she is a Senior Research Fellow in Ethnicity and Social Policy at Middlesex University. In the past she has been involved in research and teaching in the Sociology Departments of the Universities of Manchester and Surrey. Her principal academic interests are in the fields of interactionist sociology and the ethnographic study of human interactions. She has a particular research interest in the formation and negotiation of cultural identities and the processes involved in traditional representations of local identities. Her work has focused on the study of ethnic identity in minority communities and in particular Muslim communities in Greece.

**Gregory Feldman** is Assistant Professor of International Migration at the University of British Columbia. He received a doctorate in Anthropology from Syracuse University in 2001. He has publications in the *Cambridge Review of International Affairs*, *Anthropology of East Europe Review* and *Journal of Baltic Studies*. His current work critically examines the cultural logic of diplomacy, minority–State relations and State security in Europe. He has consulted for the United Nations Development Programme on ethnic integration in Estonia.

**William F. Kelleher, Jr.** is Associate Professor of Anthropology at Syracuse University and its Maxwell School of Citizenship and Public Affairs. His recent research includes work on the late twentieth-century transformations of capital and labour in a rural midwestern U.S. town dominated by transnational agricultural corporations and on race relations among university students. Along with four undergraduate students and three faculty colleagues, he is completing the book *A Hard Year Downstate: A Student Ethnography of Race and the University*. He is also finishing a book that examines the relationship between justice and reconciliation in contemporary Northern Ireland. He is the author of *The Troubles in Ballybogoin: Memory and Identity in Northern Ireland* (Ann Arbor: University of Michigan Press, 2003).

**Helen Kopnina** holds a Bachelor's degree in Cultural Anthropology (cum laude) from Brandeis University, a Master's degree in Social Sciences from the University of Amsterdam and a Ph.D. in Social Anthropology from the University of Cambridge. Presently she holds a postdoctoral position at the Free University, Amsterdam, at the Department of Culture, Organization and Management. Her research interests include Russian migration in Europe and business networks in Asia. Her current research focuses on trans-border business networks in Singapore and Malaysia.

**Sabine Mannitz** studied Ethnology, Political Science and Cultural Anthropology in Hamburg and Frankfurt on Main. She held positions as Research Officer at the Institute for Comparative Cultural and Social Anthropology at the European University in Frankfurt on the Oder (1996–1999) and at the University of Essex in Colchester, Great Britain (2000–2002). Her research interests are in the area of migration studies, ethnicity, social change and the construction of collective identities. At present she is a Researcher at the Peace Research Institute in Frankfurt on Main where she examines the implications of transnationalisation for democracy and citizenship in the EU.

**Christina Moutsou** holds a B.Sc. in History from Aristotle's University of Thessaloniki, a M.Sc. in Social Anthropology from the London School of Economics and a Ph.D. in Social Anthropology from the University of

Cambridge. She has been a Research Fellow for two years under the TMR EU Programme and a Postdoctoral Research Associate at the University of Cambridge. She trained as a Psychoanalytic Psychotherapist with the Philadelphia Association in London. Her research interests include Greek–Turkish relations, ethnic representations and the symbolic representation of Europe. She currently works on the links between anthropology and psychoanalysis. Her publications include the article 'Dreaming anthropology: unfolding intersubjectivity in complex anthropological research' (*Irish Journal of Anthropology* 2000).

**Davide Però** (D.Phil., Sussex) is Research Fellow at the Centre on Migration, Policy and Society (COMPAS) of the University of Oxford. His research focuses on migration, multiculturalism and the political Left as well as on local governance in multi-ethnic contexts. He has carried out fieldwork in Italy and Spain where he was Marie Curie Post-Doctoral Fellow.

**Cris Shore** is Professor of Anthropology at the University of Auckland, New Zealand. Since 1992, his research has focused mainly on the institutions and policies of the European Union. His recent book, *Building Europe: The Cultural Politics of European Integration* (Routledge, 2000), explores the history and effects of EU cultural policies and the organisational culture of the European Commission. His previous fieldwork focused on Italian culture and politics (*Italian Communism*, Pluto 1990). Other recent edited volumes include *The Anthropology of Europe* (Berg, 1994); *Anthropology and Cultural Studies* (Pluto, 1997); *Anthropology of Policy* (Routledge, 1997); and *Elite Cultures: Anthropological Perspectives* (Routledge, 2002). He is currently editing a volume on the anthropology of corruption.

**Jaro Stacul** obtained a Ph.D. in Social Anthropology from the University of Cambridge. He has been a Lecturer in Anthropology at the University of Wales, Swansea, and a Research Fellow at the University of Surrey. Currently he lectures at Roehampton University, London, and is Editor of the journal *Cambridge Anthropology*. His research focuses on issues of national and regional identities in western Europe (especially Italy) and on the cultural construction of the past. His publications include the book *The Bounded Field: Localism and Local Identity in an Italian Alpine Valley* (Oxford and New York: Berghahn, 2003).

**Jacqueline Waldren** received a D.Phil. in Social Anthropology from Oxford University. Currently she is a part-time Lecturer in Anthropology at the University of Oxford (Institute of Social and Cultural Anthropology) and at Oxford Brookes University (Department of Social Sciences). She is also a member of Linacre College and a Research Associate of Queen Elizabeth

House, both at the University of Oxford. She is Editor of the series *New Directions in Anthropology* for Berghahn Books (Oxford and New York). Her publications include the monograph *Insiders and Outsiders: Paradise and Reality in Mallorca* (Oxford and New York: Berghahn, 1996).

# INDEX

## A
accession, 9, 26, 41, 45, 47, 49, 54–55, 59
act of 'crossing', 14–15, 17
alienation, 54, 56, 89, 91, 112, 138, 161, 164, 166, 221
Alps, 8, 218, 226n. 7
ambassador, 49–52, 61n. 10
ambiguity of Greek identity, 125, 200, 203
Amsterdam, 9, 14, 104–7, 109–12, 114–16, 117n. 4
Anderson, Benedict, 105, 126
antagonism, 100n. 14, 112–13, 115–16, 182
anthropological writing, 4–5, 9, 12
anti-Turkishness as idiom of exclusion, 206, 208n. 8
Anzaldua, G., 161
Appadurai, Arjun, 5, 166–68
associations, 28, 62n. 14, 125–26
Aussiedler, 89
Austro-Hungarian empire, 213–14, 217
autonomist parties, 213–14, 218
autonomous work, 16, 220–21, 223–24
autonomy, 28, 213, 216–17, 220–21, 223–24, 225n. 6

## B
Balkans, 179, 181
Belfast Agreement, 153, 172
Berlin, 9, 13, 84–6, 90, 93–8, 99n. 1, 115
Berlusconi, Silvio, 222–23, 225n. 1
Bhaba, Homi, 173n. 16
Blair, Tony, 169–70
Bologna, 65–66, 68–76, 78nn. 11, 16, 18
Bologna City Council, 74

border, Irish, 154–71
Bosnia-Herzegovina, 147
Bossi, Umberto, 211
boundaries
    categorical, 25, 177, 179, 183, 193
    class, 9, 12, 37, 210
    conceptual, 8, 84, 97, 125
    cultural, 12, 107, 201, 213
    ethnic, 13, 107, 176, 178, 188, 192
    formation of, 215
    gender, 9, 14
    geographical, 9, 15, 25, 60, 177
    national/territorial, 2, 5, 23, 45, 148n. 9, 153, 157, 162, 167, 206, 214
    social, 8, 14, 16, 184, 192, 200
    spatial, 138, 147
    symbolic, 65, 176, 193
bounded communities, 7
boundedness, 9
British-Irish Agreement (1985), 160–61, 163
Brussels, 7, 14, 23, 26–29, 32, 36, 38, 120–33, 134nn. 1, 4, 8, 11, 12
Bruxellois, 132
bureaucracy, 121, 219
bureaucratic efficiency, 210

## C
Caoria, 217–19
categorical distinctions, 2
categorisations, 3, 65
Catholics, 155–62, 165–67, 169–71
centres of EU decision-making, 6, 213, 223
centres of first shelter (*see also* CPA), 73, 78n. 14
chauvinism, 210

children, 12, 24, 26, 28–29, 33–34, 36, 84, 86, 88, 94, 96, 100nn. 10, 11, 12, 106, 114, 123–25, 134n. 7, 141–43, 146
citizenship, 24–25, 30, 35, 37, 41, 43–44, 46–48, 54, 60nn. 2, 3, 61nn. 7, 9, 65, 67, 88–89, 99n. 5, 100n. 9, 124, 138–39, 145–46, 156, 172, 208n. 4
civil society, 52, 66, 69, 73–75, 91, 93, 99, 100n. 9, 165, 172
civility, 96, 98
clerical workers, 218–19
Clines, 160–61, 164, 171
coal mines, 122, 124
Cohen, Anthony P., 9, 105, 129, 211
Cold War, 2, 32, 46, 83, 87, 97, 202
collective identity, 16, 83–84, 201, 211
colonialism, 70, 154
communitarianism, 78n. 22, 115
complexity, 4, 6, 12, 15, 129
conflict, 2, 15, 49, 54, 100n. 12, 113, 121, 124–25, 137, 142, 155, 158, 166, 169, 172, 177, 191, 199–200
cosmopolitanism, 6, 97, 124–25, 143
Council of Europe, 46, 61n. 4
CPA, 73–74, 78n. 20
crossing European boundaries, 3, 6, 8–9, 12–13, 15, 17
cultural
  baggage, 36, 114
  capital, 37, 110
  homogeneity, 9, 167, 205–6
  intimacy, 14, 120–21, 133, 204
  legitimacy, 24
  pluralism, 47, 70
Cultural Studies, 77

## D

DC, 212, 214, 220
De Witte, Bruno, 24
Delors, Jacques, 5, 30
democracy, 45, 53, 55, 67, 71, 75, 93, 100n. 9, 172, 203, 207
Development Programme, 43
diaspora, 117n. 4, 125–28, 130
difference
  cultural, 13, 48, 65, 67–69, 72–73, 76–77, 92, 145, 177–78, 206, 213, 220
  ethnic, 60n. 2, 68–69, 72–73, 92, 181, 188, 192, 205–6

gender, 14, 68, 138, 148
social, 69
diplomats, 42–43, 49, 52–54, 59, 60n. 2, 189
discrimination, 92, 166
Durkheim, E., 25
Dutchification, 116

## E

eastern Europe, 84, 103, 133, 137, 139, 155, 200, 203, 205, 217
Easterners, 96–97, 203, 205, 207
economic crisis, 10n. 4, 212, 215, 217, 221, 225n. 4
economic development, 122, 216
education, 12, 23–34, 36, 39nn. 29, 35, 43, 61n. 4, 100n. 12, 114, 131, 138, 140–41, 206, 217
elites, 42, 67, 70, 77, 211
entrepreneurs, 216, 225n. 1
Estonia, 42–49, 51–56, 60, 60nn. 2, 3, 61n. 7, 62n. 12, 105
ethnic
  boundaries, 176, 178, 188, 192
  identity (*see* identity)
  integration, 12, 41–45, 47–48, 50, 52–53, 56, 60nn. 2, 3, 61nn. 5, 9
ethnicity, 4–5, 11, 47, 61n. 5, 66, 68, 76, 106–7, 115, 144, 147, 148n. 4, 177–78, 180, 182, 205, 207, 208n. 4
ethnography, 13, 15
ethnos, 88
EU (*see also* European Union), 3, 6–10, 12, 24, 26, 28–30, 32–37, 43–45, 49, 52, 54–56, 59–60, 121, 124, 128, 129–33, 197, 199, 207, 210–13, 223
EU employees, 23, 30, 121, 131–32
Eurocrats, 130
Europe
  content of, 198, 203, 210
  as rhetoric, 3, 37, 65, 198, 210
European
  Baccalaureate, 26
  boundaries, 8, 60, 120, 133
  Commission, 7, 24, 28, 30, 35, 41, 50
  education, 12, 27, 36, 39n. 35
  ethos, 5, 210, 223–25
  Idea, 30
  identity, 5–6, 12, 16, 23–24, 26, 30, 37, 38n. 4, 65, 116, 133, 176, 192,

199–200, 205, 210–11, 219, 224
Parliament, 27–30
region, 214, 217, 221–22
Schools, 10, 12, 24–37, 211
Union (*see also* EU), 2, 5, 41, 65, 103, 120–21, 124, 134n. 5, 138, 145, 148n. 1, 153–54, 192, 197
Europeanisation, 6, 24–25, 45, 64, 131, 133, 138, 192, 199, 207, 211
Europeanist anthropology, 2–3, 77n. 3
Europeanness, 2–3, 7, 14
Eurospeak, 33
everyday life, 7, 16–17, 71, 111, 133, 138, 147, 155, 161–65, 183–84, 224
exclusion, 2, 25, 64–65, 70–77, 97–98, 116, 125, 130–31, 147, 172, 201, 206, 212, 225
exile, 104, 113, 137–38, 141–43, 146
exotic, 1, 4

**F**
First World War, 217
Flemings, 121, 124, 134nn. 2, 7
flexibility, 9, 192, 200
flow, 7–8, 86, 122–23, 134n. 2
fluidity, 11, 13–14
flux, 6, 9, 17
fonctionnaires, 28
forestry, 214
FRG, 84–89, 93, 96, 98, 100n. 7

**G**
Garcia, S., 38n. 4
GDR, 83–85, 90, 93–98, 100n. 12
Gellner, Ernest, 23, 25, 38n. 7
gender, 9, 14, 66, 68, 138–39, 142–44, 146, 148, 177–78
geopolitical and economic interests, 53
geopolitical space, 9–10
German
 separation, 90
 unification, 13, 83, 85, 90
Germany, 83–93, 95–99, 99n. 5, 100n. 8, 104, 108, 124, 139–40, 148n. 1
globalisation, 7, 13, 45, 139, 211, 214
Goffman, Erving, 191
governance, 41–42, 44–45, 59, 73–75
Government of Ireland Act, 157
Grand Place, 131

grassroots discourses, 69, 72, 76, 78n. 15
Greece, 122, 127–28, 130, 134n. 3, 176, 178–80, 182–85, 192, 199, 203, 205, 207
Greek Orthodox Church, 126, 129, 199
Greeks, 121, 123–30, 134n. 7, 134n. 9, 184, 188–89, 199, 203–7
gypsies, 71–72, 181–82, 185, 187

**H**
hard work, 108, 139, 212, 218–19, 221–24, 226n. 8
Hellenic Community, 125–28, 130, 134n. 9, 134n. 10
Herzfeld, Michael, 14, 120, 133, 193n. 5, 198–99, 204, 207, 225
Hindu Punjabi, 109–10
history and memory, 162
Hobsbawm, Eric, 24, 38n. 7
Holland (*see also* Netherlands), 26
Holmes, Douglas, 64, 210
home-making, 165–66, 173n. 17
housing policy, 72–73, 78n. 18
human agency, 6–8, 16–17, 210–11, 223–24
hybridity, 125

**I**
Ida-Virumaa, 50, 62n. 12, 62n. 13
identification, 8, 13, 32, 85, 92–93, 95, 98–99, 110, 113, 115, 144, 162, 177–78, 180, 188, 206, 223, 225
identity
 Bosnian, 137, 146, 148
 collective, 16, 83–84, 201, 211
 community, 110, 201
 cultural, 76, 148n. 9
 Estonian, 46, 51
 ethnic, 49, 56, 76, 108, 145, 178, 180–81, 183, 185, 192, 201
 formation, 25, 176, 178, 182–83
 German, 98, 100n. 8
 Greek, 130, 184, 197–99, 203, 207, 208n. 4
 Greek-Pontic, 204, 207
 Italian, 212
 local (*see* local identity)
 national, 12, 36, 50, 60, 117n. 3, 201
 religious, 191
 social, 191
 Trentine, 217–18, 225n. 4

235

village, 201–2
imagined community, 126, 139, 142, 145
immigrants
   Bosnian, 14, 147
   construction of, 67–72
   economic, 88, 93, 95, 99, 207
   Greek, 126, 134n. 3
   Russian, 14–15, 105, 204
   Turkish, 7, 13, 86
immigration (*see also* migration)
   in Belgium, 121–13
   in Germany, 84–89
   in Greece, 199–200
   in Italy, 64–77, 212
   in Spain, 138–48
   policy, 60, 65–70, 74
individualism, 16, 221–22, 224
integration
   ethnic, 12, 41–45, 48–50, 52–53, 56, 60, 60n. 2, 3, 61n. 5
   European, 3, 7, 16, 24, 44, 176–77, 192
   of immigrants, 66, 76
   policy, 41, 43–45
Integration Foundation, 42–43, 49–50, 53, 60n. 1
international elite, 121, 124
intersubjectivity, 10, 15
invisibility, 106, 110–11, 117n. 5
IRA (*see also* Irish Republican Army), 157–58, 161, 164–66, 169–70, 173nn. 1, 11
Irish nationalists, 153, 156–57, 159, 166
Irish Republican Army (*see also* IRA), 160, 173n. 1
Islam, 15, 65, 128–29, 181, 184, 206, 213
Italian Communist Party (*see also* PCI), 66, 212, 214
Italian State, 212–16, 219, 221, 223–24
Italy, 64–77, 210–25

**J**
justice, 27, 65, 67, 76–77, 160, 173n. 6

**K**
key scenario, 50
kinship, 158, 185, 200, 215, 217

**L**
Labour Party, 67–68
*laip*, 220

landholding system, 220
language, 24, 26–27, 31–35, 37, 39n. 47, 42–44, 46–51, 53–56, 59, 60n. 3, 61nn. 4, 5, 7, 65, 70, 86, 88–89, 100n. 7, 117n. 3, 124, 131–32, 134n. 6, 142–43, 145–46, 181–82, 187–88, 194n. 14, 206, 213, 217–18
late modernity, 9, 219, 221, 224
Left-wing, 65, 69–71, 73–75, 77, 128–30, 212
legal status, 111, 137, 144–46
legitimising discourse, 224
Leonard, M., 37
local
   history, 167, 214, 219
   identity, 217–18, 225n. 6
local, the, 2, 17
locality, 5, 155, 162, 165–67, 169, 171, 224, 226n. 6
London, 14, 33, 37, 104–12, 114–16, 117nn. 2, 3, 4, 132, 160
Luxembourg, 26–27, 29, 38n. 5, 48

**M**
Maastricht Treaty, 212
marriage, 117n. 6, 123, 142–43, 189, 200
Marxism, 2
master status, 178, 191
Mauss, Marcel, 25
McDonald, Maryon, 7, 133
migration (*see also* immigration), 13–14, 64–68, 73–76, 77nn. 1, 6, 78n. 21, 87, 99n. 2, 103–5, 110, 122–23, 126, 138–41, 145, 147–48, 148n. 5, 215
millennium, 3–4, 11
mobility, 5–6, 10, 113, 131, 134n. 7, 143, 166
modernity, 16, 24, 120, 154–55, 210–11, 216–17, 219, 223–25
Monnet, Jean, 27, 30
movement, 6–8, 11, 14, 104–5, 113, 138–39, 155, 165, 210, 213, 223
multiculturalism, 64, 66, 68–70, 73–74, 76, 78n. 22
multilingualism, 131
Muslim minorities, 123, 176–80, 183

**N**
Nairn, Tom, 25
national
   borders, 2, 8, 96, 103

boundaries (*see* boundaries)
cohesion, 90, 98
nationalism, 5, 7, 13, 23–25, 36, 38, 41–42, 44, 51, 56, 83, 96, 98, 120, 125–26, 128, 179, 211–12
nationality, 10, 31, 61n. 5, 84–85, 87–88, 91, 99, 100n. 6, 106, 110, 123, 138, 144, 205, 207
nation-state, 37, 41, 44, 54, 56, 59–60, 61n. 9, 65, 83, 90, 97, 103, 120–22, 126, 128, 132–33, 138, 167–68, 172, 199, 212
naturalisation, 47–48, 61n. 7, 87–88, 123
Nazi-Germany, 92
negotiation of identity, 177, 184, 191
neo-liberalism, 51, 220, 223
Netherlands (*see also* Holland), 3, 29, 61n. 4
New Left, 13, 77
New York Times, 160, 171
NGO, 42, 48, 69, 74, 144, 148n. 2
non-Estonian, 12, 42–48, 51, 53–56, 59, 60n. 3
non-integrating multiculturalism, 65, 76
Nordic, 41–44, 53, 56
North/South dichotomy, 10, 218, 222
Northern Italian identity, 212
northern Italy, 210, 212–13, 218
Northern League, 212–15, 218, 222–24, 225n. 2

## O

*obshina*, 107, 112
Occidentalism, 1
Olson, J., 27
Oostlander, A., 27, 29
oppositional categories, 154
Organization for Security and Cooperation in Europe, 43, 47
Orientalism, 4
'othering', 65, 95

## P

participatory action research, 74
PASOK, 130, 134n.10
PATT, 214–15, 218, 221–22, 224
PCI (*see also* Italian Communist Party), 66–68, 70, 77n. 5, 78n. 11, 214
PDS-DS, 66, 68–71, 75
perception, 11, 14, 25, 48, 67, 134n. 8, 141, 146, 198–202
permeability of boundaries, 15
PHARE, 43, 56

policy, 12–14, 24, 34, 37, 38, 39n. 35, 41–45, 47, 52–54, 59–60, 61n. 6, 66, 71–76, 78nn. 11, 15, 18, 19, 97, 138–39, 148, 170, 180, 211
policy practices, 66, 76, 216
political crisis, 214, 216
politics, 3, 7, 13–16, 24–25, 36, 40, 65–66, 69, 75–76, 94, 121, 123, 130, 138, 147, 158, 161, 165, 196, 207, 211–12, 215, 223–25
Pomaks, 181–82, 187–89, 194n. 9
postmodern anthropology, 5, 13–14, 16
power, 5–6, 8, 11, 13–14, 16, 40, 45, 52, 76, 84, 92, 96, 113, 128, 130, 144, 165, 167, 171–72, 198, 204, 207, 210, 213–14, 220, 223, 225
processes, 2, 4–7, 14, 17, 54, 61, 75, 98, 113, 121, 138, 146–47, 154, 172, 176–78, 182, 192–93, 196, 199–200, 202
propaganda, 31, 45, 183, 214, 218, 225
property, culture of, 225
Protestants, 156–59, 169, 171
psychoanalysis, 10
psychology, 10–11, 114

## R

race, 9, 65, 77, 110, 188
rational management, 211, 215
Red Cross, 140–42, 146
refugees, 4, 13, 71–72, 85, 87, 128, 137, 149, 202, 204, 207–9
regionalist movements, 3, 213
religion, 65, 115, 128–29, 143, 177, 180–81, 184, 188, 199
representation, 1, 9, 69, 75, 125–28, 131, 133, 158, 161
Republic of Ireland, 154, 157–60, 166
Right-wing, 92, 129
Rodope, 180–81, 187
Roma, 71, 181–82, 185–88
Rome, 216, 222, 225n. 2
Ronco, 218
Royal Ulster Constabulary (*see also* RUC), 158
Russian
  migrants, 104–16, 117n. 5
  -Pontics, 203–7
  speakers, 45–47, 53–55, 59, 60n. 2, 3, 62n. 12, 108, 115
Rutelli, Francesco, 222

Ryba, R., 39n. 35

## S
Said, Edward, 25, 198
Schaerbeek, 126
school textbooks, 97
Second World War, 2, 32, 84–85, 104, 122, 124, 139
self, 11, 14, 16, 33, 56, 133, 148n. 10, 178, 184–85, 189, 200–204
self-reliance, 50–51, 219, 221, 226n. 9
September 11th, 1
shoot-to-kill policy, 170
Shore, Cris, 6, 8, 10, 12, 25, 38n. 4, 60n. 1, 64–65, 77n. 3, 130–31, 136, 210, 213, 224
Smith, Anthony, 25
Smith, J., 34, 38n. 3
social
  boundaries (*see* boundaries)
  change, 7, 137, 141
  order, 155–56, 165–66, 172
  processes, 2, 5, 17, 176–77
  relations, 8–9, 65, 73, 107, 156, 224
  worth, 155
Socialism, 68, 75–76, 84, 95, 217
solidarity, 16, 69–70, 93, 95, 105, 111, 113, 171, 211, 223–24, 225n. 1
South Tyrol, 214, 221, 225n. 3
Soviet Union, 15, 43, 46, 83, 105, 111, 113, 204
Spain, 3, 86, 122, 138–41, 147, 148n. 5
Stalker, J., 160–61, 173n. 13
Stark, D., 155, 173n. 4
State
  Italian, 78, 212–16, 219, 221, 223–24
  in Northern Ireland, 172
  Programme, 41–44, 47–49, 51–56, 60, 62n. 2
stereotyping, 15, 133, 143, 145
stigma, 117n. 5, 191, 220
Stolcke, Verena, 45, 49, 64
Strathern, Marilyn, 126, 131
students, 10, 31, 35, 38n. 5, 121, 129, 131–33, 134n. 14, 191, 202, 206
subjectivity, 10, 12–13, 25, 30, 167, 173n. 9
subsidies, 146, 212–16, 219, 225n. 9
Sultana, R., 39nn. 33, 35
Swan, D., 25, 29, 31, 33, 36, 38n. 15, 39nn. 35, 47

## T
telling, 156, 162, 173n. 8
Thatcherism, 212, 223–24, 225n. 1
tourists, 147, 148n. 2, 201–3
Treaty of Lausanne, 180–82, 193nn. 2, 3
Trentino, 213–14, 216–17, 220–21, 224, 225n. 4
Turkish
  Embassy, 125–26, 128
  immigrants (*see* immigrants)
  minority, 181, 184, 187
  mosques, 126

## U
UDR, 158
Ulster Plantation, 162
Ulster, province of, 157
uncomfortable discipline, 1
UNDP, 43, 50, 69n. 1
Unified Germany, 89, 97–99
unity in diversity, 7, 33, 120, 133

## V
Van Houtte, 26, 38, 38n. 19
Vanoi valley, 213, 219, 225n. 9
*vehiculaire*, 34
Veneto, 215, 220
violence, 142, 153, 156–57, 161–62, 165–66, 169, 172, 173nn. 2, 6, 11

## W
Wallace, W. and Smith, J., 38n. 3
Walloons, 121, 124, 134n. 2
war, 2, 32–33, 46, 53, 71–72, 83–85, 87, 90, 93, 97, 104, 122, 124, 137–42, 147–48n. 6, 153, 155, 193n. 5, 201, 216
welfare state, 219, 225n. 1
western Europe, 2, 5, 6, 14, 45, 65–66, 68, 84, 103–4, 116, 122, 130, 137, 147
western Thrace, 176, 178, 180–81, 183
work, 4, 7–9, 11, 15–17, 30, 35, 42, 49, 51–52, 62n. 12, 86, 103–4, 109, 112, 122, 124, 129, 131–32, 134n. 13, 139–42, 144–49, 154–55, 159, 161–63, 166–68, 172, 173n. 6, 178, 187, 198, 200, 205, 212, 215, 217–24, 226n. 6, 8
working-classes, 67